Daughters
of the
Revolution

Daughters of the Revolution

Classic Essays by Women

James D. Lester
Austin Peay State University

NTC Publishing Group
Lincolnwood, Illinois USA

Executive Editor: John T. Nolan
Sponsoring Editor: Marisa L. L'Heureux
Cover and interior design: Ophelia M. Chambliss
Cover art: Celia Johnson/Gerald & Cullen Rapp, Inc.
Production Manager: Rosemary Dolinski

Acknowledgments for literary selections begin on page 207, which is to
be considered an extension of the copyright page.

ISBN 0-8442-5880-6 (student text)
ISBN 0-8442-5881-4 (instructor's edition)

Published by NTC Publishing Group
© 1996 NTC Publishing Group, 4255 West Touhy Avenue
Lincolnwood (Chicago), Illinois 60646-1975 U.S.A.
Manufactured in the United States of America.

Library of Congress Cataloging-in-Publication Data

Daughters of the Revolution : classic essays by women / [edited by] James D. Lester.
    p.   cm.
  Includes index.
  ISBN 0-8442-5880-6 (pbk.)
  1. English essays—Women authors. 2. American essays—Women
authors. 3. Women—Civilization. I. Lester, James D., 1935–   .
PR1369.W66D38 1995
824.008'09287—dc20   95-11910
                                     CIP

5 6 7 8 9 VP 0 9 8 7 6 5 4 3 2 1

Contents

༄

꧁

Essays by Women of the Late 20th Century: Breaking Free   61

Preface

❧

NTC's Library of Classic Essays

This is a four-volume collection of some of the finest essays ever written, providing a broad yet in-depth overview of the development and scope of the genre. In essence, an essay is a short prose composition, usually exploring one subject and often presenting the personal view of the author. An essay may take a variety of forms (from narration to description to autobiography) and may reflect any number of moods (from critical to reflective to whimsical).

Although we recognize a few early works by Plato, Aristotle, and others as essays, it was really Michel de Montaigne, a French philosopher and writer, who substantially defined the form when he published two volumes of his own essays under the title *Essais* in 1580. Montaigne considered himself to be representative of humankind in general; thus, his essays, though they are to be read as general treatises on the human condition, are largely reflective of Montaigne's own attitudes and experiences.

The essay proved to be a most adaptable form. In the eighteenth century, both journalists and philosophers in England and pamphleteers and patriots in the American colonies quickly discovered the power of a well-crafted and provocative essay. By the middle of the nineteenth century, the essay was the form of choice for such brilliant writers as the American Ralph Waldo Emerson and the British George Eliot. In the twentieth century, the essay has become the most widely read genre—from personal essays in periodicals to scholarly essays in scientific journals to argumentative essays on the editorial pages of newspapers worldwide.

Daughters of the Revolution: Classic Essays by Women

This volume contains twenty-four classic essays that illustrate the immense contribution that women have made to the development of the genre. Organized chronologically, these essays explore an amazing diversity of topics. If, however, one of your favorites is not included here, it may well be in one of the other volumes: *Plato's Heirs: Classic Essays; Diverse Identities: Classic Multicultural Essays;* or *Of Bunsen Burners, Bones, and Belles Lettres: Classic Essays across the Curriculum.*

This volume brings you a collection of essays by women who have pondered and explored what it means to be human. It is our hope that this collection will allow you to examine who you are and better enable you to explore your place—and the place of others—in the universe.

ESSAYS BY WOMEN
OF THE 18th AND 19th CENTURIES

Joining the Fray

from A
*Vindication of
the Rights
of Woman*

MARY WOLLSTONECRAFT

Mary Wollstonecraft (1759–1797) was born in Hoxton, England. From an early age, she was forced to earn her own way in the world. Her first novel, *Mary, A Fiction* (1788), commemorated the death of her childhood friend Fanny Blood. She translated several works that were illustrated by William Blake, who himself became a literary giant. In 1792, she went to Paris to investigate for herself the French revolution; there she witnessed firsthand the Reign of Terror. In France, she met an American military captain, Gilbert Imlay, by whom she had a daughter named Fanny. She referred to herself as Mary Imlay, but there is no evidence of a marriage. Imlay ended the relationship in 1795, and Wollstonecraft tried unsuccessfully to drown herself. Later, she married William Godwin, a liberal social reformer who published his *Political Justice* in 1793. The marriage was short-lived because she died shortly after giving birth to their daughter, Mary, who was to become the wife of the poet Percy Bysshe Shelley and the author of *Frankenstein*.

In *A Vindication of the Rights of Woman* (1792), Wollstonecraft wished to "persuade women to endeavour to acquire strength, both of mind and body" and to remember that "the first object of laudable ambition is to obtain a character as a human being." She wanted women to be more than mere playthings for their husbands or, worse, mere servants. In order to contribute to society and her family and to be a true companion to her husband, Wollstonecraft believed a woman needed a good education. This essay, then, argues that a female's education should equal that awarded to males. She encouraged women to enter the professions of medicine, law, and business so that they "would not then marry for a support."

1   . . . The preposterous distinctions of rank, which render civilization a curse, by dividing the world between voluptuous tyrants and cunning envious dependents, corrupt, almost equally, every class of people, because respectability is not attached to the discharge of the relative duties of life, but to the station, and when the duties are not fulfilled the affections cannot gain sufficient strength to fortify the virtue of which they are the natural reward. Still there are some loopholes out of which a man may creep, and dare to think and act for himself; but for a woman it is an herculean task, because she has difficulties peculiar to her sex to overcome, which require almost superhuman powers.

2   A truly benevolent legislator always endeavours to make it the interest of each individual to be virtuous; and thus private virtue becoming the cement of public happiness, an orderly whole is consolidated by the tendency of all the parts towards a common centre. But the private or public virtue of woman is very problematical, for Rousseau, and a numerous list of male writers, insist that she should all her life be subjected to a severe restraint, that of propriety. Why subject her to propriety— blind propriety—if she be capable of acting from a nobler spring, if she be an heir of immortality? Is sugar always to be produced by vital blood? Is one half of the human species, like the poor African slaves, to be subjected to prejudices that brutalize them, when principles would be a surer guard, only to sweeten the cup of man? Is not this indirectly to deny woman reason? for a gift is a mockery, if it be unfit for use.

3   Women are, in common with men, rendered weak and luxurious by the relaxing pleasures which wealth procures; but added to this they are made slaves to their persons, and must render them alluring that man may lend them his reason to guide their tottering steps aright. Or should they be ambitious, they must govern their tyrants by sinister tricks, for without rights there cannot be any incumbent duties. The laws respecting woman . . . make an absurd unit of a man and his wife; and then, by the easy transition of only considering him as responsible, she is reduced to a mere cipher.

4   The being who discharges the duties of its station is independent; and, speaking of women at large, their first duty is to themselves as rational creatures, and the next, in point of importance, as citizens, is that, which includes so many, of a mother. The rank in life which dispenses with their fulfilling this duty, necessarily degrades them by making them mere dolls. Or should they turn to something more important than merely fitting drapery upon a smooth block, their minds are only occupied by some soft platonic attachment; or the actual management of an intrigue may keep their thoughts in motion; for when they neglect domestic duties, they have it not in their power to take the field and march and counter-march like soldiers, or wrangle in the senate to keep their faculties from rusting.

5   I know that, as a proof of the inferiority of the sex, Rousseau has exultingly exclaimed, How can they leave the nursery for the camp! And the camp has by some moralists been proved the school of the most heroic virtues; though I think it would puzzle a keen casuist to prove the reasonableness of the greater number of wars that have dubbed heroes. I do not mean to consider this question critically; because, having frequently viewed these freaks of ambition as the first natural mode of civilization, when the ground must be torn up, and the woods cleared by fire and sword, I do not choose to call them pests; but surely the present system of war has little connection with virtue of any denomination, being rather the school of *finesse* and effeminacy than of fortitude.

6   Yet, if defensive war, the only justifiable war, in the present advanced state of society, where virtue can show its face and ripen amidst the rigours which purify the air on the mountain's top, were alone to be adopted as just and glorious, the true heroism of antiquity might again animate female bosoms. But fair and softly, gentle reader, male or female, do not alarm thyself, for though I have compared the character of a modern soldier with that of a civilized woman, I

am not going to advise them to turn their distaff into a musket, though I sincerely wish to see the bayonet converted into a pruning-hook. I only re-created an imagination, fatigued by contemplating the vices and follies which all proceed from a feculent stream of wealth that has muddied the pure rills of natural affection, by supposing that society will some time or other be so constituted, that man must necessarily fulfil the duties of citizen, or be despised, and that while he was employed in any of the departments of civil life, his wife, also an active citizen, should be equally intent to manage her family, educate her children, and assist her neighbours.

7 But to render her really virtuous and useful, she must not, if she discharge her civil duties, want individually the protection of civil laws; she must not be dependent on her husband's bounty for her subsistence during his life, or support after his death; for how can a being be generous who has nothing of its own? or virtuous who is not free? The wife, in the present state of things, who is faithful to her husband, and neither suckles nor educates her children, scarcely deserves the name of a wife, and has no right to that of a citizen. But take away natural rights, and duties become null.

8 Women then must be considered as only the wanton solace of men, when they become so weak in mind and body that they cannot exert themselves unless to pursue some frothy pleasure, or to invent some frivolous fashion. What can be a more melancholy sight to a thinking mind, than to look into the numerous carriages that drive helter-skelter about this metropolis in a morning full of pale-faced creatures who are flying from themselves! I have often wished, with Dr Johnson, to place some of them in a little shop with half a dozen children looking up to their languid countenances for support. I am much mistaken, if some latent vigour would not soon give health and spirit to their eyes, and some lines drawn by the exercise of reason on the blank cheeks, which before were only undulated by dimples, might restore lost dignity to the character, or rather enable it to attain the true dignity of its nature. Virtue is not to be acquired even by speculation, much less by the negative supineness that wealth naturally generates.

9 Besides, when poverty is more disgraceful than even vice, is not morality cut to the quick? Still to avoid misconstruction, though I consider that women in the common walks of life are called to fulfil the duties of wives and mothers, by religion and reason, I cannot help lamenting that women of a superior cast have not a road open by which they can pursue more extensive plans of usefulness and

independence. I may excite laughter, by dropping a hint, which I mean to pursue, some future time, for I really think that women ought to have representatives, instead of being arbitrarily governed without having any direct share allowed them in the deliberations of government.

10　　But, as the whole system of representation is now, in this country, only a convenient handle for despotism, they need not complain, for they are as well represented as a numerous class of hard-working mechanics, who pay for the support of royalty when they can scarcely stop their children's mouths with bread. How are they represented whose very sweat supports the splendid stud of an heir-apparent, or varnishes the chariot of some female favourite who looks down on shame? Taxes on the very necessaries of life, enable an endless tribe of idle princes and princesses to pass with stupid pomp before a gaping crowd, who almost worship the very parade which costs them so dear. This is mere gothic grandeur, something like the barbarous useless parade of having sentinels on horseback at Whitehall, which I could never view without a mixture of contempt and indignation.

11　　How strangely must the mind be sophisticated when this sort of state impresses it! But, till these monuments of folly are levelled by virtue, similar follies will leaven the whole mass. For the same character, in some degree, will prevail in the aggregate of society; and the refinements of luxury, or the vicious repinings of envious poverty, will equally banish virtue from society, considered as the characteristic of that society, or only allow it to appear as one of the stripes of the harlequin coat, worn by the civilized man.

12　　In the superior ranks of life, every duty is done by deputies, as if duties could ever be waived, and the vain pleasures which consequent idleness forces the rich to pursue, appear so enticing to the next rank, that the numerous scramblers for wealth sacrifice everything to tread on their heels. The most sacred trusts are then considered as sinecures, because they were procured by interest, and only sought to enable a man to keep *good company*. Women, in particular, all want to be ladies. Which is simply to have nothing to do, but listlessly to go they scarcely care where, for they cannot tell what.

13　　But what have women to do in society? I may be asked, but to loiter with easy grace; surely you would not condemn them all to suckle fools and chronicle small beer! No. Women might certainly study the art of healing and be physicians as well as nurses. And midwifery, decency seems to allot to them though I am afraid the word midwife, in our dictionaries, will soon give place to *accoucheur,* and one proof of the former delicacy of the sex be effaced from the language.

14   They might also study politics, and settle their benevolence on the broadest basis; for the reading of history will scarcely be more useful than the perusal of romances, if read as mere biography; if the character of the times, the political improvements, arts, etc., be not observed. In short, if it be not considered as the history of man; and not of particular men, who filled a niche in the temple of fame, and dropped into the black rolling stream of time, that silently sweeps all before it into the shapeless void called—eternity.—For shape, can it be called, "that shape hath none"?

15   Business of various kinds, they might likewise pursue, if they were educated in a more orderly manner, which might save many from common and legal prostitution. Women would not then marry for a support, as men accept of places under Government, and neglect the implied duties; nor would an attempt to earn their own subsistence, a most laudable one! sink them almost to the level of those poor abandoned creatures who live by prostitution. For are not milliners and mantua-makers reckoned the next class? The few employments open to women, so far from being liberal, are menial; and when a superior education enables them to take charge of the education of children as governesses, they are not treated like the tutors of sons, though even clerical tutors are not always treated in a manner calculated to render them respectable in the eyes of their pupils, to say nothing of the private comfort of the individual. But as women educated like gentlewomen, are never designed for the humiliating situation which necessity sometimes forces them to fill; these situations are considered in the light of a degradation; and they know little of the human heart, who need to be told, that nothing so painfully sharpens sensibility as such a fall in life.

16   Some of these women might be restrained from marrying by a proper spirit of delicacy, and others may not have had it in their power to escape in this pitiful way from servitude; is not that Government then very defective, and very unmindful of the happiness of one-half of its members, that does not provide for honest, independent women, by encouraging them to fill respectable stations? But in order to render their private virtue a public benefit, they must have a civil existence in the State, married or single; else we shall continually see some worthy woman, whose sensibility has been rendered painfully

acute by undeserved contempt, droop like "the lily broken down by a plowshare."

17   It is a melancholy truth; yet such is the blessed effect of civilization! the most respectable women are the most oppressed; and, unless they have understandings far superior to the common run of understandings, taking in both sexes, they must, from being treated like contemptible beings, become contemptible. How many women thus waste life away the prey of discontent, who might have practised as physicians, regulated a farm, managed a shop, and stood erect, supported by their own industry, instead of hanging their heads surcharged with the dew of sensibility, that consumes the beauty to which it at first gave lustre; nay, I doubt whether pity and love are so near akin as poets feign, for I have seldom seen much compassion excited by the helplessness of females, unless they were fair; then, perhaps, pity was the soft handmaid of love, or the harbinger of lust.

18   How much more respectable is the woman who earns her own bread by fulfilling any duty, than the most accomplished beauty! —beauty did I say!—so sensible am I of the beauty of moral loveliness, or the harmonious propriety that attunes the passions of a well-regulated mind, that I blush at making the comparison; yet I sigh to think how few women aim at attaining this respectability by withdrawing from the giddy whirl of pleasure, or the indolent calm that stupefies the good sort of women it sucks in.

19   Proud of their weakness, however, they must always be protected, guarded from care, and all the rough toils that dignify the mind. If this be the fiat of fate, if they will make themselves insignificant and contemptible, sweetly to waste "life away," let them not expect to be valued when their beauty fades, for it is the fate of the fairest flowers to be admired and pulled to pieces by the careless hand that plucked them. In how many ways do I wish, from the purest benevolence, to impress this truth on my sex; yet I fear that they will not listen to a truth that dear bought experience has brought home to many an agitated bosom, nor willingly resign the privileges of rank and sex for the privileges of humanity, to which those have no claim who do not discharge its duties.

20   Those writers are particularly useful, in my opinion, who make man feel for man, independent of the station he fills, or the drapery of factitious sentiments. I then would fain convince reasonable men of the importance of some of my remarks; and prevail on them to weigh dispassionately the whole tenor of my observations. I appeal

to their understandings; and, as a fellow-creature, claim, in the name of my sex, some interest in their hearts. I entreat them to assist to emancipate their companion, to make her a *helpmeet* for them.

21   Would men but generously snap our chains, and be content with rational fellowship instead of slavish obedience, they would find us more observant daughters, more affectionate sisters, more faithful wives, more reasonable mothers—in a word, better citizens. We should then love them with true affection, because we should learn to respect ourselves; and the peace of mind of a worthy man would not be interrupted by the idle vanity of his wife, nor the babes sent to nestle in a strange bosom, having never found a home in their mother's.

Declaration of Sentiments and Resolutions: Adopted by the Seneca Falls Convention, July 19–20, 1848

ELIZABETH CADY STANTON

Elizabeth Cady Stanton (1815–1902) was an early advocate for women's rights in an age when there were few. She was born in Johnstown, New York, the daughter of a prominent attorney, congressman, and state judge. She received a superior education in physiology, geography, higher mathematics, Greek, Latin, French, music, and elocution. In 1840, she married Henry Brewster Stanton (though she omitted the word *obey* from the marriage vows). In 1848, she helped organize the first women's rights convention in Seneca Falls, New York. At the convention, her "Declaration of Sentiments" was endorsed and was later published. Patterned after the "Declaration of Independence," it protests against double standards and asks for women's rights to property, children, and the vote. Later, she collaborated with Susan B. Anthony to publish the *Revolution,* a magazine that provided a public forum for Stanton's positions on women's issues. In 1869, she formed the National Woman Suffrage Association, and she spent the latter half of the nineteenth century writing and speaking out for the women of America.

In "Declaration of Sentiments," she argues that "because women do feel themselves aggrieved, oppressed, and fraudulently deprived of their most sacred rights, we insist that they have immediate admission to all the rights and privileges which belong to them as citizens of the United States."

1   When, in the course of human events, it becomes necessary for one portion of the family of man to assume among the people of the earth a position different from that which they have hitherto occupied, but one to which the laws of nature and of nature's God entitle them, a decent respect to the opinions of mankind requires that they should declare the causes that impel them to such a course.

2   We hold these truths to be self-evident: that all men and women are created equal; that they are endowed by their Creator with certain inalienable rights; that among these are life, liberty, and the pursuit of happiness; that to secure these rights governments are instituted, deriving their just powers from the consent of the governed. Whenever any form of government becomes destructive of these ends, it is the right of those who suffer from it to refuse allegiance to it, and to insist upon the institution of a new government, laying its foundation on such principles, and organizing its powers in such form, as to them shall seem most likely to effect their safety and happiness. Prudence, indeed, will dictate that governments long established should not be changed for light and transient causes; and accordingly all experience hath shown that mankind are more disposed to suffer, while evils are sufferable, than to right themselves by abolishing the forms to which they were accustomed. But when

a long train of abuses and usurpations, pursuing invariably the same object, evinces a design to reduce them under absolute despotism, it is their duty to throw off such government, and to provide new guards for their future security. Such has been the patient sufferance of the women under this government, and such is now the necessity which constrains them to demand the equal station to which they are entitled.

3   The history of mankind is a history of repeated injuries and usurpations on the part of man toward woman, having in direct object the establishment of an absolute tyranny over her. To prove this, let facts be submitted to a candid world.

4   He has never permitted her to exercise her inalienable right to the elective franchise.

5   He has compelled her to submit to laws, in the formation of which she had no voice.

6   He has withheld from her rights which are given to the most ignorant and degraded men—both natives and foreigners.

7   Having deprived her of this first right of a citizen, the elective franchise, thereby leaving her without representation in the halls of legislation, he has oppressed her on all sides.

8   He has made her, if married, in the eye of the law, civilly dead.

9   He has taken from her all right in property, even to the wages she earns.

10   He has made her, morally, an irresponsible being, as she can commit many crimes with impunity, provided they be done in the presence of her husband. In the covenant of marriage, she is compelled to promise obedience to her husband, he becoming to all intents and purposes, her master—the law giving him power to deprive her of her liberty, and to administer chastisement.

11   He has so framed the laws of divorce, as to what shall be the proper causes, and in case of separation, to whom the guardianship of the children shall be given, as to be wholly regardless of the happiness of women—the law, in all cases, going upon a false supposition of the supremacy of man, and giving all power into his hands.

12   After depriving her of all rights as a married woman, if single, and the owner of property, he has taxed her to support a government which recognizes her only when her property can be made profitable to it.

13   He has monopolized nearly all the profitable employments, and from those she is permitted to follow, she receives but a scanty

remuneration. He closes against her all the avenues to wealth and distinction which he considers most honorable to himself. As a teacher of theology, medicine, or law, she is not known.

14   He has denied her the facilities for obtaining a thorough education, all colleges being closed against her.

15   He allows her in Church, as well as State, but a subordinate position, claiming Apostolic authority for her exclusion from the ministry, and, with some exceptions, from any public participation in the affairs of the Church.

16   He has created a false public sentiment by giving to the world a different code of morals for men and women, by which moral delinquencies which exclude women from society, are not only tolerated, but deemed of little account in man.

17   He has usurped the prerogative to Jehovah himself, claiming it as his right to assign for her a sphere of action, when that belongs to her conscience and to her God.

18   He has endeavored, in every way that he could, to destroy her confidence in her own powers, to lessen her self-respect, and to make her willing to lead a dependent and abject life.

19   Now, in view of this entire disfranchisement of one-half the people of this country, their social and religious degradation—in view of the unjust laws above mentioned, and because women do feel themselves aggrieved, oppressed, and fraudulently deprived of their most sacred rights, we insist that they have immediate admission to all the rights and privileges which belong to them as citizens of the United States.

20   In entering upon the great work before us, we anticipate no small amount of misconception, misrepresentation, and ridicule; but we shall use every instrumentality within our power to effect our object. We shall employ agents, circulate tracts, petition the State and National legislatures, and endeavor to enlist the pulpit and the press in our behalf. We hope this Convention will be followed by a series of Conventions embracing every part of the country.

[The following resolutions were discussed by Lucretia Mott, Thomas and Mary Ann McClintock, Amy Post, Catharine A. F. Stebbins, and others, and were adopted:]

21   WHEREAS, The great precept of nature is conceded to be, that "man shall pursue his own true and substantial happiness." Blackstone in his Commentaries remarks, that this law of Nature being

coeval with mankind, and dictated by God himself, is of course superior in obligation to any other. It is binding over all the globe, in all countries and at all times; no human laws are of any validity if contrary to this, and such of them as are valid, derive all their force, and all their validity, and all their authority, mediately and immediately, from this original; therefore,

22   *Resolved,* That such laws as conflict, in any way, with the true and substantial happiness of woman, are contrary to the great precept of nature and of no validity, for this is "superior in obligation to any other."

23   *Resolved,* That all laws which prevent woman from occupying such a station in society as her conscience shall dictate, or which place her in a position inferior to that of man, are contrary to the great precept of nature, and therefore of no force or authority.

24   *Resolved,* That woman is man's equal—was intended to be so by the Creator, and the highest good of the race demands that she should be recognized as such.

25   *Resolved,* That the women of this country ought to be enlightened in regard to the laws under which they live, that they may no longer publish their degradation by declaring themselves satisfied with their present position, nor their ignorance, by asserting that they have all the rights they want.

26   *Resolved,* That inasmuch as man, while claiming for himself intellectual superiority, does accord to woman moral superiority, it is preeminently his duty to encourage her to speak and teach, as she has an opportunity, in all religious assemblies.

27   *Resolved,* That the same amount of virtue, delicacy, and refinement of behavior that is required of woman in the social state, should also be required of man, and the same transgressions should be visited with equal severity on both man and woman.

28   *Resolved,* That the objection of indelicacy and impropriety, which is so often brought against woman when she addresses a public audience, comes with a very ill-grace from those who encourage, by their attendance, her appearance on the stage, in the concert, or in feats of the circus.

29   *Resolved,* That woman has too long rested satisfied in the circumscribed limits which corrupt customs and a perverted application of the Scriptures have marked out for her, and that it is time she should move in the enlarged sphere which her great Creator has assigned her.

30   *Resolved,* That it is the duty of the women of this country to secure to themselves their sacred right to the elective franchise.

31   *Resolved,* That the equality of human rights results necessarily from the fact of the identity of the race in capabilities and responsibilities.

32   *Resolved, therefore,* That, being invested by the Creator with the same capabilities, and the same consciousness of responsibility for their exercise, it is demonstrably the right and duty of woman, equally with man, to promote every righteous cause by every righteous means; and especially in regard to the great subjects of morals and religion, it is self-evidently her right to participate with her brother in teaching them, both in private and in public, by writing and by speaking, by any instrumentalities proper to be used, and in any assemblies proper to be held; and this being a self-evident truth growing out of the divinely implanted principles of human nature, any custom or authority adverse to it, whether modern or wearing the hoary sanction of antiquity, is to be regarded as a self-evident falsehood, and at war with mankind.

Only Temper

GEORGE ELIOT

George Eliot (1819–1880) was born Mary Ann Evans in Chilvers Coton, Warwickshire, England. She attended school at Attleborough, Nuneaton, and Coventry, and then, upon her mother's death in 1836, she returned home to care for her father. After her father died in 1849, she traveled to Europe and began dabbling in various writing ventures, especially translations of German texts. As an editor for the *Westminster Review,* she met many literary people, and one captured her attention. She began a relationship with George Henry Lewes in 1854, and both she and Lewes considered it a marriage even though Lewes's wife still lived in an institution for the insane. Lewes encouraged Evans to try her hand at fiction, and her first novel, *Adam Bede* (1859), appeared under the pseudonym "George Eliot." It won critical acclaim, so she followed it with other notable novels, such as *The Mill on the Floss* and *Middlemarch.*

"Only Temper" displays her essay technique and provides insight into life's emotional roller coaster. She offers her advice with a delicate but biting voice filled with humor and satire. In the essay, she creates a character, much as she did in her novels, of a temper-possessed man named Dion Touchwood. To him she ascribes various male tendencies toward flamboyant and vitriolic behavior (which often is followed by gentle, gregarious efforts to mitigate the damage caused by the bad temper). Her position is made clear: "If a man frequently passes unjust judgments, takes up false attitudes, intermits his acts of kindness with rude behavior or cruel words, and falls into the consequent vulgar error of supposing that he can make amends by labored agreeableness, I cannot consider such courses any the less ugly because they are ascribed to 'temper.' "

1 What is temper? Its primary meaning, the proportion and mode in which qualities are mingled, is much neglected in popular speech, yet even here the word often carries a reference to an habitual state or general tendency of the organism in distinction from what are held to be specific virtues and vices. As people confess to bad memory without expecting to sink in mental reputation, so we hear a man declared to have a bad temper and yet glorified as the possessor of every high quality. When he errs or in any way commits himself, his temper is accused, not his character, and it is understood that but for a brutal bearish mood he is kindness itself. If he kicks small animals, swears violently at a servant who mistakes orders, or is grossly rude to his wife, it is remarked apologetically that these things mean nothing—they are all temper.

2 Certainly there is a limit to this form of apology, and the forgery of a bill, or the ordering of goods without any prospect of paying for them, has never been set down to an unfortunate habit of sulkiness or of irascibility. But on the whole there is a peculiar exercise of indulgence towards the manifestations of bad temper which tends to encourage them, so that we are in danger of having among us a number of virtuous persons who conduct themselves detestably, just as we have hysterical patients who, with sound organs, are apparently labouring under many sorts of organic disease. Let it be admitted, however, that a man may be "a good fellow" and yet have a bad temper, so bad that we recognise his merits with reluctance, and are inclined to resent his occasionally amiable behaviour as an unfair demand on our admiration.

3 Touchwood is that kind of good fellow. He is by turns insolent, quarrelsome, repulsively haughty to innocent people who approach him with respect, neglectful of his friends, angry in the face of legiti- mate demands, procrastinating in the fulfilment of such demands, prompted to rude words and harsh looks by a moody disgust with his fellow-men in general—and yet, as everybody will assure you, the soul of honour, a steadfast friend, a defender of the oppressed, an

affectionate-hearted creature. Pity that, after a certain experience of his moods, his intimacy becomes insupportable! A man who uses his balmorals to tread on your toes with much frequency and an unmistakeable emphasis may prove a fast friend in adversity, but meanwhile your adversity has not arrived and your toes are tender. The daily sneer or growl at your remarks is not to be made amends for by a possible eulogy or defence of your understanding against depreciators who may not present themselves, and on an occasion which may never arise. I cannot submit to a chronic state of blue and green bruise as a form of insurance against an accident.

4   Touchwood's bad temper is of the contradicting pugnacious sort. He is the honourable gentleman in opposition, whatever proposal or proposition may be broached, and when others join him he secretly damns their superfluous agreement, quickly discovering that his way of stating the case is not exactly theirs. An invitation or any sign of expectation throws him into an attitude of refusal. Ask his concurrence in a benevolent measure: he will not decline to give it, because he has a real sympathy with good aims; but he complies resentfully, though where he is let alone he will do much more than any one would have thought of asking for. No man would shrink with greater sensitiveness from the imputation of not paying his debts, yet when a bill is sent in with any promptitude he is inclined to make the tradesman wait for the money he is in such a hurry to get. One sees that this antagonistic temper must be much relieved by finding a particular object, and that its worst moments must be those where the mood is that of vague resistence, there being nothing specific to oppose. Touchwood is never so little engaging as when he comes down to breakfast with a cloud on his brow, after parting from you the night before with an affectionate effusiveness at the end of a confidential conversation which has assured you of mutual understanding. Impossible that you can have committed any offence. If mice have disturbed him, that is not your fault; but, nevertheless, your cheerful greeting had better not convey any reference to the weather, else it will be met by a sneer which, taking you unawares, may give you a crushing sense that you make a poor figure with your cheerfulness, which was not asked for. Some daring person perhaps introduces another topic, and uses the delicate flattery of appealing to Touchwood for his opinion, the topic being included in his favourite studies. An indistinct muttering, with a look at the carving-knife in reply, teaches that daring person how ill he has chosen a market for

his deference. If Touchwood's behaviour affects you very closely you had better break your leg in the course of the day: his bad temper will then vanish at once: he will take a painful journey on your behalf; he will sit up with you night after night; he will do all the work of your department so as to save you from any loss in consequence of your accident; he will be even uniformly tender to you till you are well on your legs again, when he will some fine morning insult you without provocation, and make you wish that his generous goodness to you had not closed your lips against retort.

5   It is not always necessary that a friend should break his leg for Touchwood to feel compunction and endeavour to make amends for his bearishness or insolence. He becomes spontaneously conscious that he has misbehaved, and he is not only ashamed of himself, but has the better prompting to try and heal any wound he has inflicted. Unhappily the habit of being offensive "without meaning it" leads usually to a way of making amends which the injured person cannot but regard as a being amiable without meaning it. The kindnesses, the complimentary indications or assurances, are apt to appear in the light of a penance adjusted to the foregoing lapses, and by the very contrast they offer call up a keener memory of the wrong they atone for. They are not a spontaneous prompting of goodwill, but an elaborate compensation. And, in fact, Dion's atoning friendliness has a ring of artificiality. Because he formerly disguised his good feeling towards you he now expresses more than he quite feels. It is in vain. Having made you extremely uncomfortable last week he has absolutely diminished his power of making you happy to-day: he struggles against this result by excessive effort, but he has taught you to observe his fitfulness rather than to be warmed by his episodic show of regard.

6   I suspect that many persons who have an uncertain, incalculable temper flatter themselves that it enhances their fascination; but perhaps they are under the prior mistake of exaggerating the charm which they suppose to be thus strengthened; in any case they will do well not to trust in the attractions of caprice and moodiness for a long continuance or for close intercourse. A pretty woman may fan the flame of distant adorers by harassing them, but if she lets one of them make her his wife, the point of view from which he will look at her poutings and tossings and mysterious inability to be pleased will be seriously altered. And if slavery to a pretty woman, which seems among the least conditional forms of abject service, will

not bear too great a strain from her bad temper even though her beauty remain the same, it is clear that a man whose claims lie in his high character or high performances had need impress us very constantly with his peculiar value and indispensableness, if he is to test our patience by an uncertainty of temper which leaves us absolutely without grounds for guessing how he will receive our persons or humbly advanced opinions, or what line he will take on any but the most momentous occasions.

For it is among the repulsive effects of this bad temper, which is supposed to be compatible with shining virtues, that it is apt to determine a man's sudden adhesion to an opinion, whether on a personal or impersonal matter, without leaving him time to consider his grounds. The adhesion is sudden and momentary, but it either forms a precedent for his line of thought and action, or it is presently seen to have been inconsistent with his true mind. This determination of partisanship by temper has its worst effects in the career of the public man, who is always in danger of getting so enthralled by his own words that he looks into facts and questions not to get rectifying knowledge, but to get evidence that will justify his actual attitude which was assumed under an impulse dependent on something else than knowledge. There has been plenty of insistence on the evil of swearing by the words of a master, and having the judgment uniformly controlled by a "He said it;" but a much worse woe to befall a man is to have every judgment controlled by an "I said it"—to make a divinity of his own short-sightedness or passion-led aberration and explain the world in its honour. There is hardly a more pitiable degradation than this for a man of high gifts. Hence I cannot join with those who wish that Touchwood, being young enough to enter on public life, should get elected for Parliament and use his excellent abilities to serve his country in that conspicuous manner. For hitherto, in the less momentous incidents of private life, his capricious temper has only produced the minor evil of inconsistency, and he is even greatly at ease in contradicting himself, provided he can contradict you, and disappoint any smiling expectation you may have shown that the impressions you are uttering are likely to meet with his sympathy, considering that the day before he himself gave you the example which your mind is following. He is at least free from those fetters of self-justification which are the curse of parliamentary speaking, and what I rather desire for him is that he should produce the great book which he is generally pronounced capable of writing, and put his best self imperturbably on record for the advantage of society; because I should then have steady ground for bearing with his diurnal incalculableness, and could fix my gratitude as by a strong staple to that unvarying monumental service. Unhappily, Touchwood's great powers have been only so far manifested as to be believed in, not demonstrated. Everybody rates them highly, and thinks that whatever he chose to do would be done in a first-rate manner. Is it his love of disappointing complacent expectancy which has gone so far as to keep up this lamentable negation, and made him resolve not to write the comprehensive work which he would have written if nobody had expected it of him?

8   One can see that if Touchwood were to become a public man and take to frequent speaking on platforms or from his seat in the House, it would hardly be possible for him to maintain much integrity of opinion, or to avoid courses of partisanship which a healthy public sentiment would stamp with discredit. Say that he were endowed with the purest honesty, it would inevitably be dragged captive by this mysterious, Protean bad temper. There would be the fatal public necessity of justifying oratorical Temper which had got on its legs in its bitter mood and made insulting imputations, or of keeping up some decent show of consistency with opinions vented out of Temper's contradictoriness. And words would have to be followed up by acts of adhesion.

9   Certainly if a bad-tempered man can be admirably virtuous, he must be so under extreme difficulties. I doubt the possibility that a high order of character can coexist with a temper like Touchwood's. For it is of the nature of such temper to interrupt the formation of healthy mental habits, which depend on a growing harmony between perception, conviction, and impulse. There may be good feelings, good deeds—for a human nature may pack endless varieties and blessed inconsistencies in its windings—but it is essential to what is worthy to be called high character, that it may be safely calculated on, and that its qualities shall have taken the form of principles or laws habitually, if not perfectly, obeyed.

10   If a man frequently passes unjust judgments, takes up false attitudes, intermits his acts of kindness with rude behaviour or cruel words, and falls into the consequent vulgar error of supposing that he can make amends by laboured agreeableness, I cannot consider such courses any the less ugly because they are ascribed to "temper." Especially I object to the assumption that his having a fundamentally

good disposition is either an apology or a compensation for his bad behaviour. If his temper yesterday made him lash the horses, upset the curricle and cause a breakage in my rib, I feel it no compensation that to-day he vows he will drive me anywhere in the gentlest manner any day as long as he lives. Yesterday was what it was, my rib is paining me, it is not a main object of my life to be driven by Touchwood—and I have no confidence in his lifelong gentleness. The utmost form of placability I am capable of is to try and remember his better deeds already performed, and, mindful of my own offences, to bear him no malice. But I cannot accept his amends.

11   If the bad-tempered man wants to apologise he had need to do it on a large public scale, make some beneficent discovery, produce some stimulating work of genius, invent some powerful process—prove himself such a good to contemporary multitudes and future generations, as to make the discomfort he causes his friends and acquaintances a vanishing quality, a trifle even in their own estimate.

ESSAYS BY
WOMEN
OF THE EARLY 20th CENTURY

Exploring
Boundaries

Three Days to See

HELEN KELLER

Helen Keller (1880–1968) was born in Tuscumbia, Alabama, the frail daughter of Arthur and Kate Keller. She was afflicted before age two with a disease that left her deaf and blind. She describes the beginnings of her condition in her autobiography *The Story of My Life*: "They called it acute congestion of the stomach and brain. The doctor thought I could not live. Early one morning, however, the fever left just as suddenly and mysteriously as it had come. There was great rejoicing in the family that morning, but no one, not even the doctor, knew that I should never see or hear again." A few years later, Anne Sullivan arrived to help the child learn to name things, to read, to speak, and eventually to write.

In "Three Days to See" Keller expresses her dismay at the way sighted persons squander their gift. Keller urges people to awaken from lethargy and to live intensely. In this speech, published by the Utah School for the Deaf in 1934, she presents her personal preferences as guidelines for her audience, for she encourages her audience to imagine the things they might wish to see if they were blind. Then she challenges them to take action by seeing, touching, and tasting life. The essay uses a classic, three-part structure to categorize the three days to be used for seeing friends, art, and contemporary life.

1   If I were the president of a university I should establish a compulsory course in "How to Use Your Eyes." The professor would try to show his pupils how they could add joy to their lives by really seeing what passes unnoticed before them. He would try to awake their dormant and sluggish faculties.

2   Perhaps I can best illustrate my imagining what I should most like to see if I were given the use of my eyes, say, for just three days. And while I am imagining, suppose you, too, set your mind to work on the problem of how you would use your own eyes if you had only three more days to see. If with the oncoming darkness of the third night you knew that the sun would never rise for you again, how would you spend those three precious intervening days? What would you most want to let your gaze rest upon?

3   I, naturally, should want most to see the things which have become dear to me through my years of darkness. You, too, would want to let your eyes rest long on the things that have become dear to you so that you could take the memory of them with you into the night that loomed before you.

4   If, by some miracle, I were granted three seeing days, to be followed by a relapse into darkness, I should divide the period into three parts.

5   On the first day, I should want to see the people whose kindness and gentleness and companionship have made my life worth living. First I should like to gaze long upon the face of my dear teacher, Mrs. Anne Sullivan Macy, who came to me when I was a child and opened the outer world to me. I should want not merely to see the outline of her face, so that I could cherish it in my memory, but to study that face and find in it the living evidence of the sympathetic tenderness and patience with which she accomplished the difficult task of my education. I should like to see in her eyes that strength of character which has enabled her to stand firm in the face of difficulties, and that compassion for all humanity which she has revealed to me so often.

6   I do not know what it is to see into the heart of a friend through that "window of the soul," the eye. I can only "see" through my fingertips the outline of a face. I can detect laughter, sorrow, and many other obvious emotions. I know my friends from the feel of their faces. But I cannot really picture their personalities by touch. I know their personalities, of course, through other means, through the thoughts they express to me, through whatever of their actions

are revealed to me. But I am denied that deeper understanding of them which I am sure would come through sight of them, through watching their reactions to various expressed thoughts and circumstances, through noting the immediate and fleeting reactions of their eyes and countenance.

7   Friends who are near to me I know well, because through the months and years they reveal themselves to me in all their phases; but of casual friends I have only an incomplete impression, an impression gained from a handclasp, from spoken words which I take from their lips with my fingertips, or which they tap into the palm of my hand.

8   How much easier, how much more satisfying it is for you who can see to grasp quickly the essential qualities of another person by watching the subtleties of expression, the quiver of a muscle, the flutter of a hand. But does it ever occur to you to use your sight to see into the inner nature of a friend or acquaintance? Do not most of you seeing people grasp casually the outward features of a face and let it go at that?

9   For instance, can you describe accurately the faces of five good friends? Some of you can, but many cannot. As an experiment, I have questioned husbands of long standing about the color of their wives' eyes, and often they express embarrassed confusion and admit that they do not know. And, incidentally, it is a chronic complaint of wives that their husbands do not notice new dresses, new hats, and changes in household arrangements.

10   The eyes of seeing persons soon become accustomed to the routine of their surroundings, and they actually see only the startling and spectacular. But even in viewing the most spectacular sights the eyes are lazy. Court records reveal every day how inaccurately "eyewitnesses" see. A given event will be "seen" in several different ways by as many witnesses. Some see more than others, but few see everything that is within the range of their vision.

11   Oh, the things that I should see if I had the power of sight for just three days!

12   The first day would be a busy one. I should call to me all my dear friends and look long into their faces, imprinting upon my mind the outward evidences of the beauty that is within them. I should let my eyes rest, too, on the face of a baby, so that I could catch a vision of the eager, innocent beauty which precedes the individual's consciousness of the conflicts which life develops.

13   And I should like to look into the loyal, trusting eyes of my
dogs—the grave, canny little Scottie, Darkie, and the stalwart, understanding Great Dane, Helga, whose warm, tender, and playful friend-
ships are so comforting to me.

14   On that busy first day I should also view the small simple things
of my home. I want to see the warm colors in the rugs under my
feet, the pictures on the walls, the intimate trifles that transform a
house into home. My eyes would rest respectfully on the books in
raised type which I have read, but they would be more eagerly
interested in the printed books which seeing people can read, for
during the long night of my life the books I have read and those
which have been read to me have built themselves into a great shining
lighthouse, revealing to me the deepest channels of human life and
the human spirit.

15   In the afternoon of that first seeing day, I should take a long walk
in the woods and intoxicate my eyes on the beauties of the world
of Nature, trying desperately to absorb in a few hours the vast splendor which is constantly unfolding itself to those who can see. On
the way home from my woodland jaunt my path would lie near a
farm so that I might see the patient horses plowing in the field
(perhaps I should see only a tractor!) and the serene content of men
living close to the soil. And I should pray for the glory of a colorful
sunset.

16   When dusk had fallen, I should experience the double delight of
being able to see by artificial light, which the genius of man has
created to extend the power of his sight when Nature decrees darkness.

17   In the night of that first day of sight, I should not be able to
sleep, so full would be my mind of the memories of the day.

18   The next day—the second day of sight—I should arise with the
dawn and see the thrilling miracle by which night is transformed
into day. I should behold with awe the magnificent panorama of
light with which the sun awakens the sleeping earth.

19   This day I should devote to a hasty glimpse of the world, past
and present. I should want to see the pageant of man's progress, the
kaleidoscope of the ages. How can so much be compressed into one
day? Through the museums, of course. Often I have visited the New
York Museum of Natural History to touch with my hands many of
the objects there exhibited, but I have longed to see with my eyes
the condensed history of the earth and its inhabitants displayed

there—animals and the races of men pictured in their native environment; gigantic carcasses of dinosaurs and mastodons which roamed the earth long before man appeared, with his tiny stature and powerful brain, to conquer the animal kingdom; realistic presentations of the processes of evolution in animals, in man, and in the implements which man has used to fashion for himself a secure home on this planet; and a thousand and one other aspects of natural history.

20   I wonder how many readers of this article have viewed this panorama of the face of living things as pictured in that inspiring museum. Many, of course, have not had the opportunity, but I am sure that many who *have* had the opportunity have not made use of it. There, indeed, is a place to use your eyes. You who see can spend many fruitful days there, but I, with my imaginary three days of sight, could only take a hasty glimpse, and pass on.

21   My next stop would be the Metropolitan Museum of Art, for just as the Museum of Natural History reveals the material aspects of the world, so does the Metropolitan show the myriad facets of the human spirit. Throughout the history of humanity the urge to artistic expression has been almost as powerful as the urge for food, shelter, and procreation. And here, in the vast chambers of the Metropolitan Museum, is unfolded before me the spirit of Egypt, Greece, and Rome, as expressed in their art. I know well through my hands the sculptured gods and goddesses of the ancient Nile-land. I have felt copies of Parthenon friezes, and I have sensed the rhythmic beauty of charging Athenian warriors. Apollos and Venuses and the Winged Victory of Samothrace are friends of my fingertips. The gnarled, bearded features of Homer are dear to me, for he, too, knew blindness.

22   My hands have lingered upon the living marble of Roman sculpture as well as that of later generations. I have passed my hands over a plaster cast of Michelangelo's inspiring and heroic Moses; I have sensed the power of Rodin; I have been awed by the devoted spirit of Gothic wood carving. These arts which can be touched have meaning for me, but even they were meant to be seen rather than felt, and I can only guess at the beauty which remains hidden from me. I can admire the simple lines of a Greek vase, but its figured decorations are lost to me.

23   So on this, my second day of sight, I should try to probe into the soul of man through his art. The things I knew through touch I should now see. More splendid still, the whole magnificent world

of painting would be opened to me, from the Italian Primitives, with their serene religious devotion, to the Moderns, with their feverish visions. I should look deep into the canvases of Raphael, Leonardo da Vinci, Titian, Rembrandt. I should want to feast my eyes upon the warm colors of Veronese, study the mysteries of El Greco, catch a new vision of Nature from Corot. Oh, there is so much rich meaning and beauty in the art of the ages for you who have eyes to see!

24   Upon my short visit to this temple of art I should not be able to review a fraction of that great world of art which is open to you. I should be able to get only a superficial impression. Artists tell me that for a deep and true appreciation of art one must educate the eye. One must learn through experience to weigh the merits of line, of composition, of form and color. If I had eyes, how happily would I embark upon so fascinating a study! Yet I am told that, to many of you who have eyes to see, the world of art is a dark night, unexplored and unilluminated.

25   It would be with extreme reluctance that I should leave the Metropolitan Museum, which contains the key to beauty—a beauty so neglected. Seeing persons, however, do not need a Metropolitan to find this key to beauty. The same key lies waiting in smaller museums, and in books on the shelves of even small libraries. But naturally, in my limited time of imaginary sight, I should choose the place where the key unlocks the greatest treasures in the shortest time.

26   The evening of my second day of sight I should spend at a theater or at the movies. Even now I often attend theatrical performances of all sorts, but the action of the play must be spelled into my hand by a companion. But how I should like to see with my own eyes the fascinating figure of Hamlet, or the gusty Falstaff amid colorful Elizabethan trappings! How I should like to follow each movement of the graceful Hamlet, each strut of the hearty Falstaff! And since I could see only one play, I should be confronted by the many-horned dilemma, for there are scores of plays I should want to see. You who have eyes can see any you like. How many of you, I wonder, when you gaze at a play, a movie, or any spectacle, realize and give thanks for the miracle of sight which enables you to enjoy its color, grace, and movement?

27   I cannot enjoy the beauty of rhythmic movement except in a sphere restricted to the touch of my hands. I can vision only dimly the grace of a Pavlova, although I know something of the delight of rhythm, for often I can sense the beat of music as it vibrates

through the floor. I can well imagine that cadenced motion must be one of the most pleasing sights in the world. I have been able to gather something of this by tracing with my fingers the lines in sculptured marble; if this static grace can be so lovely, how much more acute must be the thrill of seeing grace in motion.

28   One of my dearest memories is of the time when Joseph Jefferson allowed me to touch his face and hands as he went through some of the gestures and speeches of his beloved Rip Van Winkle. I was able to catch thus a meager glimpse of the world of drama, and I shall never forget the delight of that moment. But, oh, how much I must miss, and how much pleasure you seeing ones can derive from watching and hearing the interplay of speech and movement in the unfolding of a dramatic performance! If I could see only one play, I should know how to picture in my mind the action of a hundred plays which I have read or had transferred to me through the medium of the manual alphabet.

29   So, through the evening of my second imaginary day of sight, the great figures of dramatic literature would crowd sleep from my eyes.

30   The following morning, I should again greet the dawn, anxious to discover new delights, for I am sure that, for those who have eyes which really see, the dawn of each day must be a perpetually new revelation of beauty.

31   This, according to the terms of my imagined miracle, is to be my third and last day of sight. I shall have no time to waste in regrets or longings; there is too much to see. The first day I devoted to my friends, animate and inanimate. The second revealed to me the history of man and Nature. Today I shall spend in the workaday world of the present, amid the haunts of men going about the business of life. And where can one find so many activities and conditions of men as in New York? So the city becomes my destination.

32   I start from my home in the quiet little suburb of Forest Hills, Long Island. Here, surrounded by green lawns, tree, and flowers, are neat little houses, happy with the voices and movements of wives and children, havens of peaceful rest for men who toil in the city. I drive across the lacy structure of steel which spans the East River, and I get a new and startling vision of the power and ingenuity of the mind of man. Busy boats chug and scurry about the river—racy speedboats, stolid, snorting tugs. If I had long days of sight ahead, I should spend many of them watching the delightful activity upon the river.

33   I look ahead, and before me rise the fantastic towers of New York, a city that seems to have stepped from the pages of a fairy story. What an awe-inspiring sight, these glittering spires, these vast banks of stone and steel—structures such as the gods might build for themselves! This animated picture is a part of the lives of millions of people every day. How many, I wonder, give it so much as a second glance? Very few, I fear. Their eyes are blind to this magnificent sight because it is so familiar to them.

34   I hurry to the top of one of those gigantic structures, the Empire State Building, for there, a short time ago, I "saw" the city below through the eyes of my secretary. I am anxious to compare my fancy with reality. I am sure I should not be disappointed in the panorama spread out before me, for to me it would be a vision of another world.

35   Now I begin my rounds of the city. First, I stand at a busy corner, merely looking at people, trying by sight of them to understand something of their lives. I see smiles, and I am happy. I see determination, and I am proud. I see suffering, and I am compassionate.

36   I stroll down Fifth Avenue. I throw my eyes out of focus so that I see no particular object but only a seething kaleidoscope of color. I am certain that the colors of women's dresses moving in a throng must be a gorgeous spectacle of which I should never tire. But perhaps if I had sight I should be like most other women—too interested in styles and the cut of individual dresses to give much attention to the splendor of color in the mass. And I am convinced, too, that I should become an inveterate window shopper, for it must be a delight to the eye to view the myriad articles of beauty on display.

37   From Fifth Avenue I make a tour of the city—to Park Avenue, to the slums, to factories, to parks where children play. I take a stay-at-home trip abroad by visiting the foreign quarters. Always my eyes are open wide to all the sights of both happiness and misery so that I may probe deep and add to my understanding of how people work and live. My heart is full of the images of people and things. My eye passes lightly over no single trifle; it strives to touch and hold closely each thing its gaze rests upon. Some sights are pleasant, filling the heart with happiness; but some are miserably pathetic. To these latter I do not shut my eyes, for they, too, are part of life. To close the eyes on them is to close the heart and mind.

38   My third day of sight is drawing to an end. Perhaps there are

many serious pursuits to which I should devote the few remaining hours, but I am afraid that on the evening of that last day I should again run away to the theater, to a hilariously funny play, so that I might appreciate the overtones of comedy in the human spirit.

39   At midnight my temporary respite from blindness would cease, and permanent night would close in on me again. Naturally in those three short days I should not have seen all I wanted to see. Only when darkness had again descended upon me should I realize how much I had left unseen. But my mind would be so crowded with glorious memories that I should have little time for regrets. Thereafter the touch of every object would bring a glowing memory of how that object looked.

40   Perhaps this short outline of how I should spend three days of sight does not agree with the program you would set for yourself if you knew that you were about to be stricken blind. I am, however, sure that if you actually faced that fate your eyes would open to things you had never seen before, storing up memories for the long night ahead. You would use your eyes as never before. Everything you saw would become dear to you. Your eyes would touch and embrace every object that came within your range of vision. Then, at last, you would really see, and a new world of beauty would open itself before you.

41   I who am blind can give one hint to those who see—one admonition to those who would make full use of the gift of sight: Use your eyes as if tomorrow you would be stricken blind. And the same method can be applied to the other senses. Hear the music of voices, the song of a bird, the mighty strains of an orchestra, as if you would be stricken deaf tomorrow. Touch each object you want to touch as if tomorrow your tactile sense would fail. Smell the perfume of flowers, taste with relish each morsel, as if tomorrow you could never smell and taste again. Make the most of every sense; glory in all the facets of pleasure and beauty which the world reveals to you through the several means of contact which Nature provides. But of all the senses; I am sure that sight must be the most delightful.

Professions for Women

VIRGINIA WOOLF

Virginia Woolf (1882–1941) was born in London, the daughter of Sir Leslie Stephen, who was renowned for his biographies of Alexander Pope, Samuel Johnson, and others. She received a good education and, in 1912, married the writer Leonard Woolf. They became one of the most celebrated literary couples in England. They were central figures in the Bloomsbury Group of literary figures and artists. The Woolfs also founded Hogarth Press, which published not only their own works but the works of many notable British writers.

Woolf wrote a number of innovative novels: *Mrs. Dalloway* (1925), *To the Lighthouse* (1927), *Orlando* (1928), *The Waves* (1931), and *Between the Acts* (1941). She also wrote many essays, both critical and meditative, which were collected, in part, in *The Common Reader* (1925), *The Second Common Reader* (1933), and *The Death of the Moth and Other Essays* (1942), which was published after her suicide in 1941.

The Death of the Moth and Other Essays contains selections from her unpublished essays, short stories, and sketches. "Professions for Women" is based on a speech delivered in 1931 to a society of women professionals that was formed to support the employment of women. Woolf reminisces about her own experiences as a professional writer, especially two barriers that she and all women must overcome. The first barrier she describes as the Angel in the House, which is a personification of the good girl who urges her to "be sympathetic; be tender; flatter; deceive" and above all to never "let anybody guess that you have a mind of your own." Woolf had to drive away that demon so that she could write effective criticism. The second barrier is a feminine reluctance to open her heart and soul in her novels, to release the libido, to say "something about the body, about the passion, which it was unfitting for her as a woman to say." Thus, she charges her audience of women to speak openly and honestly about themselves and to follow the dictates of their own minds by ignoring the whispers of the Angel in the House.

1   When your secretary invited me to come here, she told me that your Society is concerned with the employment of women and she suggested that I might tell you something about my own professional experiences. It is true I am a woman; it is true I am employed; but what professional experiences have I had? It is difficult to say. My profession is literature; and in that profession there are fewer experiences for women than in any other, with the exception of the stage— fewer, I mean, that are peculiar to women. For the road was cut many years ago—by Fanny Burney, by Aphra Behn, by Harriet Martineau, by Jane Austen, by George Eliot—many famous women, and many more unknown and forgotten, have been before me, making the path smooth, and regulating my steps. Thus, when I came to write, there were very few material obstacles in my way. Writing was a reputable and harmless occupation. The family peace was not broken by the scratching of a pen. No demand was made upon the family purse. For ten and sixpence one can buy paper enough to write all the plays of Shakespeare—if one has a mind that way. Pianos and models, Paris, Vienna, and Berlin, masters and mistresses, are not needed by a writer. The cheapness of writing paper is, of course, the reason why women have succeeded as writers before they have succeeded in the other professions.

2   But to tell you my story—it is a simple one. You have only got to figure to yourselves a girl in a bedroom with a pen in her hand. She had only to move that pen from left to right—from ten o'clock to one. Then it occurred to her to do what is simple and cheap enough after all—to slip a few of those pages into an envelope, fix

a penny stamp in the corner, and drop the envelope into the red box at the corner. It was thus that I became a journalist; and my effort was rewarded on the first day of the following month—a very glorious day it was for me—by a letter from an editor containing a cheque for one pound ten shillings and sixpence. But to show you how little I deserve to be called a professional woman, how little I know of the struggles and difficulties of such lives, I have to admit that instead of spending that sum upon bread and butter, rent, shoes and stockings, or butcher's bills, I went out and bought a cat—a beautiful cat, a Persian cat, which very soon involved me in bitter disputes with my neighbors.

3   What could be easier than to write articles and to buy Persian cats with the profits? But wait a moment. Articles have to be about something. Mine, I seem to remember, was about a novel by a famous man. And while I was writing this review, I discovered that if I were going to review books I should need to do battle with a certain phantom. And the phantom was a woman, and when I came to know her better I called her after the heroine of a famous poem. The Angel in the House. It was she who used to come between me and my paper when I was writing reviews. It was she who bothered me and wasted my time and so tormented me that at last I killed her. You who come of a younger and happier generation may not have heard of her—you may not know what I mean by The Angel in the House. I will describe her as shortly as I can. She was intensely sympathetic. She was immensely charming. She was utterly unselfish. She excelled in the difficult arts of family life. She sacrificed herself daily. If there was chicken, she took the leg; if there was a draught she sat in it—in short she was so constituted that she never had a mind or a wish of her own, but preferred to sympathize always with the minds and wishes of others. Above all—I need not say it—she was pure. Her purity was supposed to be her chief beauty— her blushes, her great grace. In those days—the last of Queen Victoria—every house had its Angel. And when I came to write I encountered her with the very first words. The shadow of her wings fell on my page; I heard the rustling of her skirts in the room. Directly, that is to say, I took my pen in my hand to review that novel by a famous man, she slipped behind me and whispered: "My dear, you are a young woman. You are writing about a book that has been written by a man. Be sympathetic; be tender; flatter; deceive; use all the arts and wiles of our sex. Never let anybody guess that

you have a mind of your own. Above all, be pure." And she made as if to guide my pen. I now record the one act for which I take some credit to myself, though the credit rightly belongs to some excellent ancestors of mine who left me a certain sum of money—shall we say five hundred pounds a year?—so that it was not necessary for me to depend solely on charm for my living. I turned upon her and caught her by the throat. I did my best to kill her. My excuse if I were to be had up at a court of law, would be that I acted in self-defence. Had I not killed her she would have killed me. She would have plucked the heart out of my writing. For as I found directly I put pen to paper, you cannot review even a novel without having a mind of your own, without expressing what you think to be the truth about human relations, morality, sex. And all these questions, according to the Angel of the House cannot be dealt with freely and openly by women; they must charm, they must conciliate, they must—to put it bluntly—tell lies if they are to succeed. Thus, whenever I felt the shadow of her wing or the radiance of her halo upon my page, I took up the inkpot and flung it at her. She died hard. Her fictitious nature was of great assistance to her. It is far harder to kill a phantom than a reality. She was always creeping back when I thought I had despatched her. Though I flatter myself that I killed her in the end, the struggle was severe; it took much time that had better have been spent upon learning Greek grammar; or in roaming the world in search of adventures. But it was a real experience; it was an experience that was bound to befall all women writers at that time. Killing the Angel in the House was part of the occupation of a woman writer.

4   But to continue my story. The Angel was dead; what then remained? You may say that what remained was a simple and common object—a young woman in a bedroom with an inkpot. In other words, now that she had rid herself of falsehood, that young woman had only to be herself. Ah, but what is "herself"? I mean, what is a woman? I assure you, I do not know. I do not believe that you know. I do not believe that anybody can know until she has expressed herself in all the arts and professions open to human skill. That indeed is one of the reasons why I have come here—out of respect for you, who are in process of showing us by your experiments what a woman is, who are in process of providing us, by your failures and successes, with that extremely important piece of information.

5   But to continue the story of my professional experiences. I made one pound ten and six by my first review; and I bought a Persian

cat with the proceeds. Then I grew ambitious. A Persian cat is all very well, I said; but a Persian cat is not enough. I must have a motor-car. And it was thus that I became a novelist—for it is a very strange thing that people will give you a motor-car if you will tell them a story. It is a still stranger thing that there is nothing so delightful in the world as telling stories. It is far pleasanter than writing reviews of famous novels. And yet, if I am to obey your secretary and tell you my professional experiences as a novelist, I must tell you about a very strange experience that befell me as a novelist. And to understand it you must try first to imagine a novelist's state of mind. I hope I am not giving away professional secrets if I say that a novelist's chief desire is to be as unconscious as possible. He has to induce in himself a state of perpetual lethargy. He wants life to proceed with the utmost quiet and regularity. He wants to see the same faces, to read the same books, to do the same things day after day, month after month, while he is writing, so that nothing may break the illusion in which he is living—so that nothing may disturb or disquiet the mysterious nosings about, feelings round, darts, dashes, and sudden discoveries of that very shy and illusive spirit, the imagination. I suspect that this state is the same both for men and women. Be that as it may, I want you to imagine me writing a novel in a state of trance. I want you to figure to yourselves a girl sitting with a pen in her hand, which for minutes, and indeed for hours, she never dips into the inkpot. The image that comes to my mind when I think of this girl is the image of a fisherman lying sunk in dreams on the verge of a deep lake with a rod held out over the water. She was letting her imagination sweep unchecked round every rock and cranny of the world that lies submerged in the depths of our unconscious being. Now came the experience that I believe to be far commoner with women writers than with men. The line raced through the girl's fingers. Her imagination had rushed away. It had sought the pools, the depths, the dark places where the largest fish slumber. And then there was a smash. There was an explosion. There was foam and confusion. The imagination had dashed itself against something hard. The girl was roused from her dream. She was indeed in a state of the most acute and difficult distress. To speak without figure, she had thought of something, something about the body, about the passion, which it was unfitting for her as a woman to say. Men, her reason told her, would be shocked. The consciousness of what men will say of a woman who speaks the truth about her passions had roused her from her artist's state of consciousness. She could write no more. The trance was over. Her imagination could work no longer. This I believe to be a very common experience with women writers—they are impeded by the extreme conventionality of the other sex. For though men sensibly allow themselves great freedom in these respects, I doubt that they realize or can control the extreme severity with which they condemn such freedom in women.

6   These then were two very genuine experiences of my own. These were two of the adventures of my professional life. The first—killing the Angel in the House—I think I solved. She died. But the second, telling the truth about my own experiences as a body, I do not think I solved. I doubt that any woman has solved it yet. The obstacles against her are still immensely powerful—and yet they are very diffi-cult to define. Outwardly, what is simpler than to write books? Outwardly, what obstacles are there for a woman rather than for a man? Inwardly, I think, the case is very different; she has still many ghosts to fight, many prejudices to overcome. Indeed it will be a long time still, I think, before a woman can sit down to write a book without finding a phantom to be slain, a rock to be dashed against. And if this is so in literature, the freest of all professions for women, how is it in the new professions which you are now for the first time entering?

7   Those are the questions that I should like, had I time, to ask you. And indeed, if I have laid stress upon these professional experiences of mine, it is because I believe that they are, though in different forms, yours also. Even when the path is nominally open—when there is nothing to prevent a woman from being a doctor, a lawyer, a civil servant—there are many phantoms and obstacles, as I believe, looming in her way. To discuss and define them is I think of great value and importance; for thus only can the labour be shared, the difficulties be solved. But besides this, it is necessary also to discuss the ends and the aims for which we are fighting, for which we are doing battle with these formidable obstacles. Those aims cannot be taken for granted; they must be perpetually questioned and examined. The whole position, as I see it—here in this hall surrounded by women practising for the first time in history I know not how many different professions—is one of extraordinary interest and impor-tance. You have won rooms of your own in the house hitherto exclusively owned by men. You are able, though not without great

labour and effort, to pay the rent. You are earning your five hundred pounds a year. But this freedom is only a beginning; the room is your own, but it is still bare. It has to be furnished; it has to be decorated; it has to be shared. How are you going to furnish it, how are you going to decorate it? With whom are you going to share it, and upon what terms? These, I think are questions of the utmost importance and interest. For the first time in history you are able to ask them; for the first time you are able to decide for yourselves what the answers should be. Willingly would I stay and discuss those questions and answers—but not tonight. My time is up; and I must cease.

How It Feels to Be Colored Me

ZORA NEALE HURSTON

Zora Neale Hurston (1901–1960) was born in Eatonville, Florida. She attended Howard University from 1923 to 1924 but ultimately earned a B.A. degree from Barnard College in 1928. Though she lived principally in Fort Pierce, Florida, she traveled extensively and held a variety of jobs—librarian at the Library of Congress, instructor of drama at Bethune-Cookman College and at North Carolina College for Negroes (now known as North Carolina Central University), staff writer at Paramount Studios, and as assistant to the writer Fannie Hurst.

While at Barnard College, Hurston studied anthropology under Franz Boas, who encouraged her to study black mythology. She plunged into the task with zeal. Her folklore study, *Mules and Men* (1935), featured in introduction by Boas. Her novels also provide insight into black myth and legend, especially *Their Eyes Were Watching God* (1937) and *Moses, Man of the Mountain* (1939).

Hurston wrote "How It Feels to Be Colored Me" in 1928 while completing her studies at Barnard. She describes the day when she came to understand that she was black. For thirteen years she lived in Eatonville, Florida, the first all-black incorporated town in the United States. At age thirteen, however, she was sent to Jacksonville, Florida, to care for the young children of her brothers. There, in an integrated community, she discovered what it meant to be black, but she argues, "I do not belong to the sobbing school of Negrohood who hold that nature somehow has given them a lowdown dirty deal and whose feelings are all hurt about it." She argues that most of the time she has no sense of race, "I am *me*."

1   I am colored but I offer nothing in the way of extenuating circumstances except the fact that I am the only Negro in the United States whose grandfather on the mother's side was *not* an Indian chief.

2   I remember the very day that I became colored. Up to my thirteenth year I lived in the little Negro town of Eatonville, Florida. It is exclusively a colored town. The only white people I knew passed through the town going to or coming from Orlando. The native whites rode dusty horses, the Northern tourists chugged down the sandy village road in automobiles. The town knew the Southerners and never stopped cane chewing when they passed. But the Northerners were something else again. They were peered at cautiously from behind curtains by the timid. The more venturesome would come out on the porch to watch them go past and got just as much pleasure out of the tourists as the tourists got out of the village.

3   The front porch might seem a daring place for the rest of the town, but it was a gallery seat for me. My favorite place was atop the gatepost. Proscenium box for a born first-nighter. Not only did I enjoy the show, but I didn't mind the actors knowing that I liked it. I usually spoke to them in passing. I'd wave at them and when they returned my salute, I would say something like this: "Howdy-do-well-I-thank-you-where-you-goin'?" Usually automobile or the horse paused at this, and after a queer exchange of compliments, I would probably "go a piece of the way" with them, as we say in farthest Florida. If one of my family happened to come to the front in time to see me, of course negotiations would be rudely broken off. But even so, it is clear that I was the first "welcome-to-our-state" Floridian, and I hope the Miami Chamber of Commerce will please take notice.

4   During this period, white people differed from colored to me only in that they rode through town and never lived there. They liked to hear me "speak pieces" and sing and wanted to see me dance the parse-me-la, and gave me generously of their small silver for doing these things, which seemed strange to me for I wanted to do them so much that I needed bribing to stop. Only they didn't know it. The

colored people gave no dimes. They deplored any joyful tendencies in me, but I was their Zora nevertheless. I belonged to them, to the nearby hotels, to the county—everybody's Zora.

5   But changes came in the family when I was thirteen, and I was sent to school in Jacksonville. I left Eatonville, the town of the oleanders, as Zora. When I disembarked from the river-boat at Jacksonville, she was no more. It seemed that I had suffered a sea change. I was not Zora of Orange County any more, I was now a little colored girl. I found it out in certain ways. In my heart as well as in the mirror, I became a fast brown—warranted not to rub nor run.

6   But I am not tragically colored. There is no great sorrow dammed up in my soul, nor lurking behind my eyes. I do not mind at all. I do not belong to the sobbing school of Negrohood who hold that nature somehow has given them a lowdown dirty deal and whose feelings are all hurt about it. Even in the helter-skelter skirmish that is my life, I have seen that the world is to the strong regardless of a little pigmentation more or less. No, I do not weep at the world—I am too busy sharpening my oyster knife.

7   Someone is always at my elbow reminding me that I am the granddaughter of slaves. It fails to register depression with me. Slavery is sixty years in the past. The operation was successful and the patient is doing well, thank you. The terrible struggle that made me an American out of a potential slave said "On the line!" The Reconstruction said "Get set!"; and the generation before said "Go!" I am off to a flying start and I must not halt in the stretch to look behind and weep. Slavery is the price I paid for civilization, and the choice was not with me. It is a bully adventure and worth all that I have paid through my ancestors for it. No one on earth ever had a greater chance for glory. The world to be won and nothing to be lost. It is thrilling to think—to know that for any act of mine, I shall get twice as much praise or twice as much blame. It is quite exciting to hold the center of the national stage, with the spectators not knowing whether to laugh or to weep.

8   The position of my white neighbor is much more difficult. No brown specter pulls up a chair beside me when I sit down to eat. No dark ghost thrusts its leg against mine in bed. The game of keeping what one has is never so exciting as the game of getting.

9   I do not always feel colored. Even now I often achieve the unconscious Zora of Eatonville before the Hegira. I feel most colored when I am thrown against a sharp white background.

10   For instance at Barnard. "Beside the waters of the Hudson" I
feel my race. Among the thousand white persons, I am a dark rock
surged upon, and overswept, but through it all, I remain myself.
When covered by the waters, I am; and the ebb but reveals me again.

11   Sometimes it is the other way around. A white person is set down
in our midst, but the contrast is just as sharp for me. For instance, when
I sit in the drafty basement that is The New World Cabaret with a white
person, my color comes. We enter chatting about any little nothing
that we have in common and are seated by the jazz waiters. In the
abrupt way that jazz orchestras have, this one plunges into a number.
It loses no time in circumlocutions, but gets right down to business.
It constricts the thorax and splits the heart with its tempo and narcotic
harmonies. This orchestra grows rambunctious, rears on its hind legs
and attacks the tonal veil with primitive fury, rending it, clawing it until
it breaks through to the jungle beyond. I follow those heathen—follow
them exultingly. I dance wildly inside myself; I yell within, I whoop; I
shake my assegai above my head, I hurl it true to the mark *yeeeeooww!*
I am in the jungle and living in the jungle way. My face is painted red
and yellow and my body is painted blue. My pulse is throbbing like a
war drum. I want to slaughter something—give pain, give death to
what, I do not know. But the piece ends. The men of the orchestra
wipe their lips and rest their fingers. I creep back slowly to the veneer
we call civilization with the last tone and find the white friend sitting
motionless in his seat, smoking calmly.

12   "Good music they have here," he remarks, drumming the table
with his fingertips.

13   Music. The great blobs of purple and red emotion have not touched
him. He has only heard what I felt. He is far away and I see him but
dimly across the ocean and the continent that have fallen between us.
He is so pale with his whiteness then and I am *so* colored.

14   At certain times I have no race, I am *me*. When I set my hat at a
certain angle and saunter down Seventh Avenue, Harlem City, feeling
as snooty as the lions in front of the Forty-Second Street Library,
for instance. So far as my feelings are concerned, Peggy Hopkins
Joyce on the Boule Mich with her gorgeous raiment, stately carriage,
knees knocking together in a most aristocratic manner, has nothing
on me. The cosmic Zora emerges. I belong to no race nor time. I
am the eternal feminine with its string of beads.

15   I have no separate feeling about being an American citizen and colored. I am merely a fragment of the Great Soul that surges within the boundaries. My country, right or wrong.

16   Sometimes, I feel discriminated against, but it does not make me angry. It merely astonishes me. How *can* any deny themselves the pleasure of my company? It's beyond me.

17   But in the main, I feel like a brown bag of miscellany propped against a wall. Against a wall in company with other bags, white, red and yellow. Pour out the contents, and there is discovered a jumble of small things priceless and worthless. A first-water diamond, an empty spool, bits of broken glass, lengths of string, a key to a door long since crumbled away, a rusty knife-blade, old shoes saved for a road that never was and never will be, a nail bent under the weight of things too heavy for any nail, a dried flower or two still a little fragrant. In your hand is the brown bag. On the ground before you is the jumble it held—so much like the jumble in the bags, could they be emptied, that all might be dumped in a single heap and the bags refilled without altering the content of any greatly. A bit of colored glass more or less would not matter. Perhaps that is how the Great Stuffer of Bags filled them in the first place—who knows?

Women: A House Divided

MARGARET MEAD

Margaret Mead (1901–1979) was one of America's most respected anthropologists for more than fifty years. Her book *Coming of Age in Samoa* (1928), which examined the maturation of Samoans from adolescence to adulthood, won great acclaim and launched her career. She taught at Columbia University for many years. Among her other books are *Culture and Commitment* (1970) and *Blackberry Winter: A Memoir* (1972).

"Women: A House Divided," first published in 1970, is a challenge to the women's movement. Mead questions whether women, as they change their roles in the social structure, can find satisfaction. She notes that women can have public roles, private roles, or try to balance the two. As an anthropologist, Mead suggests that, traditionally, "most women put their families first." As a consequence, working mothers must confront their own guilt and criticism from others. Mead argues that the women's movement has one thing working in its favor—time. She suggests that, over several generations, women need to adjust themselves and their children to a new social reality.

1   How far ahead are you thinking?

2   As the demands for immediate changes in women's lives become

more strident and angry, this is a question every woman must ask herself and try to answer honestly. For the time span within which change is projected will make a great difference, I believe. Concentration on the very near future—a decade or two—will certainly bring about some very necessary reforms, but it will also obscure the basic issue—how women will face living in a world in which homemaking and childbearing are no longer the central focus of their lives. Change in our time can be only a step toward preparing our daughters and our daughters' daughters to think and act in new ways.

3   There are other questions as well.

4   Married or single, working or not working today, women must begin to think in terms of a basic choice: Public role and private role—which is the more important? In an emergency which would you sacrifice? If your child was sick or unhappy, would you leave him in someone else's care, as a man must do? If your husband's job took him to another country, would you give up a promising career to go with him? Would you go far away from friends and relatives for your career?

5   However important, responsible and fulfilling a woman's work may be, the answer is quite predictable. Most women put their families first. And few will think them wrong. This is the choice women have been brought up to make and men have been taught to expect. It is the unusual woman, the woman wholly committed to her career or an impersonal goal, on whom criticism descends.

6   Up to the present the dilemma is one most women have managed to avoid. One way of doing it has been by defining their work as an adjunct to their personal lives. Even today, when over one third of the women living in husband-wife homes—about 15 million married women—are working, this remains true. The kinds of positions women hold and the money they are paid are, at least in part, a reflection of women's own definitions of the place of work in their lives and of the reciprocal belief among men that giving a woman a career job is a high risk.

7   Only a change in viewpoint will enable women to take full advantage of the opportunities they now are so ardently seeking.

8   Looking ahead, another question each woman must ask herself is: How do you feel about other women?

9   Two generations ago the few women who chose work over a home cared a great deal about feminine solidarity. Set apart from the women who stayed home and the men among whom they

worked, they had need to count on one another. Today, I think, women place far less reliance on other women for friendship or companionship. The picture most women have of a wider world outside the home is one in which they will spend their days together with men. But will they?

10 Women students complain—and rightly so—that women are far underrepresented at the upper level of the academic, the professional and the business world. A principal demand of every feminist group is that women be given equal opportunity with men to rise to the top. But are they prepared for a world in which women are active at every level?

11 Given the choice of a man or a woman, how many girls today would elect to study under a woman? How many women in business would choose to work for another woman? How many wives today willingly trust another woman with the care of their children? How many women enthusiastically accept another woman as a companion for recreation?

12 Perhaps the most valuable aspect of the new women's protest groups is the rediscovery that women can think and work together and find common ground for action. However, the continual fracturing of these groups suggests that women as a group do not easily achieve working solidarity.

13 The point is not that we have to look forward to some new division of the sexes in social life or in the working world. The point is rather that women as individuals want to be treated as people—as full human beings. For the present men are the principal target; it is they who are accused of treating women as second-class citizens. For some they are "the enemy." But we shall become full human beings, I think, only when we ourselves can treat one another as full human beings, worthy of other women's trust and respect.

14 This must include, as well, a new regard for women's traditional occupations, within and outside the home. Otherwise there is a very real danger that we shall lose what is most precious in human life—the ability to give devoted and cherishing care to other human beings—just at the time in human history when it is most imperative that we learn how to expand our capacity for caring and to translate it into ways of protecting the earth itself.

15 Women are in a peculiar position today. On the one hand they downgrade the things they know best how to do. But on the other hand they are extremely unwilling to share with others the tasks they

do in their homes. The truth is, women are trapped in their present conception of a home as a very private place from which everyone but their husbands and children are excluded. How much of a trap it is comes out in the only solution to conflict between home and work many wives and mothers have to offer: Why can't my husband stay home in an emergency? Take care of a sick child for a day? Wait for the plumber? It doesn't occur to them that this is no solution. It would only put a man, instead of a woman, in the position of relinquishing outside responsibilities.

16   Such a solution looks only to the past. As long as a woman's care for her family represented her major social responsibility, her greatest opportunity for achieving a measure of independence and self-expression lay in having a home in which she was the chief executive. This we have achieved. In most American homes there are no mothers-in-law, no daughters-in-law, no maiden aunts or dependent sisters. Even daughters often leave home as soon as they are grown. There are no servants with status. At most there may be a cleaning woman with her own (usually mistaken) ideas of where to set down the ashtrays or how to arrange a bouquet. And now wives and mothers, though they reign supreme, look down on homemaking tasks.

17   By denigrating the tasks that women have done for their families we also have demeaned all those who could replace us in our homes. On this crucial point women's freedom to choose what they will do and women's view of other women are joined.

18   Looking to the future, beyond the day when women long to leave their homes out of discontent, we can find a way to reverse this trend. For then making a home for one's own family or for the family of a woman who has made a different choice will also be a matter of choice. Some women will choose to become engineers and doctors and lawyers and physicists and biochemists. And some will prefer to care for homes and little children. Whether this is a possibility that can be realized depends essentially on women's attitudes *now* toward women's roles as homemakers and caretakers of people. Will a woman biochemist, for instance, learn a new willingness to share her homemaking role with another woman who is professionally trained as a homemaker?

19   As women's sense of their freedom to make choices grows, the importance of what women have done and been in the past will acquire a new visibility. For this reason women have a special responsibility to accord dignity to women's work, to recognize the fact that the fields of women's traditional activities involve high-level skills,

not only drudgery, and to prize those who, given a chance to do so, learn them as professionals.

20   Some forms of so-called women's work, of course, already are highly professionalized. The time has come when homemaking too should move in this direction. It is quite possible that just as today young men are choosing to be teachers of small children—with the greatest future benefit to early-childhood education—so also eventually some men will choose other, formerly feminine caretaking roles as a profession. In another generation it may well be that people will speak not only of "mothering" but also of "fathering" and "parenting" as special talents to be sought out and developed in many individuals.

21   Women's attitudes toward other women are no less important in the redefinition of women's relationships to men, in the development of new styles of work and in the openness each may have to the other's interpretations of phenomena. In the past, distrusting their own abilities and viewpoints, women have been overeager to accept men's judgments or they have been overresistant to any modification of their own judgments about social legislation, the handling of crime, priorities in national goals or the uses made of the earth's resources.

22   But in time, as men and women begin to work together as intellectual equals on the multiple problems of public life, women will have new insights to offer and new solutions to propose. Then the feminine preference for persons, for caretaking and conservation, for intimacy of understanding *combined with* the masculine preference for working with things, for mastery and exploitation, for rational objectivity, can enrich our perceptions of the world. For women this will involve a change of scale; for men, a greater trust in intuitive—subjective—processes.

23   No one can possibly predict how long it will take for partnerships of this kind to come to fruition. Nor can one begin to guess what new viewpoints about human behavior and the nature of civilization will grow out of such new associations of men and women.

24   But I think it is safe to say that the outcome depends on women's willingness to work for immediate change within a framework of more than one generation. What women have to give is not heritable in the sense that it is built into the female organism. It is, instead, learning that has been passed on from mother to child for hundreds of generations. It can be lost by women who deny their past. It can

be distorted by women who deny the realities of a changing world. It can be safely learned and modified by daughters who sense their mothers are moving imaginatively in the direction their children—sons and daughters—will take in making a new social reality, given time.

To Dispel Fears of Live Burial

JESSICA MITFORD

Jessica Mitford was born in 1917 in England to a wealthy and established family. While her brother was sent to Eton, Mitford and her sisters were educated at home by their mother. Nonetheless, she flourished and developed into an outstanding investigative sociologist and a fine writer. She moved to the United States in 1939 and became a citizen in 1944. She has written for such distinguished magazines as *Harper's, McCall's,* and *Atlantic Monthly.* Among her successful books are *Lifeitselfmanship* (1959), *Daughters and Rebels* (1960), and *A Fine Old Conflict* (1977). *Kind and Unusual Punishment* (1973) was Mitford's attempt to expose and denounce the American penal system. However, the book that made her famous was *The American Way of Death* (1963), which is a devastating study of death and burial in the United States.

"To Dispel Fears of Live Burial," which is taken from *The American Way of Death*, shows Mitford's brilliant investigative research and her unique writing style, which is laced with wit, brutal honesty, and unswerving bluntness. Mitford awakens her readers to the process hidden behind closed doors in funeral parlors. Her detailed analysis caused an outcry from morticians across the country but, in truth, had little effect on the processes she described or the public's apathy toward them. Through it all, she set a standard for investigative reporting long before it became the media norm in the 1980s and 1990s.

1   Embalming is indeed a most extraordinary procedure, and one must wonder at the docility of Americans who each year pay hundreds of millions of dollars for its perpetuation, blissfully ignorant of what it is all about, what is done, how it is done. Not one in ten thousand has any idea of what actually takes place. Books on the subject are extremely hard to come by. They are not to be found in most libraries or bookshops.

2   In an era when huge television audiences watch surgical operations in the comfort of their living rooms, when, thanks to the animated cartoon, the geography of the digestive system has become familiar territory even to the nursery school set, in a land where the satisfaction of curiosity about almost all matters is a national pastime, the secrecy surrounding embalming can, surely, hardly be attributed to the inherent gruesomeness of the subject. Custom in this regard has within this century suffered a complete reversal. In the early days of American embalming, when it was performed in the home of the deceased, it was almost mandatory for some relative to stay by the embalmer's side and witness the procedure. Today, family members who might wish to be in attendance would certainly be dissuaded by the funeral director. All others, except apprentices, are excluded by law from the preparation room.

3   A close look at what does actually take place may explain in large measure the undertaker's intractable reticence concerning a procedure that has become his major *raison d'être*. It is possible he fears that public information about embalming might lead patrons to wonder if they really want this service? If the funeral men are loath to discuss the subject outside the trade, the reader may, understandably, be equally loath to go on reading at this point. For those who have the stomach for it, let us part the formaldehyde curtain. . . .

4   The body is first laid out in the undertaker's morgue—or rather, Mr. Jones is reposing in the preparation room—to be readied to bid the world farewell.

5   The preparation room in any of the better funeral establishments has the tiled and sterile look of a surgery, and indeed the embalmer-restorative artist who does his chores there is beginning to adopt the term "dermasurgeon" (appropriately corrupted by some mortician-writers as "demisurgeon") to describe his calling. His equipment, consisting of scalpels, scissors, augers, forceps, clamps, needles, pumps, tubes, bowls and basins, is crudely imitative of the surgeon's as is his technique, acquired in a nine- or twelve-month post-high-

school course in an embalming school. He is supplied by an advanced chemical industry with a bewildering array of fluids, sprays, pastes, oils, powders, creams, to fix or soften tissue, shrink or distend it as needed, dry it here, restore the moisture there. There are cosmetics, waxes and paints to fill the cover features, even plaster of Paris to replace entire limbs. There are ingenious aids to prop and stabilize the cadaver: A Vari-Pose Head Rest, the Edwards Arm and Hand Positioner, the Repose Block (to support the shoulders during the embalming), and the Throop Foot Positioner, which resembles an old-fashioned stocks.

6   Mr. John H. Eckels, president of the Eckels College of Mortuary Science, thus describes the first part of the embalming procedure: "In the hands of a skilled practitioner, this work may be done in a comparatively short time and without mutilating the body other than by slight incision—so slight that it scarcely would cause serious inconvenience if made upon a living person. It is necessary to remove the blood, and doing this not only helps in the disinfecting, but removes the principal cause of disfigurements due to discoloration."

7   Another textbook discusses the all-important time element: "The earlier this is done, the better, for every hour that elapses between death and embalming will add to the problems and complications encountered. . . ." Just how soon should one get going on the embalming? The author tells us, "On the basis of such scanty information made available to this profession through its rudimentary and haphazard system of technical research, we must conclude that the best results are to be obtained if the subject is embalmed before life is completely extinct—that is, before cellular death has occurred. In the average case, this would mean within an hour after somatic death." For those who feel that there is something a little rudimentary, not to say haphazard, about this advice, a comforting thought is offered by another writer. Speaking of fears entertained in early days of premature burial, he points out, "One of the effects of embalming by chemical injection, however, has been to dispel fears of live burial." How true; once the blood is removed, chances of live burial are indeed remote.

8   To return to Mr. Jones, the blood is drained out through the veins and replaced by embalming fluid pumped in through the arteries. As noted in *The Principles and Practices of Embalming*, "Every operator has a favorite injection and drainage point—a fact which becomes a handicap only if he fails or refuses to forsake his favorites when

conditions demand it." Typical favorites are the carotid artery, femoral artery, jugular vein, subclavian vein. There are various choices of embalming fluid. If Flextone is used, it will produce a "mild, flexible rigidity. The skin retains a velvety softness, the tissues are rubbery and pliable. Ideal for women and children." It may be blended with B. and G. Products Company's Lyf-Lyk tint, which is guaranteed to reproduce "nature's own skin texture . . . the velvety appearance of living tissue." Suntone comes in three separate tints: Suntan; Special Cosmetic Tint, a pink shade "especially indicated for young female subjects"; and Regular Cosmetic Tint, moderately pink.

9   About three to six gallons of dyed and perfumed solution of formaldehyde, glycerin, borax, phenol, alcohol and water are soon circulating through Mr. Jones, whose mouth has been sewn together with a "needle directed upward between the upper lip and gum and brought out through the left nostril," with the corners raised slightly "for a more pleasant expression." If he should be bucktoothed, his teeth are cleaned with Bon Ami and coated with colorless nail polish. His eyes, meanwhile, are closed with flesh-tinted eye caps and eye cement.

10   The next step is to have at Mr. Jones with a thing called a trocar. This is a long, hollow needle attached to a tube. It is jabbed into the abdomen, poked around the entrails and chest cavity, the contents of which are pumped out and replaced with "cavity fluid." This done, and the hole in the abdomen sewn up, Mr. Jones's face is heavily creamed (to protect the skin from burns which may be caused by leakage of the chemicals), and he is covered with a sheet and left unmolested for a while. But not for long—there is more, much more, in store for him. He has been embalmed, but not yet restored, and the best time to start the restorative work is eight to ten hours after embalming, when the tissues have become firm and dry.

11   The object of all this attention to the corpse, it must be remembered, is to make it presentable for viewing in an attitude of healthy repose. "Our customs require the presentation of our dead in the semblance of normality . . . unmarred by the ravages of illness, disease or mutilation," says Mr. J. Sheridan Mayer in his *Restorative Art*. This is rather a large order since few people die in the full bloom of health, unravaged by illness and unmarked by some disfigurement. The funeral industry is equal to the challenge: "In some cases the gruesome appearance of a mutilated or disease-ridden subject may be quite discouraging. The task of restoration may seem impossible

and shake the confidence of the embalmer. This is the time for intestinal fortitude and determination. Once the formative work is begun and affected tissues are cleaned or removed, all doubts of success vanish. It is surprising and gratifying to discover the results which may be obtained."

12   The embalmer, having allowed an appropriate interval to elapse, returns to the attack, but now he brings into play the skill and equipment of sculptor and cosmetician. Is a hand missing? Casting one in plaster of Paris is a simple matter. "For replacement purposes, only a cast of the back of the hand is necessary; this is within the ability of the average operator and is quite adequate." If a lip or two, a nose or an ear should be missing, the embalmer has at hand a variety of restorative waxes with which to model replacements. Pores and skin texture are simulated by stippling with a little brush, and over this cosmetics are laid on. Head off? Decapitation cases are rather routinely handled. Ragged edges are trimmed, and head joined to torso with a series of splints, wires and sutures. It is a good idea to have a little something at the neck—a scarf or high collar—when time for viewing comes. Swollen mouth? Cut out tissue as needed from inside the lips. If too much is removed, the surface contour can easily be restored by padding with cotton. Swollen necks and cheeks are reduced by removing tissue through vertical incisions made down each side of the neck. "When the deceased is casketed, the pillow will hide the suture incisions . . . as an extra precaution against leakage, the suture may be painted with liquid sealer."

13   The opposite condition is more likely to present itself—that of emaciation. His hypodermic syringe now loaded with massage cream, the embalmer seeks out and fills the hollowed and sunken areas by injection. In this procedure the backs of the hands and fingers and the under-chin area should not be neglected.

14   Positioning the lips is a problem that recurrently challenges the ingenuity of the embalmer. Closed too tightly, they tend to give a stern, even disapproving expression. Ideally, embalmers feel, the lips should give the impression of being ever so slightly parted, the upper lip protruding slightly for a more youthful appearance. This takes some engineering, however, as the lips tend to drift apart. Lip drift can sometimes be remedied by pushing one or two straight pins through the inner margin of the lower lip and then inserting them between the two front upper teeth. If Mr. Jones happens to have no teeth, the pins can just as easily be anchored in his Armstrong

Face Former and Denture Replacer. Another method to maintain lip closure is to dislocate the lower jaw, which is then held in its new position by a wire run through holes which have been drilled through the upper and lower jaws at the midline. As the French are fond of saying, *il faut souffrir pour être belle.**

15   If Mr. Jones has died of jaundice, the embalming fluid will very likely turn him green. Does this deter the embalmer. Not if he has intestinal fortitude. Masking pastes and cosmetics are heavily laid on, burial garments and casket interiors are color-correlated with particular care, and Jones is displayed beneath rose-colored lights. Friends will say, "How *well* he looks." Death by carbon monoxide, on the other hand, can be rather a good thing from the embalmer's viewpoint: "One advantage is the fact that this type of discoloration is an exaggerated form of a natural pink coloration." This is nice because the healthy glow is already present and needs but little attention.

16   The patching and filling completed, Mr. Jones is now shaved, washed and dressed. Cream-based cosmetic, available in pink, flesh, suntan, brunette and blond, is applied to his hands and face, his hair is shampooed and combed (and, in the case of Mrs. Jones, set), his hands manicured. For the horny-handed son of toil special care must be taken; cream should be applied to remove ingrained grime, and the nails cleaned. "If he were not in the habit of having them manicured in life, trimming and shaping is advised for better appearance—never questioned by kin."

17   Jones is now ready for casketing (this is the present participle of the verb "to casket"). In this operation, his right shoulder should be depressed slightly "to turn the body a bit to the right and soften the appearance of lying flat on the back." Positioning the hands is a matter of importance, and special rubber positioning blocks may be used. The hands should be cupped slightly for a more lifelike, relaxed appearance. Proper placement of the body requires a delicate sense of balance. It should lie as high as possible in the casket, yet not so high that the lid, when lowered, will hit the nose. On the other hand, we are cautioned, placing the body too low "creates the impression that the body is in a box."

18   Jones is next wheeled into the appointed slumber room where a

---

*   It is necessary to suffer to be beautiful.

few last touches may be added—his favorite pipe placed in his hand or, if he was a great reader, a book propped into position. (In the case of little Master Jones a Teddy bear may be clutched.) Here he will hold open house for a few days, visiting hours 10 A.M. to 9 P.M.

Breaking Free

Writing a Woman's Life

CAROLYN HEILBRUN

Carolyn Heilbrun was born in 1926 and earned a B.A. at Wellesley College and both an M.A. and a Ph.D. at Columbia University. She then became a member of Columbia's faculty and gained distinction as a scholar in Victorian and modern British literature. She has also gained recognition for her work in feminist theory, especially with such books as *Reinventing Womanhood* (1981), *Toward a Recognition of Androgyny: Aspects of Male and Female in Literature* (1982), and *Hamlet's Mother and Other Women* (1990). Her 1988 book, *Writing a Woman's Life*, explores the four options for writing about a life: autobiography, fiction, biography, or, in the words of her preface, "the woman may write her own life in advance of living it, unconsciously, and without recognizing or naming the process."

The essay reprinted here is one chapter of *Writing a Woman's Life*. In it, Heilbrun explores her theory that "women write under an assumed name far more often than do men, and have done so since the early nineteenth century." She admits here that she used the pen name "Amanda Cross" to write commercial detective stories, such as *Poetic Justice* (1979), *In the Last Analysis* (1981), *Death in a Tenured Position* (1986), and *The James Joyce Murder* (1987). She used the pseudonym, in part, to avoid censure from her colleagues at Columbia University, but she also did it to create an alter ego and to give herself "another possibility of female destiny" and "an escape from gender." She says the use of a pen name provides a way for women to enact "the dangerous adventures of a woman's life, unconstrained by female propriety." In addition, the pen name gave her secrecy, and, she insists, "secrecy is power."

> [*Marilyn Monroe*] *was a female impersonator; we are all trained to be female impersonators.*
> Gloria Steinem

1   We must recognize what the past suggests: women are well beyond youth when they begin, often unconsciously, to create another story. Not even then do they recognize it as another story. Usually they believe that the obvious reasons for what they are doing are the only ones; only in hindsight, or through a biographer's imaginative eyes, can the concealed story be surmised. I have decided, in order to illustrate the way such a story might be uncovered, to use myself as an example, analyzing the reasons why I adopted and for years kept wholly secret the pseudonym of Amanda Cross, under which, beginning in 1964, I published detective stories. Not until I had been asked repeatedly to account publicly for my decision to write detective novels under a pseudonym did I realize that the explanation I had always offered, and believed, was perhaps insufficient.

2   I have the impression—and I want to emphasize that it is no more than an impression—that, despite a few famous male exceptions, women write under an assumed name far more often than do men, and have done so since the early nineteenth century. Women write under pseudonyms for profound reasons that require scrupulous examination. As Gilbert and Gubar put it, "the [woman's] pseudonym began to function more prominently as a name of power, the mark of a private christening into a second self, a rebirth into linguistic primacy" (1987, 241).

3   Certainly I was not without coldly practical reasons when I decided to write detective novels as Amanda Cross. There was no question in my mind then, nor is there any now, that had those responsible for my promotion to tenure in the English department of the university where I teach known of the novels, they would have counted them heavily against me; I would probably have been rejected. As it

happens, the professor who came up for tenure before me had written several novels—serious ones, not items of "popular culture"—and was turned down, as he supposed then, for being a novelist. I don't intend to analyze the motives behind this harsh response to English professors' forays into fiction, but harsh it is. So the practical reasons for writing under a pseudonym were clear. One had one's "real" identity, and if one chose to indulge in frivolities, however skillful, one did it under another name than that reserved for proper scholarship.

4   I no longer think that this was the whole explanation. I think now that there are layers within layers of significance to a woman's decision to write under a pseudonym, but the most important reason for her doing so is that the woman author is, consciously or not, creating an alter ego as she writes, another possibility of female destiny. So full of anxiety were women, before the current women's movement, when imagining alternate destinies that they wished to hide their authorial identity from prying eyes.

5   Charlotte Brontë, after writing to her publisher that she was "neither man nor woman," went on to say, "I come before you as an author only. It is the sole standard by which you have a right to judge me—the sole ground on which I accept your judgment." She felt, correctly no doubt, that certain scenes she had created that were considered "unfeminine" had been judged so only because she was a woman; a man would have been able to "get away with it." She wished to bring *Villette* out under what Margot Peters calls "the sheltering shadow of an incognito" (Peters, 256, 352). She had, in fact, an overwhelming desire for anonymity. And, indeed, even her best friends secretly, or not so secretly, found her novels "coarse" and unbecoming in their presentation of passion. When Matthew Arnold disliked *Villette* because it was so full of hunger, rebellion, rage, he was at the same time identifying its strengths, but these were unbearably presumptuous in a woman writer.

6   George Sand, too, chose a name other than her own, but, as we have seen, before the pseudonym came male impersonation, the freedom of moving like a boy. George Eliot, too, as we know, sought the safety of anonymity.

7   But what has all this to do with an assistant professor of English in 1964 who was hardly as restricted as those three literary giants? What does a woman setting out in the early 1960s to write a detective story have to do with the problems of women in the nineteenth century, before women had any legal identity or, indeed, any rights

at all? How could someone worried about promotion in a profession, enjoying all the freedoms of action by then won for women, if not quite all the liberties of dress and movement the next decade would bring, compare herself to these women so constrained, so much the prisoners of powerful convention, so lacking a tradition of female accomplishment?

8   I believe that women have long searched, and continue to search, for an identity "other" than their own. Caught in the conventions of their sex, they have sought an escape from gender. A woman author who was not content to expound the titillations of romance, or to live out Freud's family romance, had two means of escape. One was to hide her identity as an author within the shelter of anonymity, the safety of secrecy, to write while protecting the quotidian self leading her appropriate life. The other way was to create in her writings women characters, and sometimes male characters, who might openly enact the dangerous adventures of a woman's life, unconstrained by female propriety. Some, like Charlotte Brontë, did both. George Eliot, whose "significant other," George Henry Lewes, protected her from all assaults from public, publisher, or reviewer, did not re-create new female destinies, but examined with genius and wisdom the life of her times. Willa Cather lived a private life meticulously protected from scrutiny, and, in the words of Louise Bogan, when she was awarded Princeton's first honorary degree to a woman, Cather "well knew that she had accomplished, in the last decade or so, a miracle which would cause any university now extant to forget and forgive her sex" (Schroeter, 126). We know, however, that she dressed as a boy when in college, and was able so successfully to ghostwrite S. S. McClure's autobiography, with its account of male adventures, that not even his family suspected that he had not written it himself. She could neither fit, within the expectations for her sex, into a life that allowed the enactment of her dreams, nor discover in the public sphere a place where she could be wholly herself.

9   We return from this account of great names to the life of a woman in her late thirties in the year 1963. Why did she determine to write a detective novel? It certainly was not because time was hanging heavy on her hands: she had three children under the age of eight, a large dog, newly acquired, a husband who had gone back for his Ph.D. in economics, and a full-time job. Her motives were both clear and clouded. She "knew" then what her "single" motive was:

she had run out of English detective novels, having read them all many times. She felt an enormous need to enter the world of fiction that the English detective-novel writers were no longer providing, or were unable to provide in sufficient numbers. Why not try to write one?

10   Many people have had the same thought; few enough have acted on it, for the very good reason that writing a detective novel is a lot of work, much easier to conceive than to carry through, to abandon than to complete. Only recently have I asked myself whether the urge to write them instead of reading them is, after all, a sufficient explanation, given the circumstances.

11   I believe now that I must have wanted, with extraordinary fervor, to create a space for myself. This was, physically, almost impossible. The cost of renting an apartment in New York City was certainly insignificant then compared to now, but for us the need for each child to have a room took precedence over my needs. I used to notice, visiting in the suburbs where so many of my contemporaries lived in those days (and from which our holdout was considered almost as eccentric as my working), that there would be a den, and a finished basement, and a laundry, and, in fact, a room for everyone but the wife/mother, who, it was assumed, had the whole house. Anne Sexton has written a very good poem about this point, which shocked many people at the time:

Housewife

Some women marry houses.
It's another kind of skin; it has a heart,
a mouth, a liver and bowel movements.
The walls are permanent and pink.
See how she sits on her knees all day,
faithfully washing herself down.
Men enter by force, drawn back like Jonah
into their fleshy mothers.
A woman *is* her mother.
That's the main thing.*

---

*"Housewife" from ALL MY PRETTY ONES. Copyright © 1962 by Anne Sexton. Copyright © renewed 1990 by Linda G. Sexton. Reprinted by permission of Houghton Mifflin Co. All rights reserved.

If there was no space for a woman in the suburban dream house, how unlikely that there would be space in a small city apartment. So I sought, I now guess, psychic space.

12   But I also sought another identity, another role. I sought to create an individual whose destiny offered more possibility than I could comfortably imagine for myself. Charlotte Brontë, that genius, in creating Jane Eyre, was not more hungry or rebellious than I. Our talents are not comparable, but our impulses are. Writing even the most minor of novels, formula fiction as it is called, nonetheless teaches one a great deal about the ways of genius. (It has often occurred to me that all teachers of literature ought to have written and published a work of fiction in order to understand something fundamental about what they teach, but that is another matter.)

13   Many women writers used a male protagonist in their first novels: George Eliot, Charlotte Brontë, Willa Cather, May Sarton, to name a few; and among the famous women who wrote detective stories in what have come to be called the golden twenties, all featured male detectives. Some, later, created women sleuths to act with their male detectives, or instead of them—Christie's Miss Marple. Tey's Miss Pym, Sayers's Harriet Vane; indeed, a number of male detective writers also had temporary female sleuths—and the logical thing for me to have done, looking back, would have been to create a male detective. I do remember trying, very briefly, to do so, and abandoning the attempt with great haste. Here again we have a good surface reason: I simply didn't know enough about how men thought, as opposed to spoke, and I had read enough modern novels written by women but with male protagonists—Nadine Gordimer had recently written one—to know that male sexuality, to go no further, was a problem. And one did not create detectives, even in the dreary 1950s and early 1960s, wholly without sexual thoughts or experience. (Women writers in the nineteenth century had certain minor advantages.) But there was more to it than that. In our post-Freudian days—and mine was a generation that bowed down before Freud and paid constant homage—abandoning one's womanhood fictionally meant exposing oneself to terrible accusations and suspicions, far too risky for one working as hard as I was to maintain a proper wife, mother, role-playing mask. These days, when, I am glad to say, there are many women mystery writers creating sexually active women detectives, both lesbian and hetero, it is hard to think oneself back to that situation, but it was very real indeed.

14   I created a fantasy. Without children, unmarried, unconstrained by the opinions of others, rich and beautiful, the newly created Kate Fansler now appears to me a figure out of never-never land. That she seems less a fantasy figure these days—when she is mainly criticized for drinking and smoking too much, and for having married—says more about the changing mores, and my talents as prophet, than about my intentions at the time. I wanted to give her everything and see what she could do with it. Of course, she set out on a quest (the male plot), she became a knight (the male role), she rescued a (male) princess. Later I found Denise Levertov's lines:

> In childhood dream-play I was always
> the knight or squire, not
> the lady:
> quester, petitioner, win or lose, not
> she who was sought.*

(That Kate had the help of a man is neither here nor there. We all need help. She was dependent not on any male individual but on the New York police force and the D.A.'s office, without which action was impossible.) Kate was gutsy. She also held a few opinions I now consider retrograde (such as her faith in Freud's conviction that the complaints of sexual abuse on the part of his women patients were all fantasy), but she has changed with time, she's learned, and that's all one can ask of anybody.

15   The question I am most often asked is how and why I chose the name "Amanda Cross." This was, or seemed at the time, a matter of no significance. My husband and I had once been stranded in a deserted part of Nova Scotia; while we awaited rescue, we contemplated a road sign reading "MacCharles Cross." My husband, attempting cheer, remarked that if either of us ever wanted a pseudonym, that would be a good one. I remembered that moment in 1963 when I finished my first detective novel, but was told that my book had obviously been written by a woman and that I should use a woman's first name. I chose "Amanda," under the (as it turned out, entirely mistaken) impression that no one since Noel Coward's

---

*Denise Levertov: "Relearning the Alphabet" (excerpt) from POEMS 1968–1972. Copyright © 1970 by Denise Levertov. Reprinted by permission of New Directions Publishing Corporation.

early plays had had that name. In recent years, I have heard many other explanations of my choice of pseudonym: that I stole Agatha Christie's initials; that the word *cross* carries many meanings of conflict, tension, and choice, which I wanted; that the phrase *a-man-da-cross* is not without significance, and so on. I accept all of them, even the one claiming it was after Katherine Hepburn's role of Amanda in *Adam's Rib*. I didn't see that movie until a few years ago, on television. Certainly if I had, the name would have appealed to me for that reason. A word or name must bear, I agree with Coleridge, all the meanings that connotations attach to it.

16   I had a very good reason for secrecy, but as I now perceive, the secrecy itself was wonderfully attractive. Secrecy is power. True, one gives up recognition and publicity and fame, should any be coming one's way, but for me that was not difficult. I do not care for publicity and, because I have a regular paying job, I can afford, as a writer of detective novels, to avoid it. I think that secrecy gave me a sense of control over my destiny that nothing else in my life, in those pre-tenure, pre-women's-movement days, afforded.

17   (I might mention, in passing, that the secret was easily kept, because I told no one other than my husband, my agent, and my publisher. Doris Lessing, in her recent stunt of publishing novels under a pseudonym, the motives for which I shall abjure examining, found that her secret was easily kept because she did not tell any friends or acquaintances; so my instincts were proved right. But there was one awful moment. My first novel was nominated for the Edgar, awarded annually by the Mystery Writers of America for the best first novel. As E. B. White has said, it is a very satisfactory thing to win a prize before a large group of people. But winning would have blown my cover, and I prayed to lose: I was absolutely unambivalent. As it turned out, the prize was won by the first of the Rabbi novels, which was a vast relief to me.)

18   Meanwhile, creating Kate Fansler and her quests, I was recreating myself. Women come to writing, I believe, simultaneously with self-creation. Sand went to Paris and dressed as a boy. Colette was locked in a room by her husband to become his ghostwriter; that was what her self demanded to take the terrible risk of writing. Even when the writing self was strengthened, only after great trouble could she leave her husband and find her own name, a single name, peculiarly marked by both feminine and—because it was her father's name—patriarchal significance.

19   Let me add that for female writers this act of self-creation comes later in life than for such a one as Keats. George Eliot was thirty-eight at the time her first fiction was published. So was Willa Cather. Virginia Woolf was in her thirties. This is by no means a universal rule with women writers, but it is frequent enough to be worth noticing. Acting to confront society's expectations for oneself requires either the mad daring of youth, or the colder determination of middle age. Men tend to move on a fairly predictable path to achievement; women transform themselves only after an awakening. And that awakening is identifiable only in hindsight.

20   There were aspects of my double life that were fun. Before the Amanda Cross secret was out, I found myself corresponding under both identities and, in one instance, writing different letters to the same person under both names. James Sandoe, well-known professor of drama and critic of mystery stories, decided on different occasions to write to Amanda Cross about her novels and to Carolyn Heilbrun about androgyny and her essay on Dorothy Sayers. Eventually I admitted to him the identity of his two correspondents.

21   We are only just beginning, I think, to understand the way autobiography works in fiction, and fiction in autobiography. Consider, for example, the question of mothers in novels. Florence Nightingale, writing of her despair at a life without occupation or purpose, commented on how young women pass their time by reading novels in which "the heroine has generally no family ties (almost invariably no mother), or, if she has, they do not interfere with her entire independence." The heroines of most novels by women have either no mothers, or mothers who are ineffectual and unsatisfactory. Think of George Eliot; think of Jane Austen; think of the Brontës. As a rule, the women in these novels are very lonely; they have no women friends, though they sometimes have a sister who is a friend.

22   What was the function of mothers toward daughters before the current women's movement, before, let us say, 1970? Whatever the drawbacks, whatever the frustrations or satisfactions of the mother's life, her mission was to prepare the daughter to take her place in the patriarchal succession, that is, to marry, to bear children (preferably sons), and to encourage her husband to succeed in the world. But for many women, mothers and daughters alike, there moved in their imaginations dreams of some other life: of personal accomplishment, of the understanding and control of hard facts and complex problems,

of a place in a community where women were in sufficient numbers to render the accomplished woman neither lonely nor an anomaly. Above all, the dream of taking control of one's life without the intrusion of a mother's patriarchal wishes for her daughter, without the danger of injuring the much loved and pitied mother.

23   When, safely hidden behind anonymity, I invented Kate Fansler, I gave her parents, already dead, whom she could freely dislike, and create herself against, although they had been good enough to leave her with a comfortable income. (So Samuel Butler, writing *The Way of All Flesh*, recommended that all children be deserted at birth, wrapped in a generous portion of pound notes.) Carolyn Heilbrun had, in fact, great affection for her parents, great admiration for her father and a sense of affectionate protectiveness toward her mother. But they were conservative people; they could not understand her wish to remake the world and discover the possibility of different destinies for women within it. Amanda Cross could write, in the popular, unimportant form of detective fiction, the destiny she hoped for women, if not exactly, any longer, for herself: the alternate life she wished to inscribe upon the female imagination.

24   It is of the very first importance to realize, however, that Carolyn Heilbrun in 1963 was not dissatisfied with her life. She was not, like Florence Nightingale, or Charlotte Brontë isolated at Haworth, dreaming of some event to rescue her. She believed then, as now, that her life was a full and satisfactory one, with every promise of becoming more so. When she sought psychic space, it was not from personal frustration but rather from a wish, characteristic of almost every woman writer who did not write erotic romances, for more space, less interruption, more possibility of adventure and the companionship of wiser women through these adventures, greater risk and a more fearless affronting of destiny than seemed possible in the 1950s and early 1960s.

25   How much of this wish to transform female destiny was conscious? None of it. I suspect that if I had been told then that my depriving Kate Fansler of parents indicated any ambivalence on my part toward my parents, I would have disputed that conclusion with vigor. All the conscious reasons for writing were good ones; they operated, they were sufficient to explain my actions. Yet the real reasons permitted me, as other women have found ways to permit themselves, to write my own life on a level far below consciousness, making it possible for me to experience what I would not have had the courage

to undertake in full awareness. I think Virginia Woolf, for example, early realized, deeply if unconsciously, that the narratives provided for women were insufficient for her needs. Her life and her works, the equal to any by her contemporaries, have been until recently less studied academically because we quite literally did not have the language, the theory, or the perceptions with which to analyze them. All her novels struggle against narrative and the old perceptions of the world. She felt in herself a powerful need for a love we have come to call maternal, a love that few men are able to offer (outside of romance) and that women have been carefully trained not to seek in other women. Virginia Woolf found a nurturing man to live with, and she found women to love her. She needed to be loved, and she knew it. Most of us women, I think, transform our need to be loved into a need to love, expecting, therefore, of men and of children, more than they, caught in their own lives, can give us. But Woolf, whether from need or genius, or both, knew that when Chloe and Olivia worked side by side in a laboratory, when women had a room of their own and money of their own (which is power), the old story of woman's destiny, the old marriage plot, would give way to another story for women, a quest plot.

26   So women like Carolyn Heilbrun in 1963, and writers of an earlier time, seeking some place outside Freud's family romance, wrote out, under other names or in hidden stories, their revolutionary hopes.

27   Women have long been nameless. They have not been persons. Handed by a father to another man, the husband, they have been objects of circulation, exchanging one name for another. That is why the story of Persephone and Demeter is the story of all women who marry: why death and marriage, as Nancy Miller pointed out in *The Heroine's Text,* were the only two possible ends for women in novels, and were, frequently, the same end. For the young woman died as a subject, ceased as an entity. For this reason, then, women who began to write another story often wrote it under another name. They were inventing something so daring that they could not risk, in their own person, the frightful consequences.

28   Let me return, after these grand statements about famous women and female destiny, to my two names adopted so cavalierly twenty-five years ago. Something happened to both Carolyn and Amanda: the women's movement. Carolyn began writing in a more personal, for her more courageous, manner, recognizing that women could not speak to other women as men had always spoken, as though

from on high. She wrote of herself, she told her own story, she risked exposure; going public was still a chancy thing for a woman, but not as chancy as it had been, because there were more women doing it.

29   And Amanda became more openly courageous too: she wrote of feminist matters, and let her heroine continue to smoke and drink, despite frequent protests from readers. I think too much drinking is a fearful affliction, and I don't smoke, but Kate Fansler has stuck to her martinis and cigarettes as a sort of camouflage for her more revolutionary opinions and actions. For some reason, I was reluctant to reform her, to tell her how to behave. My hope, of course, is that younger women will imitate her, not in smoking and drinking, not necessarily in marrying or declining to have children, but rather in daring to use her security in order to be brave on behalf of other women, and to discover new stories for women. She is, oddly, no longer a fantasy figure but an aging woman who battles despair and, one hopes with a degree of wit and humor, finds in the constant analysis of our ancient patriarchal ways, and in sheer effrontery, a reason to endure.

30   Kate Fansler has aged less rapidly than do mortals, but inexorably. And it is she, rather than the persona "Amanda Cross," who has come to be a presence in my life. When I have not written about her for a while, she makes her presence known. Biographers have sometimes written, as have fiction writers, of the palpable existence of their subjects. I remember reading once that Simenon, when he had ignored Maigret for many months, would find him waiting around corners, silently confronting his creator, demanding incarnation, or at least attention. So it has been with Kate. And when I recently promised not to begin a new detective novel until I had finished another, different kind of book, she would not let me be. So for the first time I wrote short stories about her, told by her niece Leighton Fansler as a kind of Watson. Though I have often thought in the past that I would write no more detective novels, I now think that I shall probably be forced to write them as long as Kate is there to nudge me.

31   Kate Fansler has taught me many things. About marriage, first of all. I could see no reason for her to marry: there was no question of children. But, insisting upon marrying, she taught me that a relationship has a momentum, it must change and develop, and will tend to move toward the point of greatest commitment. I don't wholly understand this, but I accept it, learning that the commitment

of marriage, which I had taken for granted, has its unique force. But it is about aging that she has taught me most. She is still attractive, but no longer beautiful, and unconcerned with her looks. Her clothes she regards as a costume one dons for the role one will play in the public sphere. Her beauty was the only attribute I regretted bestowing, and age has tempered that, although, unlike her creator, she is still a fantasy figure in being eternally slim. But most important, she has become braver as she has aged, less interested in the opinions of those she does not cherish, and has come to realize that she has little to lose, little any longer to risk, that age above all, both for those with children and those without them, is the time when there is very little "they" can do for you, very little reason to fear, or hide, or not attempt brave and important things. Lear said, "I will do such things, what they are yet I know not, but they shall be the terrors of the earth." He said this in impotent rage in his old age, but Kate Fansler has taught me to say it in the bravery and power of age.

Graduation

MAYA ANGELOU

Born Marguerita Johnson in 1928 in St. Louis, Missouri, Maya Angelou spent most of her childhood in Stamps, Arkansas. Angelou studied dance in San Francisco and won a role in a touring troupe of *Porgy & Bess* that visited Europe and Africa for the State Department. Later, she taught dance in Rome and Tel Aviv, and she wrote for newspapers in Cairo and Ghana. Along the way, she developed a fluency in French, Spanish, Italian, Arabic, and Fanti.

Back in the United States, she collaborated with Godfrey Cambridge to produce, direct, and star in *Cabaret for Freedom*. She then starred in Genet's *The Blacks*. For a time, she worked with Martin Luther King, Jr., as northern coordinator for the Southern Christian Leadership Conference. In addition, she wrote and produced a ten-part TV series on traditions of American life.

She has written several autobiographical works, including *I Know Why the Caged Bird Sings* (1970), *Gather Together in My Name* (1974), *Singin' and Swingin' and Gettin' Merry Like Christmas* (1976), *The Heart of a Woman* (1981), *All God's Children Need Traveling Shoes* (1986), and *Wouldn't Take Nothing for My Journey Now* (1994). She also has several books of poetry, including *Just Give Me a Cool Drink of Water 'Fore I Die* (1971), *Oh Pray My Wings Are Gonna Fit Me Well* (1975), *And Still I Rise* (1978), and *Shaker, Why Don't You Sing?* (1983).

"Graduation" appeared in *I Know Why the Caged Bird Sings*. In it she describes her graduation day, a time of joy and celebration but also a time of agony. Angelou displays her anger with the white bureaucrat Donleavy whose demeaning words "fell like bricks around the auditorium and too many settled in my belly." However, her classmate Henry Reed shows the group how to transcend the occasion, enabling her to say, "I was a proud member of the wonderful, beautiful Negro race."

1   The children in Stamps trembled visibly with anticipation. Some adults were excited too, but to be certain, the whole young population had come down with graduation epidemic. Large classes were graduating from both the grammar school and the high school. Even those who were years removed from their own day of glorious release were anxious to help with preparations as a kind of dry run. The junior students who were moving into the vacating classes' chairs were tradition-bound to show their talents for leadership and management. They strutted through the school and around the campus exerting pressure on the lower grades. Their authority was so new that occasionally if they pressed a little too hard it had to be overlooked. After all, next term was coming, and it never hurt a sixth grader to have a play sister in the eighth grade, or a tenth-year student to be able to call a twelfth grader Bubba. So all was endured in a spirit of shared understanding. But the graduating classes themselves were the nobility. Like travelers with exotic destinations on their minds, the graduates were remarkably forgetful. They came to school without their books, or tablets or even pencils. Volunteers fell over themselves to secure replacements for the missing equipment. When accepted, the willing workers might or might not be thanked, and it was of no importance to the pregraduation rites. Even teachers were respectful of the now quiet and aging seniors, and tended to speak to them, if not as equals, as beings only slightly lower than themselves. After tests were returned and grades given, the student body, which acted like an extended family, knew who did well, who excelled, and what piteous ones had failed.

2   Unlike the white high school, Lafayette County Training School distinguished itself by having neither lawn, nor hedges, nor tennis court, nor climbing ivy. Its two buildings (main classrooms, the grade school and home economics) were set on a dirt hill with no fence to limit either its boundaries or those of bordering farms. There was a large expanse to the left of the school which was used alternately

as a baseball diamond or a basketball court. Rusty hoops on the swaying poles represented the permanent recreational equipment, although bats and balls could be borrowed from the P.E. teacher if the borrower was qualified and if the diamond wasn't occupied.

3   Over this rocky area relieved by a few shady tall persimmon trees the graduating class walked. The girls often held hands and no longer bothered to speak to the lower students. There was a sadness about them, as if this old world was not their home and they were bound for higher ground. The boys, on the other hand, had become more friendly, more outgoing. A decided change from the closed attitude they projected while studying for finals. Now they seemed not ready to give up the old school, the familiar paths and classrooms. Only a small percentage would be continuing on to college—one of the South's A & M (agricultural and mechanical) schools, which trained Negro youths to be carpenters, farmers, handymen, masons, maids, cooks and baby nurses. Their future rode heavily on their shoulders, and blinded them to the collective joy that had pervaded the lives of the boys and girls in the grammar school graduating class.

4   Parents who could afford it had ordered new shoes and ready-made clothes for themselves from Sears and Roebuck or Montgomery Ward. They also engaged the best seamstresses to make the floating graduating dresses and to cut down secondhand pants which would be pressed to a military slickness for the important event.

5   Oh, it was important, all right. Whitefolks would attend the ceremony, and two or three would speak of God and home, and the Southern way of life, and Mrs. Parsons, the principal's wife, would play the graduation march while the lower-grade graduates paraded down the aisles and took their seats below the platform. The high school seniors would wait in empty classrooms to make their dramatic entrance.

6   In the Store I was the person of the moment. The birthday girl. The center. Bailey had graduated the year before, although to do so he had had to forfeit all pleasures to make up for his time lost in Baton Rouge.

7   My class was wearing butter-yellow piqué dresses, and Momma launched out on mine. She smocked the yoke into tiny crisscrossing puckers, then shirred the rest of the bodice. Her dark fingers ducked in and out of the lemony cloth as she embroidered raised daisies around the hem. Before she considered herself finished she had added a crocheted cuff on the puff sleeves, and a pointy crocheted collar.

8   I was going to be lovely. A walking model of all the various styles of fine hand sewing and it didn't worry me that I was only twelve years old and merely graduating from the eighth grade. Besides, many teachers in Arkansas Negro schools had only that diploma and were licensed to impart wisdom.

9   The days had become longer and more noticeable. The faded beige of former times had been replaced with strong and sure colors. I began to see my classmates' clothes, their skin tones, and the dust that waved off pussy willows. Clouds that lazed across the sky were objects of great concern to me. Their shiftier shapes might have held a message that in my new happiness and with a little bit of time I'd soon decipher. During that period I looked at the arch of heaven so religiously my neck kept a steady ache. I had taken to smiling more often, and my jaws hurt from the unaccustomed activity. Between the two physical sore spots, I suppose I could have been uncomfortable, but that was not the case. As a member of the winning team (the graduating class of 1940) I had outdistanced unpleasant sensations by miles. I was headed for the freedom of open fields.

10   Youth and social approval allied themselves with me and we trammeled memories of slights and insults. The wind of our swift passage remodeled my features. Lost tears were pounded to mud and then to dust. Years of withdrawal were brushed aside and left behind, as hanging ropes of parasitic moss.

11   My work alone had awarded me a top place and I was going to be one of the first called in the graduating ceremonies. On the classroom blackboard, as well as on the bulletin board in the auditorium, there were blue stars and white stars and red stars. No absences, no tardinesses, and my academic work was among the best of the year. I could say the preamble to the Constitution even faster than Bailey. We timed ourselves often: "Wethepeopleof-theUnitedStatesinordertoformamoreperfectunion . . ." I had memorized the Presidents of the United States from Washington to Roosevelt in chronological as well as alphabetical order.

12   My hair pleased me too. Gradually the black mass had lengthened and thickened, so that it kept at last to its braided pattern, and I didn't have to yank my scalp off when I tried to comb it.

13   Louise and I had rehearsed the exercises until we tired out ourselves. Henry Reed was class valedictorian. He was a small, very black boy with hooded eyes, a long, broad nose and an oddly shaped head. I had admired him for years because each term he and I vied for the

best grades in our class. Most often he bested me, but instead of being disappointed I was pleased that we shared top places between us. Like many Southern Black children, he lived with his grandmother, who was as strict as Momma and as kind as she knew how to be. He was courteous, respectful and soft-spoken to elders, but on the playground he chose to play the roughest games. I admired him. Anyone, I reckoned, sufficiently afraid or sufficiently dull could be polite. But to be able to operate at a top level with both adults and children was admirable.

14   His valedictory speech was entitled "To Be or Not to Be." The rigid tenth-grade teacher had helped him write it. He'd been working on the dramatic stresses for months.

15   The weeks until graduation were filled with heady activities. A group of small children were to be presented in a play about buttercups and daisies and bunny rabbits. They could be heard throughout the building practicing their hops and their little songs that sounded like silver bells. The older girls (nongraduates, of course) were assigned the task of making refreshments for the night's festivities. A tangy scent of ginger, cinnamon, nutmeg and chocolate wafted around the home economics building as the budding cooks made samples for themselves and their teachers.

16   In every corner of the workshop, axes and saws split fresh timber as the woodshop boys made sets and stage scenery. Only the graduates were left out of the general bustle. We were free to sit in the library at the back of the building or look in quite detachedly, naturally, on the measures being taken for our event.

17   Even the minister preached on graduation the Sunday before. His subject was, "Let your light so shine that men will see your good works and praise your Father, Who is in Heaven." Although the sermon was purported to be addressed to us, he used the occasion to speak to backsliders, gamblers and general ne'er-do-wells. But since he had called our names at the beginning of the service we were mollified.

18   Among Negroes the tradition was to give presents to children going only from one grade to another. How much more important this was when the person was graduating at the top of the class. Uncle Willie and Momma had sent away for a Mickey Mouse watch like Bailey's. Louise gave me four embroidered handkerchiefs. (I gave her three crocheted doilies.) Mrs. Sneed, the minister's wife, made me an underskirt to wear for graduation, and nearly

every customer gave me a nickel or maybe even a dime with the instruction "Keep on moving to higher ground," or some such encouragement.

19   Amazingly the great day finally dawned and I was out of bed before I knew it. I threw open the back door to see it more clearly, but Momma said, "Sister, come away from that door and put your robe on."

20   I hoped the memory of that morning would never leave me. Sunlight was itself still young, and the day had none of the insistence maturity would bring it in a few hours. In my robe and barefoot in the backyard, under cover of going to see about my new beans, I gave myself up to the gentle warmth and thanked God that no matter what evil I had done in my life He had allowed me to live to see this day. Somewhere in my fatalism I had expected to die, accidentally, and never have the chance to walk up the stairs in the auditorium and gracefully receive my hard-earned diploma. Out of God's merciful bosom I had won reprieve.

21   Bailey came out in his robe and gave me a box wrapped in Christmas paper. He said he had saved his money for months to pay for it. It felt like a box of chocolates, but I knew Bailey wouldn't save money to buy candy when we had all we could want under our noses.

22   He was as proud of the gift as I. It was a soft-leather-bound copy of a collection of poems by Edgar Allan Poe, or, as Bailey and I called him, "Eap." I turned to "Annabel Lee" and we walked up and down the garden rows, the cool dirt between our toes, reciting the beautifully sad lines.

23   Momma made a Sunday breakfast although it was only Friday. After we finished the blessing, I opened my eyes to find the watch on my plate. It was a dream of a day. Everything went smoothly and to my credit. I didn't have to be reminded or scolded for anything. Near evening I was too jittery to attend to chores, so Bailey volunteered to do all before his bath.

24   Days before, we had made a sign for the Store, and as we turned out the lights Momma hung the cardboard over the doorknob. It read clearly: CLOSED. GRADUATION.

25   My dress fitted perfectly and everyone said that I looked like a sunbeam in it. On the hill, going toward the school, Bailey walked behind with Uncle Willie, who muttered, "Go on, Ju." He wanted him to walk ahead with us because it embarrassed him to have to

walk so slowly. Bailey said he'd let the ladies walk together, and the men would bring up the rear. We all laughed, nicely.

26   Little children dashed by out of the dark like fireflies. Their crepe-paper dresses and butterfly wings were not made for running and we heard more than one rip, dryly, and the regretful "uh uh" that followed.

27   The school blazed without gaiety. The windows seemed cold and unfriendly from the lower hill. A sense of ill-fated timing crept over me, and if Momma hadn't reached for my hand I would have drifted back to Bailey and Uncle Willie, and possibly beyond. She made a few slow jokes about my feet getting cold, and tugged me along to the now-strange building.

28   Around the front steps, assurance came back. There were my fellow "greats," the graduating class. Hair brushed back, legs oiled, new dresses and pressed pleats, fresh pocket handkerchiefs and little handbags, all homesewn. Oh, we were up to snuff, all right. I joined my comrades and didn't even see my family go in to find seats in the crowded auditorium.

29   The school band struck up a march and all classes filed in as had been rehearsed. We stood in front of our seats, as assigned, and on a signal from the choir director, we sat. No sooner had this been accomplished than the band started to play the national anthem. We rose again and sang the song, after which we recited the pledge of allegiance. We remained standing for a brief minute before the choir director and the principal signaled to us, rather desperately I thought, to take our seats. The command was so unusual that our carefully rehearsed and smooth-running machine was thrown off. For a full minute we fumbled for our chairs and bumped into each other awkwardly. Habits change or solidify under pressure, so in our state of nervous tension we had been ready to follow our usual assembly pattern: the American national anthem, then the pledge of allegiance, then the song every Black person I knew called the Negro National Anthem. All done in the same key, with the same passion and most often standing on the same foot.

30   Finding my seat at last, I was overcome with a presentiment of worse things to come. Something unrehearsed, unplanned, was going to happen, and we were going to be made to look bad. I distinctly remember being explicit in the choice of pronoun. It was "we," the graduating class, the unit, that concerned me then.

31   The principal welcomed "parents and friends" and asked the Bap-

tist minister to lead us in prayer. His invocation was brief and punchy, and for a second I thought we were getting back on the high road to right action. When the principal came back to the dais, however, his voice had changed. Sounds always affected me profoundly and the principal's voice was one of my favorites. During assembly it melted and lowed weakly into the audience. It had not been in my plan to listen to him, but my curiosity was piqued and I straightened up to give him my attention.

32   He was talking about Booker T. Washington, our "late great leader," who said we can be as close as the fingers on the hand, etc. . . . Then he said a few vague things about friendship and the friendship of kindly people to those less fortunate than themselves. With that his voice nearly faded, thin, away. Like a river diminishing to a stream and then to a trickle. But he cleared his throat and said, "Our speaker tonight, who is also our friend, came from Texarkana to deliver the commencement address, but due to the irregularity of the train schedule, he's going to, as they say, 'speak and run.' " He said that we understood and wanted the man to know that we were most grateful for the time he was able to give us and then something about how we were willing always to adjust to another's program, and without more ado—"I give you Mr. Edward Donleavy."

33   Not one but two white men came through the door off-stage. The shorter one walked to the speaker's platform, and the tall one moved over to the center seat and sat down. But that was our principal's seat, and already occupied. The dislodged gentleman bounced around for a long breath or two before the Baptist minister gave him his chair, then with more dignity than the situation deserved, the minister walked off the stage.

34   Donleavy looked at the audience once (on reflection, I'm sure that he wanted only to reassure himself that we were really there), adjusted his glasses and began to read from a sheaf of papers.

35   He was glad "to be here and to see the work going on just as it was in the other schools."

36   At the first "Amen" from the audience I willed the offender to immediate death by choking on the word. But Amens and Yes, sir's began to fall around the room like rain through a ragged umbrella.

37   He told us of the wonderful changes we children in Stamps had in store. The Central School (naturally, the white school was Central) had already been granted improvements that would be in use in the fall. A well-known artist was coming from Little Rock to teach art

to them. They were going to have the newest microscopes and chemistry equipment for their laboratory. Mr. Donleavy didn't leave us long in the dark over who made these improvements available to Central High. Nor were we to be ignored in the general betterment scheme he had in mind.

38   He said that he had pointed out to people at a very high level that one of the first-line football tacklers at Arkansas Agricultural and Mechanical College had graduated from good old Lafayette County Training School. Here fewer Amen's were heard. Those few that did break through lay dully in the air with the heaviness of habit.

39   He went on to praise us. He went on to say how he had bragged that "one of the best basketball players at Fisk sank his first ball right here at Lafayette County Training School."

40   The white kids were going to have a chance to become Galileos and Madame Curies and Edisons and Gauguins, and our boys (the girls weren't even in on it) would try to be Jesse Owenses and Joe Louises.

41   Owens and the Brown Bomber were great heroes in our world, but what school official in the white-goddom of Little Rock had the right to decide that those two men must be our only heroes? Who decided that for Henry Reed to become a scientist he had to work like George Washington Carver, as a bootblack, to buy a lousy microscope? Bailey was obviously always going to be too small to be an athlete, so which concrete angel glued to what country seat had decided that if my brother wanted to become a lawyer he had to first pay penance for his skin by picking cotton and hoeing corn and studying correspondence books at night for twenty years?

42   The man's dead words fell like bricks around the auditorium and too many settled in my belly. Constrained by hard-learned manners I couldn't look behind me, but to my left and right the proud graduating class of 1940 had dropped their heads. Every girl in my row had found something new to do with her handkerchief. Some folded the tiny squares into love knots, some into triangles, but most were wadding them, then pressing them flat on their yellow laps.

43   On the dais, the ancient tragedy was being replayed. Professor Parsons sat, a sculptor's reject, rigid. His large, heavy body seemed devoid of will or willingness, and his eyes said he was no longer with us. The other teachers examined the flag (which was draped stage right) or their notes, or the windows which opened on our now-famous playing diamond.

44   Graduation, the hush-hush magic time of frills and gifts and congratulations and diplomas, was finished for me before my name was called. The accomplishment was nothing. The meticulous maps, drawn in three colors of ink, learning and spelling decasyllabic words, memorizing the whole of *The Rape of Lucrece*—it was for nothing. Donleavy had exposed us.

45   We were maids and farmers, handymen and washerwomen, and anything higher that we aspired to was farcical and presumptuous.

46   Then I wished that Gabriel Prosser and Nat Turner had killed all whitefolks in their beds and that Abraham Lincoln had been assassinated before the signing of the Emancipation Proclamation, and that Harriet Tubman had been killed by that blow on her head and Christopher Columbus had drowned in the *Santa María*.

47   It was awful to be Negro and have no control over my life. It was brutal to be young and already trained to sit quietly and listen to charges brought against my color with no chance of defense. We should all be dead. I thought I should like to see us all dead, one on top of the other. A pyramid of flesh with the whitefolks on the bottom, as the broad base, then the Indians with their silly tomahawks and teepees and wigwams and treaties, the Negroes with their mops and recipes and cotton sacks and spirituals sticking out of their mouths. The Dutch children should all stumble in their wooden shoes and break their necks. The French should choke to death on the Louisiana Purchase (1803) while silkworms ate all the Chinese with their stupid pigtails. As a species, we were an abomination. All of us.

48   Donleavy was running for election, and assured our parents that if he won we could count on having the only colored paved playing field in that part of Arkansas. Also—he never looked up to acknowledge the grunts of acceptance—also, we were bound to get some new equipment for the home economics building and the workshop.

49   He finished, and since there was no need to give any more than the most perfunctory thank-you's, he nodded to the men on the stage, and the tall white man who was never introduced joined him at the door. They left with the attitude that now they were off to something really important. (The graduation ceremonies at Lafayette County Training School had been a mere preliminary.)

50   The ugliness they left was palpable. An uninvited guest who wouldn't leave. The choir was summoned and sang a modern arrangement of "Onward, Christian Soldiers," with new words per-

taining to graduates seeking their place in the world. But it didn't work. Elouise, the daughter of the Baptist minister, recited "Invictus," and I could have cried at the impertinence of "I am the master of my fate, I am the captain of my soul."

51 My name had lost its ring of familiarity and I had to be nudged to go and receive my diploma. All my preparations had fled. I neither marched up to the stage like a conquering Amazon, nor did I look in the audience for Bailey's nod of approval. Marguerite Johnson, I heard the name again, my honors were read, there were noises in the audience of appreciation, and I took my place on the stage as rehearsed.

52 I thought about colors I hated: ecrù, puce, lavender, beige and black.

53 There was shuffling and rustling around me, then Henry Reed was giving his valedictory address, "To Be or Not to Be." Hadn't he heard the whitefolks? We couldn't _be_, so the question was a waste of time. Henry's voice came out clear and strong. I feared to look at him. Hadn't he got the message? There was no "nobler in the mind" for Negroes because the world didn't think we had minds, and they let us know it. "Outrageous fortune"? Now, that was a joke. When the ceremony was over I had to tell Henry Reed some things. That is, if I still cared. Not "rub," Henry, "erase." "Ah, there's the erase." Us.

54 Henry had been a good student in elocution. His voice rose on tides of promise and fell on waves of warnings. The English teacher had helped him to create a sermon winging through Hamlet's soliloquy. To be a man, a doer, a builder, a leader, or to be a tool, an unfunny joke, a crusher of funky toadstools. I marveled that Henry could go through with the speech as if we had a choice.

55 I had been listening and silently rebutting each sentence with my eyes closed; then there was a hush, which in an audience warns that something unplanned is happening. I looked up and saw Henry Reed, the conservative, the proper, the A student, turn his back to the audience and turn to us (the proud graduating class of 1940) and sing, nearly speaking,

> "Lift ev'ry voice and sing
> Till earth and heaven ring
> Ring with the harmonies of Liberty . . ."

It was the poem written by James Weldon Johnson. It was the

music composed by J. Rosamond Johnson. It was the Negro national anthem. Out of habit we were singing it.

56   Our mothers and fathers stood in the dark hall and joined the hymn of encouragement. A kindergarten teacher led the small children onto the stage and the buttercups and daisies and bunny rabbits marked time and tried to follow:

> "Stony the road we trod
> Bitter the chastening rod
> Felt in the days when hope, unborn, had died.
> Yet with a steady beat
> Have not our weary feet
> Come to the place for which our fathers sighed?"

57   Every child I knew had learned that song with his ABC's and along with "Jesus Loves Me This I Know." But I personally had never heard it before. Never heard the words, despite the thousands of times I had sung them. Never thought they had anything to do with me.

58   On the other hand, the words of Patrick Henry had made such an impression on me that I had been able to stretch myself tall and trembling and say, "I know not what course others may take, but as for me, give me liberty or give me death."

59   And now I heard, really for the first time:

> "We have come over a way that with tears
> has been watered,
> We have come, treading our path through
> the blood of the slaughtered."*

60   While echoes of the song shivered in the air, Henry Reed bowed his head, said "Thank you," and returned to his place in the line. The tears that slipped down many faces were not wiped away in shame.

61   We were on top again. As always, again. We survived. The depths had been icy and dark, but now a bright sun spoke to our souls. I was no longer simply a member of the proud graduating class of

*"Lift Ev'ry Voice and Sing"—words by James Weldon Johnson and music by J. Rosamond Johnson. Copyright by Edward B. Marks Music Corporation. Used by permission.

1940; I was a proud member of the wonderful, beautiful Negro race.

62   Oh, Black known and unknown poets, how often have your auctioned pains sustained us? Who will compute the lonely nights made less lonely by your songs, or the empty pots made less tragic by your tales?

63   If we were a people much given to revealing secrets, we might raise monuments and sacrifice to the memories of our poets, but slavery cured us of that weakness. It may be enough, however, to have it said that we survive in exact relationship to the dedication of our poets (include preachers, musicians and blues singers).

On Self-Respect

JOAN DIDION

Joan Didion was born in 1934 in Sacramento, California. Didion says that she found comfort in books during her childhood, for she moved with her family constantly from one army base to another during World War II. She gained some of her writing skills by copying passages from Joseph Conrad and Ernest Hemingway. At the University of California at Berkeley, she first published in the campus magazine *Occident*. Later, in New York, she wrote for *Vogue*. She returned to California in 1964 to write a series of columns on social issues for *The Saturday Evening Post*. She gained critical acclaim when these essays were published in 1968 under the title *Slouching Towards Bethlehem*, which makes an allusion to "The Second Coming" by William Butler Yeats, a poem that predicts the future as a frightening, amoral beast slouching towards Bethlehem to be born.

A novelist, essayist, and screenwriter, Didion has lived and worked primarily in California, which provides the setting for her satiric and ironic commentary on the American scene. She collaborated on the movies *A Star Is Born* (1976) and *True Confession* (1981). Her novels include *Play It as It Lays* (1970), *A Book of Common Prayer* (1976), and *Democracy* (1984).

In *Slouching Towards Bethlehem*, Didion is preoccupied with the popular culture of southern California—its turmoil, drugs, passion, and frenzy. Her essay "On Self-Respect" seems to search for an answer to that human frenzy, and she finds it in the concept of good character. The essay begins with her reflections about her failure to be elected to Phi Beta Kappa, the distinguished honor society. The event "marked the end of something, and innocence may well be the word for it." She came to recognize that self-respect did not include the approval of her peers; it did include courage, discipline, and the willingness to accept risk.

1   Once, in a dry season, I wrote in large letters across two pages of a notebook that innocence ends when one is stripped of the delusion that one likes oneself. Although now, some years later, I marvel that a mind on the outs with itself should have nonetheless made painstaking record of its every tremor, I recall with embarrassing clarity the flavor of those particular ashes. It was a matter of misplaced self-respect.

2   I had not been elected to Phi Beta Kappa. This failure could scarcely have been more predictable or less ambiguous (I simply did not have the grades), but I was unnerved by it; I had somehow thought myself a kind of academic Raskolnikov, curiously exempt from the cause-effect relationships which hampered others. Although even the humorless nineteen-year-old that I was must have recognized that the situation lacked real tragic stature, the day that I did not make Phi Beta Kappa nonetheless marked the end of something, and innocence may well be the word for it. I lost the conviction that lights would always turn green for me, the pleasant certainty that those rather passive virtues which had won me approval as a child automatically guaranteed me not only Phi Beta Kappa keys but happiness, honor, and the love of a good man; lost a certain touching faith in the totem power of good manners, clean hair, and proven competence on the Stanford-Binet scale. To such doubtful amulets had my self-respect been pinned, and I faced myself that day with the nonplused apprehension of someone who has come across a vampire and has no crucifix at hand.

3   Although to be driven back upon oneself is an uneasy affair at best, rather like trying to cross a border with borrowed credentials, it seems to me now the one condition necessary to the beginnings of real self-respect. Most of our platitudes notwithstanding, self-deception remains the most difficult deception. The tricks that work on others count for nothing in that very well-lit back alley where one keeps assignations with oneself: no winning smiles will do here, no prettily drawn lists of good intentions. One shuffles flashily but

in vain through one's marked cards—the kindness done for the wrong reason, the apparent triumph which involved no real effort, the seemingly heroic act into which one had been shamed. The dismal fact is that self-respect has nothing to do with the approval of others—who are, after all, deceived easily enough; has nothing to do with reputation, which, as Rhett Butler told Scarlett O'Hara, is something people with courage can do without.

4   To do without self-respect, on the other hand, is to be an unwilling audience of one to an interminable documentary that details one's failings, both real and imagined, with fresh footage spliced in for every screening. *There's the glass you broke in anger, there's the hurt on X's face; watch now, this next scene, the night Y came back from Houston, see how you muff this one.* To live without self-respect is to lie awake some night, beyond the reach of warm milk, phenobarbital, and the sleeping hand on the coverlet, counting up the sins of commission and omission, the trusts betrayed, the promises subtly broken, the gifts irrevocably wasted through sloth or cowardice or carelessness. However long we postpone it, we eventually lie down alone in that notoriously uncomfortable bed, the one we make ourselves. Whether or not we sleep in it depends, of course, on whether or not we respect ourselves.

5   To protest that some fairly improbable people, some people who *could not possibly respect themselves*, seem to sleep easily enough is to miss the point entirely, as surely as those people miss it who think that self-respect has necessarily to do with not having safety pins in one's underwear. There is a common superstition that "self-respect" is a kind of charm against snakes, something that keeps those who have it locked in some unblighted Eden, out of strange beds, ambivalent conversations, and trouble in general. It does not at all. It has nothing to do with the face of things, but concerns instead a separate peace, a private reconciliation. Although the careless, suicidal Julian English in *Appointment in Samarra* and the careless, incurably dishonest Jordan Baker in *The Great Gatsby* seem equally improbable candidates for self-respect, Jordan Baker had it, Julian English did not. With that genius for accommodation more often seen in women than in men, Jordan took her own measure, made her own peace, avoided threats to that peace: "I hate careless people," she told Nick Carraway. "It takes two to make an accident."

6   Like Jordan Baker, people with self-respect have the courage of their mistakes. They know the price of things. If they choose to commit

adultery, they do not then go running, in an access of bad conscience, to receive absolution from the wronged parties; nor do they complain unduly of the unfairness, the undeserved embarrassment, of being named corespondent. In brief, people with self-respect exhibit a certain toughness, a kind of moral nerve; they display what was once called *character,* a quality which, although approved in the abstract, sometimes loses ground to other, more instantly negotiable virtues. The measure of its slipping prestige is that one tends to think of it only in connection with homely children and United States senators who have been defeated, preferably in the primary, for reelection. Nonetheless, character—the willingness to accept responsibility for one's own life—is the source from which self-respect springs.

7   Self-respect is something that our grandparents, whether or not they had it, knew all about. They had instilled in them, young, a certain discipline, the sense that one lives by doing things one does not particularly want to do, by putting fears and doubts to one side, by weighing immediate comforts against the possibility of larger, even intangible, comforts. It seemed to the nineteenth century admirable, but not remarkable, that Chinese Gordon put on a clean white suit and held Khartoum against the Mahdi; it did not seem unjust that the way to free land in California involved death and difficulty and dirt. In a diary kept during the winter of 1846, an emigrating twelve-year-old named Narcissa Cornwall noted coolly: "Father was busy reading and did not notice that the house was being filled with strange Indians until Mother spoke about it." Even lacking any clue as to what Mother said, one can scarcely fail to be impressed by the entire incident: the father reading, the Indians filing in, the mother choosing the words that would not alarm, the child duly recording the event and noting further that those particular Indians were not, "fortunately for us," hostile. Indians were simply part of the *donnée.*

8   In one guise or another, Indians always are. Again, it is a question of recognizing that anything worth having has its price. People who respect themselves are willing to accept the risk that the Indians will be hostile, that the venture will go bankrupt, that the liaison may not turn out to be one in which *every day is a holiday because you're married to me.* They are willing to invest something of themselves; they may not play at all, but when they do play, they know the odds.

9   That kind of self-respect is a discipline, a habit of mind that can never be faked but can be developed, trained, coaxed forth. It was

once suggested to me that, as an antidote to crying, I put my head in a paper bag. As it happens, there is a sound physiological reason, something to do with oxygen, for doing exactly that, but the psychological effect alone is incalculable: it is difficult in the extreme to continue fancying oneself Cathy in *Wuthering Heights* with one's head in a Food Fair bag. There is a similar case for all the small disciplines, unimportant in themselves; imagine maintaining any kind of swoon, commiserative or carnal, in a cold shower.

10   But those small disciplines are available only insofar as they represent larger ones. To say that Waterloo was won on the playing fields of Eton is not to say that Napoleon might have been saved by a crash program in cricket; to give formal dinners in the rain forest would be pointless did not the candlelight flickering on the liana call forth deeper, stronger disciplines, values instilled long before. It is a kind of ritual, helping us to remember who and what we are. In order to remember it, one must have known it.

11   To have that sense of one's intrinsic worth which constitutes self-respect is potentially to have everything: the ability to discriminate, to love and to remain indifferent. To lack it is to be locked within oneself, paradoxically incapable of either love or indifference. If we do not respect ourselves, we are on the one hand forced to despise those who have so few resources as to consort with us, so little perception as to remain blind to our fatal weaknesses. On the other, we are peculiarly in thrall to everyone we see, curiously determined to live out—since our self-image is untenable—their false notions of us. We flatter ourselves by thinking this compulsion to please others an attractive trait: a gist for imaginative empathy, evidence of our willingness to give. *Of course* I will play Francesca to your Paolo, Helen Keller to anyone's Annie Sullivan: no expectation is too misplaced, no role too ludicrous. At the mercy of those we cannot but hold in contempt, we play roles doomed to failure before they are begun, each defeat generating fresh despair at the urgency of divining and meeting the next demand made upon us.

12   It is the phenomenon sometimes called "alienation from self." In its advanced stages, we no longer answer the telephone, because someone might want something; that we could say *no* without drowning in self-reproach is an idea alien to this game. Every encounter demands too much, tears the nerves, drains the will, and the specter of something as small as an unanswered letter arouses such disproportionate guilt that answering it becomes out of the question.

To assign unanswered letters their proper weight, to free us from the expectations of others, to give us back to ourselves—there lies the great, the singular power of self-respect. Without it, one eventually discovers the final turn of the screw: one runs away to find oneself, and finds no one at home.

Ruth's Song (Because She Could Not Sing It)

GLORIA STEINEM

Gloria Steinem was born in 1934 in Toledo, Ohio. She earned a B.A. degree at Smith College and pursued graduate study at the University of Delhi and the University of Calcutta, India. In India, she joined social activists and became a member of a group called Radical Humanists. With members of that group, she witnessed caste riots and gained sympathy for the minority classes. Back in the United States, she began her writing career in New York City as contributing editor to *Glamour* magazine from 1962 to 1969. In 1968, she cofounded *New York* magazine. In 1972, she cofounded and became editor of *Ms.* magazine.

Steinem's political science studies in India gave her a sense of dismay about the wide gulf between the wealthy and the poor and the discrepancies between the lifestyles of various classes—white and black, male and female, privileged and underprivileged. *Ms.* magazine gave her the forum she needed, and she emerged as a powerful pioneer in the feminist movement of the 1970s and 1980s.

Steinem's parents divorced when she was ten, so she assumed responsibility for herself and her mentally ill mother. "Ruth's Song

(Because She Could Not Sing It)" describes Steinem's relationship with her mother. For twenty years, her mother did not receive proper mental health care, and Steinem suggests the reason: "Like women alcoholics who drink in their kitchens while costly programs are constructed for executives who drink, or like the homemakers subdued with tranquilizers while male patients get therapy and personal attention instead, my mother was not an important worker." Yet the reminiscence discloses one important fact: Ruth's song had a strong impact on her daughter.

1   Happy or unhappy, families are all mysterious. We have only to imagine how differently we would be described—and will be, after our deaths—by each of the family members who believe they know us. The only question is, Why are some mysteries more important than others?

2   The fate of my Uncle Ed was a mystery of importance in our family. We lavished years of speculation on his transformation from a brilliant young electrical engineer to the town handyman. What could have changed this elegant, Lincolnesque student voted "Best Dressed" by his classmates to the gaunt, unshaven man I remember? Why did he leave a young son and a first wife of the "proper" class and religion, marry a much less educated woman of the "wrong" religion, and raise a second family in a house near an abandoned airstrip; a house whose walls were patched with metal signs to stop the wind? Why did he never talk about his transformation?

3   For years, I assumed that some secret and dramatic events of a year he spent in Alaska had made the difference. Then I discovered that the trip had come after his change and probably been made because of it. Strangers he worked for as a much-loved handyman talked about him as one more tragedy of the Depression, and it was true that Uncle Ed's father, my paternal grandfather, had lost his money in the stock-market crash and died of (depending on who was telling the story) pneumonia or a broken heart. But the crash of 1929 also had come long after Uncle Ed's transformation. Another theory was that he was afflicted with a mental problem that lasted

most of his life, yet he was supremely competent at his work, led an independent life, and asked for help from no one.

4   Perhaps he had fallen under the spell of a radical professor in the early days of the century, the height of this country's romance with socialism and anarchism. That was the theory of another uncle on my mother's side. I do remember that no matter how much Uncle Ed needed money, he would charge no more for his work than materials plus 10 percent, and I never saw him in anything other than ancient boots and overalls held up with strategic safety pins. Was he really trying to replace socialism-in-one-country with socialism-in-one-man? If so, why did my grandmother, a woman who herself had run for the school board in coalition with anarchists and socialists, mistrust his judgment so much that she left his share of her estate in trust, even though he was over fifty when she died? And why did Uncle Ed seem uninterested in all other political words and acts? Was it true instead that, as another relative insisted, Uncle Ed had chosen poverty to disprove the myths of Jews and money?

5   Years after my uncle's death, I asked a son in his second family if he had the key to this family mystery. No, he said. He had never known his father any other way. For that cousin, there had been no question. For the rest of us, there was to be no answer.

6   For many years I also never imagined my mother any way other than the person she had become before I was born. She was just a fact of life when I was growing up; someone to be worried about and cared for; an invalid who lay in bed with eyes closed and lips moving in occasional response to voices only she could hear; a woman to whom I brought an endless stream of toast and coffee, bologna sandwiches and dime pies, in a child's version of what meals should be. She was a loving, intelligent, terrorized woman who tried hard to clean our littered house whenever she emerged from her private world, but who could rarely be counted on to finish one task. In many ways, our roles were reversed: I was the mother and she was the child. Yet that didn't help her, for she still worried about me with all the intensity of a frightened mother, plus the special fears of her own world full of threats and hostile voices.

7   Even then I suppose I must have known that, years before she was thirty-five and I was born, she had been a spirited, adventurous young woman who struggled out of a working-class family and into college, who found work she loved and continued to do, even after

she was married and my older sister was there to be cared for. Certainly, our immediate family and nearby relatives, of whom I was by far the youngest, must have remembered her life as a whole and functioning person. She was thirty before she gave up her own career to help my father run the Michigan summer resort that was the most practical of his many dreams, and she worked hard there as everything from bookkeeper to bar manager. The family must have watched this energetic, fun-loving, book-loving woman turn into someone who was afraid to be alone, who could not hang on to reality long enough to hold a job, and who could rarely concentrate enough to read a book.

8   Yet I don't remember any family speculation about the mystery of my mother's transformation. To the kind ones and those who liked her, this new Ruth was simply a sad event, perhaps a mental case, a family problem to be accepted and cared for until some natural process made her better. To the less kind or those who had resented her earlier independence, she was a willful failure, someone who lived in a filthy house, a woman who simply would not pull herself together.

9   Unlike the case of my Uncle Ed, exterior events were never suggested as reason enough for her problems. Giving up her own career was never cited as her personal parallel of the Depression. (Nor was there discussion of the Depression itself, though my mother, like millions of others, had made potato soup and cut up blankets to make my sister's winter clothes.) Her fears of dependence and poverty were no match for my uncle's possible political beliefs. The real influence of newspaper editors who had praised her reporting was not taken as seriously as the possible influence of one radical professor.

10   Even the explanation of mental illness seemed to contain more personal fault when applied to my mother. She had suffered her first "nervous breakdown," as she and everyone else called it, before I was born and when my sister was about five. It followed years of trying to take care of a baby, be the wife of a kind but financially irresponsible man with show-business dreams, and still keep her much-loved job as reporter and newspaper editor. After many months in a sanatorium, she was pronounced recovered. That is, she was able to take care of my sister again, to move away from the city and the job she loved, and to work with my father at the isolated rural lake in Michigan he was trying to transform into a resort worthy of the big dance bands of the 1930s.

11   But she was never again completely without the spells of depres-

sion, anxiety, and visions into some other world that eventually were to turn her into the nonperson I remember. And she was never again without a bottle of dark, acrid-smelling liquid she called "Doc Howard's medicine": a solution of chloral hydrate that I later learned was the main ingredient of "Mickey Finns" or "knockout drops," and that probably made my mother and her doctor the pioneers of modern tranquilizers. Though friends and relatives saw this medicine as one more evidence of weakness and indulgence, to me it always seemed an embarrassing but necessary evil. It slurred her speech and slowed her coordination, making our neighbors and my school friends believe she was a drunk. But without it, she would not sleep for days, even a week at a time, and her feverish eyes began to see only that private world in which wars and hostile voices threatened the people she loved.

12   Because my parents had divorced and my sister was working in a faraway city, my mother and I were alone together then, living off the meager fixed income that my mother got from leasing her share of the remaining land in Michigan. I remember a long Thanksgiving weekend spent hanging on to her with one hand and holding my eighth-grade assignment of *Tale of Two Cities* in the other, because the war outside our house was so real to my mother that she had plunged her hand through a window, badly cutting her arm in an effort to help us escape. Only when she finally agreed to swallow the medicine could she sleep, and only then could I end the terrible calm that comes with crisis and admit to myself how afraid I had been.

13   No wonder that no relative in my memory challenged the doctor who prescribed this medicine, asked if some of her suffering and hallucinating might be due to overdose or withdrawal, or even consulted another doctor about its use. It was our relief as well as hers.

14   But why was she never returned even to that first sanatorium? Or to help that might come from other doctors? It's hard to say. Partly, it was her own fear of returning. Partly, it was too little money, and a family's not-unusual assumption that mental illness is an inevitable part of someone's personality. Or perhaps other family members had feared something like my experience when, one hot and desperate summer between the sixth and seventh grade, I finally persuaded her to let me take her to the only doctor from those sanatorium days whom she remembered without fear.

15   Yes, this brusque old man told me after talking to my abstracted,

timid mother for twenty minutes: She definitely belongs in a state hospital. I should put her there right away. But even at that age, *Life* magazine and newspaper exposés had told me what horrors went on inside those hospitals. Assuming there to be no other alternative, I took her home and never tried again.

16   In retrospect, perhaps the biggest reason my mother was cared for but not helped for twenty years was the simplest: Her functioning was not that necessary to the world. Like women alcoholics who drink in their kitchens while costly programs are constructed for executives who drink, or like the homemakers subdued with tranquilizers while male patients get therapy and personal attention instead, my mother was not an important worker. She was not even the caretaker of a very young child, as she had been when she was hospitalized the first time. My father had patiently brought home the groceries and kept our odd household going until I was eight or so and my sister went away to college. Two years later when wartime gas rationing closed his summer resort and he had to travel to buy and sell in summer as well as winter, he said: How can I travel and take care of your mother? How can I make a living? He was right. It was impossible to do both. I did not blame him for leaving once I was old enough to be the bringer of meals and answerer of my mother's questions. ("Has your sister been killed in a car crash?" "Are there German soldiers outside?") I replaced my father, my mother was left with one more way of maintaining a sad status quo, and the world went on undisturbed.

17   That's why our lives, my mother's from forty-six to fifty-three, and my own from ten to seventeen, were spent alone together. There was one sane winter in a house we rented to be near my sister's college in Massachusetts, then one bad summer spent house-sitting in suburbia while my mother hallucinated and my sister struggled to hold down a summer job in New York. But the rest of those years were lived in Toledo where both my mother and father had been born, and on whose city newspapers an earlier Ruth had worked.

18   First we moved into a basement apartment in a good neighborhood. In those rooms behind a furnace, I made one last stab at being a child. By pretending to be much sicker with a cold than I really was, I hoped my mother would suddenly turn into a sane and cheerful woman bringing me chicken soup à la Hollywood. Of course, she could not. It only made her feel worse that she could not. I stopped pretending.

19   But for most of those years, we lived in the upstairs of the house my mother had grown up in and that her parents left her—a deteriorating farmhouse engulfed by the city, with poor but newer houses stacked against it and a major highway a few feet from its sagging front porch. For a while, we could rent the two downstairs apartments to a newlywed factory worker and a local butcher's family. Then the health department condemned our ancient furnace for the final time, sealing it so tight that even my resourceful Uncle Ed couldn't produce illegal heat.

20   In that house, I remember:

21   . . . lying in the bed my mother and I shared for warmth, listening on the early morning radio to the royal wedding of Princess Elizabeth and Prince Philip being broadcast live, while we tried to ignore and thus protect each other from the unmistakable sounds of the factory worker downstairs beating up and locking out his pregnant wife.

22   . . . hanging paper drapes I had bought in the dime store; stacking books and papers in the shape of two armchairs and covering them with blankets; evolving my own dishwashing system (I waited until all the dishes were dirty, then put them in the bathtub); and listening to my mother's high praise for these housekeeping efforts to bring order from chaos, though in retrospect I think they probably depressed her further.

23   . . . coming back from one of the Eagles' Club shows where I and other veterans of a local tap-dancing school made ten dollars a night for two shows, and finding my mother waiting with a flashlight and no coat in the dark cold of the bus stop, worried about my safety walking home.

24   . . . in a good period, when my mother's native adventurousness came through, answering a classified ad together for an amateur acting troupe that performed Biblical dramas in churches, and doing several very corny performances of *Noah's Ark* while my proud mother shook metal sheets backstage to make thunder.

25   . . . on a hot summer night, being bitten by one of the rats that shared our house and its back alley. It was a terrifying night that turned into a touching one when my mother, summoning courage from some unknown reservoir of love, became a calm, comforting parent who took me to a hospital emergency room despite her terror at leaving home.

26   . . . coming home from a local library with the three books a week into which I regularly escaped, and discovering that for once there

was no need to escape. My mother was calmly planting hollyhocks in the vacant lot next door.

27   But there were also times when she woke in the early winter dark, too frightened and disoriented to remember that I was at my usual after-school job, and so called the police to find me. Humiliated in front of my friends by sirens and policemen, I would yell at her—and she would bow her head in fear and say "I'm sorry, I'm sorry, I'm sorry," just as she had done so often when my otherwise-kindhearted father had yelled at her in frustration. Perhaps the worst thing about suffering is that it finally hardens the hearts of those around it.

28   After there were many, many times when I badgered her until her shaking hands had written a small check to cash at the corner grocery and I could leave her alone while I escaped to the comfort of well-heated dime stores that smelled of fresh doughnuts, or to air-conditioned Saturday-afternoon movies that were windows on a very different world.

29   But my ultimate protection was this: I was just passing through, a guest in the house; perhaps this wasn't my mother at all. Though I knew very well that I was her daughter, I sometimes imagined that I had been adopted and that my real parents would find me, a fantasy I've since discovered is common. (If children wrote more and grownups less, being adopted might be seen not only as a fear but also as a hope.) Certainly, I didn't mourn the wasted life of this woman who was scarcely older than I am now. I worried only about the times when she got worse.

30   Pity takes distance and a certainty of surviving. It was only after our house was bought for demolition by the church next door, and after my sister had performed the miracle of persuading my father to give me a carefree time before college by taking my mother with him to California for a year, that I could afford to think about the sadness of her life. Suddenly, I was far away in Washington, living with my sister and sharing a house with several of her friends. While I finished high school and discovered to my surprise that my classmates felt sorry for me because my mother *wasn't* there, I also realized that my sister, at least in her early childhood, had known a very different person who lived inside our mother, an earlier Ruth.

31   She was a woman I met for the first time in a mental hospital near Baltimore, a humane place with gardens and trees where I visited her each weekend of the summer after my first year away in college. Fortunately, my sister hadn't been able to work and be our mother's

caretaker, too. After my father's year was up, my sister had carefully researched hospitals and found the courage to break the family chain.

32   At first, this Ruth was the same abstracted, frightened woman I had lived with all those years; though now all the sadder for being approached through long hospital corridors and many locked doors. But gradually she began to talk about her past life, memories that doctors there must have been awakening. I began to meet a Ruth I had never known.

33   . . . A tall, spirited, auburn-haired high-school girl who loved basketball and reading; who tried to drive her uncle's Stanley Steamer when it was the first car in the neighborhood; who had a gift for gardening and who sometimes, in defiance of convention, wore her father's overalls; a girl with the courage to go to dances even though her church told her that music itself was sinful, and whose sense of adventure almost made up for feeling gawky and unpretty next to her daintier, dark-haired sister.

34   . . . A very little girl, just learning to walk, discovering the body places where touching was pleasurable, and being punished by her mother who slapped her hard across the kitchen floor.

35   . . . A daughter of a handsome railroad-engineer and a school-teacher who felt she had married "beneath her"; the mother who took her two daughters on Christmas trips to faraway New York on an engineer's free railroad pass and showed them the restaurants and theaters they should aspire to—even though they could only stand outside them in the snow.

36   . . . A good student at Oberlin College, whose freethinking traditions she loved, where friends nicknamed her "Billy"; a student with a talent for both mathematics and poetry, who was not above putting an invisible film of Karo syrup on all the john seats in her dormitory the night of a big prom; a daughter who had to return to Toledo, live with her family, and go to a local university when her ambitious mother—who had scrimped and saved, ghostwritten a minister's sermons, and made her daughters' clothes in order to get them to college at all—ran out of money. At home, this Ruth became a part-time bookkeeper in a lingerie shop for the very rich, commuting to classes and listening to her mother's harsh lectures on the security of becoming a teacher; but also a young woman who was still rebellious enough to fall in love with my father, the editor of her university newspaper, a funny and charming young man who was a terrible

student, had no intention of graduating, put on all the campus dances, and was unacceptably Jewish.

37   I knew from family lore that my mother had married my father twice: once secretly, after he invited her to become the literary editor of his campus newspaper, and once a year later in a public ceremony, which some members of both families refused to attend as the "mixed marriage" of its day.

38   And I knew that my mother had gone on to earn a teaching certificate. She had used it to scare away truant officers during the winters when, after my father closed the summer resort for the season, we lived in a house trailer and worked our way to Florida or California and back by buying and selling antiques.

39   But only during those increasingly adventurous weekend outings from the hospital—going shopping, to lunch, to the movies—did I realize that she had taught college calculus for a year in deference to her mother's insistence that she have teaching "to fall back on." And only then did I realize she had fallen in love with newspapers along with my father. After graduating from the university paper, she wrote a gossip column for a local tabloid, under the name "Duncan MacKenzie," since women weren't supposed to do such things, and soon had earned a job as society reporter on one of Toledo's two big dailies. By the time my sister was four or so, she had worked her way up to the coveted position of Sunday editor.

40   It was a strange experience to look into those brown eyes I had seen so often and realize suddenly how much they were like my own. For the first time, I realized that she might really be my mother.

41   I began to think about the many pressures that might have led up to that first nervous breakdown: leaving my sister whom she loved very much with a grandmother whose values my mother didn't share; trying to hold on to a job she loved but was being asked to leave by her husband; wanting very much to go with a woman friend to pursue their own dreams in New York; falling in love with a co-worker at the newspaper who frightened her by being more sexually attractive, more supportive of her work than my father, and perhaps the man she should have married; and finally, nearly bleeding to death with a miscarriage because her own mother had little faith in doctors and refused to get help.

42   Did those months in the sanatorium brainwash her in some Freud-ian or very traditional way into making what were, for her, probably

the wrong choices? I don't know. It almost doesn't matter. Without extraordinary support to the contrary, she was already convinced that divorce was unthinkable. A husband could not be left for another man, and certainly not for a reason as selfish as a career. A daughter could not be deprived of her father and certainly not be uprooted and taken off to an uncertain future in New York. A bride was supposed to be virginal (not "shopworn," as my euphemistic mother would have said), and if your husband turned out to be kind, but innocent of the possibility of a woman's pleasure, then just be thankful for kindness.

43   Of course, other women have torn themselves away from work and love and still survived. But a story my mother told me years later has always symbolized for me the formidable forces arrayed against her.

> "It was early spring, nothing was open yet. There was nobody for miles around. We had stayed at the lake that winter, so I was alone a lot while your father took the car and traveled around on business. You were a baby. Your sister was in school, and there was no phone. The last straw was that the radio broke. Suddenly it seemed like forever since I'd been able to talk with anyone—or even hear the sound of another voice.
>
> "I bundled you up, took the dog, and walked out to the Brooklyn road. I thought I'd walk the four or five miles to the grocery store, talk to some people, and find somebody to drive me back. I was walking along with Fritzie running up ahead in the empty road—when suddenly a car came out of nowhere and down the hill. It hit Fritzie head on and threw him over to the side of the road. I yelled and screamed at the driver, but he never slowed down. He never looked at us. He never even turned his head.
>
> "Poor Fritzie was all broken and bleeding, but he was still alive. I carried him and sat down in the middle of the road, with his head cradled in my arms. I was going to *make* the next car stop and help.

"But no car ever came. I sat there for hours, I don't know how long, with you in my lap and holding Fritzie, who was whimpering and looking up at me for help. It was dark by the time he finally died. I pulled him over to the side of the road and walked back home with you and washed the blood out of my clothes.

"I don't know what it was about that one day—it was like a breaking point. When your father came home, I said: 'From now on, I'm going with you. I won't bother you. I'll just sit in the car. But I can't bear to be alone again.' "

44   I think she told me that story to show she had tried to save herself, or perhaps she wanted to exorcise a painful memory by saying it out loud. But hearing it made me understand what could have turned her into the woman I remember: a solitary figure sitting in the car, perspiring through the summer, bundled up in winter, waiting for my father to come out of this or that antique shop, grateful just not to be alone. I was there, too, because I was too young to be left at home, and I loved helping my father wrap and unwrap the newspaper around the china and small objects he had bought at auctions and was selling to dealers. It made me feel necessary and grown-up. But sometimes it was hours before we came back to the car again and to my mother who was always patiently, silently waiting.

45   At the hospital and later when Ruth told me stories of her past, I used to say, "But why didn't you leave? Why didn't you take the job? Why didn't you marry the other man?" She would always insist it didn't matter, she was lucky to have my sister and me. If I pressed hard enough, she would add, "If I'd left you never would have been born."

46   I always thought but never had the courage to say: *But you might have been born instead.*

47   I'd like to tell you that this story has a happy ending. The best I can do is one that is happier than its beginning.

48   After many months in that Baltimore hospital, my mother lived on her own in a small apartment for two years while I was in college and my sister married and lived nearby. When she felt the old terrors coming back, she returned to the hospital at her own request. She

was approaching sixty by the time she emerged from there and from a Quaker farm that served as a halfway house, but she confounded her psychiatrists' predictions that she would be able to live outside for shorter and shorter periods. In fact, she never returned. She lived more than another twenty years, and for six of them, she was well enough to stay in a rooming house that provided both privacy and company. Even after my sister and her husband moved to a larger house and generously made two rooms into an apartment for her, she continued to have some independent life and many friends. She worked part-time as a "salesgirl" in a china shop; went away with me on yearly vacations and took one trip to Europe with relatives; went to women's club meetings; found a multiracial church that she loved; took meditation courses; and enjoyed many books. She still could not bear to see a sad movie, to stay alone with any of her six grandchildren while they were babies, to live without many tranquilizers, or to talk about those bad years in Toledo. The old terrors were still in the back of her mind, and each day was a fight to keep them down.

49   It was the length of her illness that had made doctors pessimistic. In fact, they could not identify any serious mental problem and diagnosed her only as having "an anxiety neurosis": low self-esteem, a fear of being dependent, a terror of being alone, a constant worry about money. She also had spells of what now would be called agoraphobia, a problem almost entirely confined to dependent women: fear of going outside the house, and incapacitating anxiety attacks in unfamiliar or public places.

50   Would you say, I asked one of her doctors, that her spirit had been broken? "I guess that's as good a diagnosis as any," he said. "And it's hard to mend anything that's been broken for twenty years."

51   But once out of the hospital for good, she continued to show flashes of the different woman inside; one with a wry kind of humor, a sense of adventure, and a love of learning. Books on math, physics, and mysticism occupied a lot of her time. ("Religion," she used to say firmly, "begins in the laboratory.") When she visited me in New York during her sixties and seventies, she always told taxi drivers that she was eighty years old ("so they will tell me how young I look"), and convinced theater ticket sellers that she was deaf long before she really was ("so they'll give us seats in the front row"). She made friends easily, with the vulnerability and charm of a person who feels

entirely dependent on the approval of others. After one of her visits, every shopkeeper within blocks of my apartment would say, "Oh yes, I know your mother!" At home, she complained that people her own age were too old and stodgy for her. Many of her friends were far younger than she. It was as if she were making up for her own lost years.

52   She was also overly appreciative of any presents given to her—and that made giving them irresistible. I loved to send her clothes, jewelry, exotic soaps, and additions to her collection of tarot cards. She loved receiving them, though we both knew they would end up stored in boxes and drawers. She carried on a correspondence in German with our European relatives, and exchanges with many other friends, all written in her painfully slow, shaky handwriting. She also loved giving gifts. Even as she worried about money and figured out how to save pennies, she would buy or make carefully chosen presents for grandchildren and friends.

53   Part of the price she paid for this much health was forgetting. A single reminder of those bad years in Toledo was enough to plunge her into days of depression. There were times when this fact created loneliness for me, too. Only two of us had lived most of my childhood. Now, only one of us remembered. But there were also times in later years when, no matter how much I pled with reporters *not* to inter-view our friends and neighbors in Toledo, *not* to say that my mother had been hospitalized, they published things that hurt her very much and sent her into a downhill slide.

54   On the other hand, she was also her mother's daughter, a person with a certain amount of social pride and pretension, and some of her objections had less to do with depression than false pride. She complained bitterly about one report that we had lived in a house trailer. She finally asked angrily: "Couldn't they at least say 'vacation mobile home'?" Divorce was still a shame to her. She might cheerfully tell friends, "I don't know *why* Gloria says her father and I were divorced—we never were." I think she justified this to herself with the idea that they had gone through two marriage ceremonies, one in secret and one in public, but been divorced only once. In fact, they were definitely divorced, and my father had briefly married someone else.

55   She was very proud of my being a published writer, and we gener-ally shared the same values. After her death, I found a mother-daughter morals quiz I once had written for a women's magazine.

In her unmistakably shaky writing, she had recorded her own answers, her entirely accurate imagination of what my answers would be, and a score that concluded our differences were less than those "normal for women separated by twenty-odd years." Nonetheless, she was quite capable of putting a made-up name on her name tag when going to a conservative women's club where she feared our shared identity would bring controversy or even just questions. When I finally got up the nerve to tell her I was signing a 1972 petition of women who publicly said we had had abortions and were demanding the repeal of laws that made them illegal and dangerous, her only reply was sharp and aimed to hurt back. "Every starlet says she's had an abortion," she said. "It's just a way of getting publicity." I knew she agreed that abortion should be a legal choice, but I also knew she would never forgive me for embarrassing her in public.

56   In fact, her anger and a fairly imaginative ability to wound with words increased in her last years when she was most dependent, most focused on herself, and most likely to need the total attention of others. When my sister made a courageous decision to go to law school at the age of fifty, leaving my mother in a house that not only had many loving teenage grandchildren in it but a kindly older woman as a paid companion besides, my mother reduced her to frequent tears by insisting that this was a family with no love in it, no home-cooked food in the refrigerator; not a real family at all. Since arguments about home cooking wouldn't work on me, my punishment was creative and different. She was going to call up *The New York Times*, she said, and tell them that this was what feminism did: it left old sick women all alone.

57   Some of this bitterness brought on by failing faculties was eventually solved by a nursing home near my sister's house where my mother not only got the twenty-four-hour help her weakening body demanded, but the attention of affectionate nurses besides. She charmed them, they loved her, and she could still get out for an occasional family wedding. If I ever had any doubts about the debt we owe to nurses, those last months laid them to rest.

58   When my mother died just before her eighty-second birthday in a hospital room where my sister and I were alternating the hours in which her heart wound slowly down to its last sounds, we were alone together for a few hours while my sister slept. My mother seemed bewildered by her surroundings and the tubes that invaded her body, but her consciousness cleared long enough for her to say: "I want

to go home. Please take me home." Lying to her one last time, I said I would. "Okay, honey," she said. "I trust you." Those were her last understandable words.

59   The nurses let my sister and me stay in the room long after there was no more breath. She had asked us to do that. One of her many fears came from a story she had been told as a child about a man whose coma was mistaken for death. She also had made out a living will requesting that no extraordinary measures be used to keep her alive, and that her ashes be sprinkled in the same stream as my father's.

60   Her memorial service was in the Episcopalian church that she loved because it fed the poor, let the homeless sleep in its pews, had members of almost every race, and had been sued by the Episcopalian hierarchy for having a woman priest. Most of all, she loved the affection with which its members had welcomed her, visited her at home, and driven her to services. I think she would have liked the Quaker-style informality with which people rose to tell their memories of her. I know she would have loved the presence of many friends. It was to this church that she donated some of her remaining Michigan property in the hope that it could be used as a multiracial camp, thus getting even with those people in the tiny nearby town who had snubbed my father for being Jewish.

61   I think she also would have been pleased with her obituary. It emphasized her brief career as one of the early women journalists and asked for donations to Oberlin's scholarship fund so others could go to this college she loved so much but had to leave.

62   I know I will spend the next years figuring out what her life has left in me.

63   I realize that I've always been more touched by old people than by children. It's the talent and hopes locked up in a failing body that get to me; a poignant contrast that reminds me of my mother, even when she was strong.

64   I've always been drawn to any story of a mother and a daughter on their own in the world. I saw *A Taste of Honey* several times as both a play and a film, and never stopped feeling it. Even *Gypsy* I saw over and over again, sneaking in backstage for the musical and going to the movie as well. I told myself that I was learning the tap-dance routines, but actually my eyes were full of tears.

65   I once fell in love with a man only because we both belonged to that large and secret club of children who had "crazy mothers." We traded stories of the shameful houses to which we could never invite our friends. Before he was born, his mother had gone to jail for her pacifist convictions. Then she married the politically ambitious young lawyer who had defended her, stayed home, and raised many sons. I fell out of love when he confessed that he wished I wouldn't smoke or swear, and he hoped I wouldn't go on working. His mother's plight had taught him self-pity—nothing else.

66   I'm no longer obsessed, as I was for many years, with the fear that I would end up in a house like that one in Toledo. Now, I'm obsessed instead with the things that I could have done for my mother while she was alive, or the things I should have said.

67   I still don't understand why so many, many years passed before I saw my mother as a person and before I understood that many of the forces in her life are patterns women share. Like a lot of daughters, I suppose I couldn't afford to admit that what had happened to my mother was not all personal or accidental, and therefore could happen to me.

68   One mystery has finally cleared. I could never understand why my mother hadn't been helped by Pauline, her mother-in-law; a woman she seemed to love more than her own mother. This paternal grandmother had died when I was five, before my mother's real problems began but long after that "nervous breakdown," and I knew Pauline was once a suffragist who addressed Congress, marched for the vote, and was the first woman member of a school board in Ohio. She must have been a courageous and independent woman, yet I could find no evidence in my mother's reminiscences that Pauline had encouraged or helped my mother toward a life of her own.

69   I finally realized that my grandmother never changed the politics of her own life, either. She was a feminist who kept a neat house for a husband and four antifeminist sons, a vegetarian among five male meat eaters, and a woman who felt so strongly about the dangers of alcohol that she used only paste vanilla; yet she served both meat and wine to the men of the house and made sure their lives and comforts were continued undisturbed. After the vote was won, Pauline seems to have stopped all feminist activity. My mother greatly admired the fact that her mother-in-law kept a spotless house and prepared a week's meals at a time. Whatever her own internal tor-

ments, Pauline was to my mother a woman who seemed able to "do it all." "Whither thou goest, I shall go," my mother used to say to her much-loved mother-in-law, quoting the Ruth of the Bible. In the end, her mother-in-law may have added to my mother's burdens of guilt.

70   Perhaps like many later suffragists, my grandmother was a public feminist and a private isolationist. That may have been heroic in itself, the most she could be expected to do, but the vote and a legal right to work were not the only kind of help my mother needed.

71   The world still missed a unique person named Ruth. Though she longed to live in New York and in Europe, she became a woman who was afraid to take a bus across town. Though she drove the first Stanley Steamer, she married a man who never let her drive.

72   I can only guess what she might have become. The clues are in moments of spirit or humor.

73   After all the years of fear, she still came to Oberlin with me when I was giving a speech there. She remembered everything about its history as the first college to admit blacks and the first to admit women, and responded to students with the dignity of a professor, the accuracy of a journalist, and a charm that was all her own.

74   When she could still make trips to Washington's wealth of libraries, she became an expert genealogist, delighting especially in finding the rogues and rebels in our family tree.

75   Just before I was born, when she had cooked one more enormous meal for all the members of some famous dance band at my father's resort and they failed to clean their plates, she had taken a shotgun down from the kitchen wall and held it over their frightened heads until they had finished the last crumb of strawberry shortcake. Only then did she tell them the gun wasn't loaded. It was a story she told with great satisfaction.

76   Though sex was a subject she couldn't discuss directly, she had a great appreciation of sensuous men. When a friend I brought home tried to talk to her about cooking, she was furious. ("He came out in the kitchen and talked to me about *stew!*") But she forgave him when we went swimming. She whispered, "He has wonderful legs!"

77   On her seventy-fifth birthday, she played softball with her grandsons on the beach, and took pride in hitting home runs into the ocean.

78   Even in the last year of her life, when my sister took her to visit a neighbor's new and luxurious house, she looked at the vertical

stripes of a very abstract painting in the hallway and said, tartly, "Is that the price code?"

79 She worried terribly about being socially accepted herself, but she never withheld her own approval for the wrong reasons. Poverty or style or lack of education couldn't stand between her and a new friend. Though she lived in a mostly white society and worried if I went out with a man of the "wrong" race, just as she had once married a man of the "wrong" religion, she always accepted each person as an individual.

80 "Is he *very* dark?" she once asked worriedly about a friend. But when she met this very dark person, she only said afterward, "What a kind and nice man!"

81 My father was the Jewish half of the family, yet it was my mother who taught me to have pride in that tradition. It was she who encouraged me to listen to a radio play about a concentration camp when I was little. "You should know that this can happen," she said. Yet she did it just enough to teach, never enough to frighten.

82 It was she who introduced me to books and a respect for them, to poetry that she knew by heart, and to the idea that you could never criticize someone unless you "walked miles in their shoes."

83 It was she who sold that Toledo house, the only home she had, with the determination that the money be used to start me in college. She gave both her daughters the encouragement to leave home for four years of independence that she herself had never had.

84 After her death, my sister and I found a journal that she had kept of her one cherished and belated trip to Europe. It was a trip she had described very little when she came home: she always deplored people who talked boringly about their personal travels and showed slides. Nonetheless, she had written a descriptive essay called "Grandma Goes to Europe." She still must have thought of herself as a writer. Yet she showed this long journal to no one.

85 I miss her, but perhaps no more in death than I did in life. Dying seems less sad than having lived too little. But at least we're now asking questions about all the Ruths and all our family mysteries.

86 If her song inspires that, I think she would be the first to say: It was worth the singing.

Femininity

SUSAN
BROWNMILLER

Susan Brownmiller was born in Brooklyn in 1935. She was educated at Cornell University and the Jefferson School of Social Studies. After a brief period as an actress, Brownmiller shifted her attentions to writing and worked at various magazines, including *Newsweek, The Village Voice,* and *Coronet.* She cofounded two organizations: Women Against Pornography and New York Radical Feminists. In 1975, she published *Against Our Will: Men, Women, and Rape,* a book that argues that "rape is nothing more or less than a conscious process of intimidation by which *all men* keep *all women* in a state of fear." The book was serialized in four magazines and became a Book-of-the-Month Club selection. It won immediate awards and propelled her to *Time's* list of Women of the Year for 1975.

Femininity, published in 1984, examines the public view of women, which Brownmiller believes places limitations on all women. In 1989, Brownmiller published *Waverly Place,* a novel about the murder of a mother and her child by a brutal man who had abused them both physically and mentally. She has continued to write nonfiction pieces on feminist issues for a variety of publications.

The essay "Femininity" is an excerpt from her 1984 book of the same title. Brownmiller establishes her tone early by describing men as being like knives or forks, "straight-edged, sharply pronged, and formidable," while women are like spoons, "softly curved" and able to hold the "food in a rounded well." She argues that femininity "is a romantic sentiment, a nostalgic tradition of imposed limitations." Underlying the essay and, for that matter, the book is this thesis: "Femininity pleases men because it makes them appear more masculine by contrast; and, in truth, conferring an extra portion of unearned gender distinction on men, an unchallenged space in which to breathe freely and feel stronger, wiser, more competent, is femininity's special gift.''

We had a game in our house called ''setting the table'' and I was Mother's helper. Forks to the left of the plate, knives and spoons to the right. Placing the cutlery neatly, as I recall, was one of my first duties, and the event was alive with meaning. When a knife or a fork dropped on the floor, that meant a man was unexpectedly coming to dinner. A falling spoon announced the surprise arrival of a female guest. No matter that these visitors never arrived on cue, I had learned a rule of gender identification. Men were straight-edged, sharply pronged and formidable, women were softly curved and held the food in a rounded well. It made perfect sense, like the division of pink and blue that I saw in babies, an orderly way of viewing the world. Daddy, who was gone all day at work and who loved to putter at home with his pipe, tobacco and tool chest, was knife and fork. Mommy and Grandma, with their ample proportions and pots and pans, were grownup soup spoons, large and capacious. And I was a teaspoon, small and slender, easy to hold and just right for pudding, my favorite dessert.

Being good at what was expected of me was one of my earliest projects, for not only was I rewarded, as most children are, for doing things right, but excellence gave pride and stability to my childhood existence. Girls were different from boys, and the expression of that difference seemed mine to make clear. Did my loving, anxious mother, who dressed me in white organdy pinafores and Mary Janes and who cried hot tears when I got them dirty, give me my first instruction? Of course. Did my doting aunts and uncles with their gifts of pretty dolls and miniature tea sets add to my education? Of course. But even without the appropriate toys and clothes, lessons in the art of being feminine lay all around me and I absorbed them all: the fairy tales that were read to me at night, the brightly colored advertisements I pored over in magazines before I learned to decipher the words, the movies I saw, the comic books I hoarded, the radio soap operas I happily followed whenever I had to stay in bed with a cold. I loved being a little girl, or rather I loved being a fairy princess, for that was who I thought I was.

3   As I passed through a stormy adolescence to a stormy maturity, femininity increasingly became an exasperation, a brilliant, subtle esthetic that was bafflingly inconsistent at the same time that it was minutely, demandingly concrete, a rigid code of appearance and behavior defined by do's and don't-do's that went against my rebellious grain. Femininity was a challenge thrown down to the female sex, a challenge no proud, self-respecting young woman could afford to ignore, particularly one with enormous ambition that she nursed in secret, alternately feeding or starving its inchoate life in tremendous confusion.

4   "Don't lose your femininity" and "Isn't it remarkable how she manages to retain her femininity?" had terrifying implications. They spoke of a bottom-line failure so irreversible that nothing else mattered. The pinball machine has registered "tilt," the game had been called. Disqualification was marked on the forehead of a woman whose femininity was lost. No records would be entered in her name, for she had destroyed her birthright in her wretched, ungainly effort to imitate a man. She walked in limbo, this hapless creature, and it occurred to me that one day I might see her when I looked in the mirror. If the danger was so palpable that warning notices were freely posted, wasn't it possible that the small bundle of resentments I carried around in secret might spill out and place the mark on my own forehead? Whatever quarrels with femininity I had I kept to myself; whatever handicaps femininity imposed, they were mine to deal with alone, for there was no women's movement to ask the tough questions, or to brazenly disregard the rules.

5   Femininity, in essence, is a romantic sentiment, a nostalgic tradition of imposed limitations. Even as it hurries forward in the 1980s, putting on lipstick and high heels to appear well dressed, it trips on the ruffled petticoats and hoopskirts of an era gone by. Invariably and necessarily, femininity is something that women had more of in the past, not only in the historic past of prior generations, but in each woman's personal past as well—in the virginal innocence that is replaced by knowledge, in the dewy cheek that is coarsened by age, in the "inherent nature" that a woman seems to misplace so forgetfully whenever she steps out of bounds. Why should this be so? The XX chromosomal message has not been scrambled, the estrogen-dominated hormonal balance is generally as biology

intended, the reproductive organs, whatever use one has made of them, are usually in place, the breasts of whatever size are most often where they should be. But clearly, biological femaleness is not enough.

6　Femininity always demands more. It must constantly reassure its audience by a willing demonstration of difference, even when one does not exist in nature, or it must seize and embrace a natural variation and compose a rhapsodic symphony upon the notes. Suppose one doesn't care to, has other things on her mind, is clumsy or tone-deaf despite the best instruction and training? To fail at the feminine difference is to appear not to care about men, and to risk the loss of their attention and approval. To be insufficiently feminine is viewed as a failure in core sexual identity, or as a failure to care sufficiently about oneself, for a woman found wanting will be appraised (and will appraise herself) as mannish or neutered or simply unattractive, as men have defined these terms.

7　We are talking, admittedly, about an exquisite esthetic. Enormous pleasure can be extracted from feminine pursuits as a creative outlet or purely as relaxation; indeed, indulgence for the sake of fun, or art, or attention, is among femininity's great joys. But the chief attraction (and the central paradox, as well) is the competitive edge that femininity seems to promise in the unending struggle to survive, and perhaps to triumph. The world smiles favorably on the feminine woman: it extends little courtesies and minor privilege. Yet the nature of this competitive edge is ironic, at best, for one works at femininity by accepting restrictions, by limiting one's sights, by choosing an indirect route, by scattering concentration and not giving one's all as a man would to his own, certifiably masculine, interests. It does not require a great leap of imagination for a woman to understand the feminine principle as a grand collection of compromises, large and small, that she simply must make in order to render herself a successful woman. If she has difficulty in satisfying femininity's demands, if its illusions go against her grain, or if she is criticized for her shortcomings and imperfections, the more she will see femininity as a desperate strategy of appeasement, a strategy she may not have the wish or the courage to abandon, for failure looms in either direction.

8　It is fashionable in some quarters to describe the feminine and masculine principles as polar ends of the human continuum, and to sagely profess that both polarities exist in all people. Sun and moon,

yin and yang, soft and hard, active and passive, etcetera, may indeed
be opposites, but a linear continuum does not illuminate the problem.
(Femininity, in all its contrivances, is a very active endeavor.) What,
then, is the basic distinction? The masculine principle is better understood as a driving ethos of superiority designed to inspire straightfor-
ward, confident success, while the feminine principle is composed
of vulnerability, the need for protection, the formalities of compliance
and the avoidance of conflict—in short, an appeal of dependence
and good will that gives the masculine principle its romantic validity
and its admiring applause.

9   Femininity pleases men because it makes them appear more masculine by contrast; and, in truth, conferring an extra portion of unearned
gender distinction on men, an unchallenged space in which to breathe
freely and feel stronger, wiser, more competent, is femininity's special
gift. One could say that masculinity is often an effort to please women,
but masculinity is known to please by displays of mastery and competence while femininity pleases by suggesting that these concerns,
except in small matters, are beyond its intent. Whimsy, unpredictabil-
ity and patterns of thinking and behavior that are dominated by
emotion, such as tearful expressions of sentiment and fear, are
thought to be feminine precisely because they lie outside the established route to success.

10   If in the beginnings of history the feminine woman was defined
by her physical dependency, her inability for reasons of reproductive
biology to triumph over the forces of nature that were the tests of
masculine strength and power, today she reflects both an economic
and emotional dependency that is still considered "natural," romantic and attractive. After an unsettling fifteen years in which many
basic assumptions about the sexes were challenged, the economic
disparity did not disappear. Large numbers of women—those with
small children, those left high and dry after a mid-life divorce—need
financial support. But even those who earn their own living share
a universal need for connectedness (call it love, if you wish). As
unprecedented numbers of men abandon their sexual interest in
women, others, sensing opportunity, choose to demonstrate their
interest through variety and a change in partners. A sociological fact
of the 1980s is that female competition for two scarce
resources—men and jobs—is especially fierce.

11   So it is not surprising that we are currently witnessing a renewed
interest in femininity and an unabashed indulgence in feminine pur-

suits. Femininity serves to reassure men that women need them and care about them enormously. By incorporating the decorative and the frivolous into its definition of style, femininity functions as an effective antidote to the unrelieved seriousness, the pressure of making one's way in a harsh, difficult world. In its mandate to avoid direct confrontation and to smooth over the fissures of conflict, femininity operates as a value system of niceness, a code of thoughtfulness and sensitivity that in modern society is sadly in short supply.

There is no reason to deny that indulgence in the art of feminine illusion can be reassuring to a woman, if she happens to be good at it. As sexuality undergoes some dizzying revisions, evidence that one is a woman "at heart" (the inquisitor's question) is not without worth. Since an answer of sorts may be furnished by piling on additional documentation, affirmation can arise from such identifiable but trivial feminine activities as buying a new eyeliner, experimenting with the latest shade of nail color, or bursting into tears at the outcome of a popular romance novel. Is there anything destructive in this? Time and cost factors, a deflection of energy and an absorption in fakery spring quickly to mind, and they need to be balanced, as in a ledger book, against the affirming advantage.

Where Is the Love?

JUNE JORDAN

June Jordan was born in 1936 in New York City and educated at Barnard College and the University of Chicago. She is a poet, essayist, novelist, biographer, songwriter, and dramatist. She has served as visiting writer-in-residence at several colleges and universities and lectured at many schools. She is currently a professor of Afro-American studies and Women's studies at the University of California, Berkeley.

Her *Civil Wars* (1981), from which "Where Is the Love?" is taken, is a collection of essays, articles, and lectures. Toni Cade Bambara, in a *Ms.* review, calls *Civil Wars* "a chilling but profoundly hopeful vision of living in the USA. Jordan's vibrant spirit manifests itself throughout this collection. . . . What is fundamental to that spirit is caring, commitment, a deep-rooted belief in the sanctity of life."

"Where Is the Love?" began as a speech to the 1978 National Black Writers Conference. It next appeared as an essay in *Essence* magazine and was then included in *Civil Wars*. In the face of prejudice against women and against blacks, she says, "The love devolving from my quest for self-love and self-respect and self-determination must be, as I see it, something you can verify in the ways that I present myself to others, and in the ways that I approach people different from myself." Ultimately, she affirms that she must "learn to love myself well enough to love you (whoever you are)" so that love will be reciprocal and growing.

1   The 1978 National Black Writers Conference at Howard University culminated with an extremely intense public seminar entitled *Feminism and the Black Woman Writer*. This was an historic, unprecedented event tantamount to conceding that, under such a heading, there might be something to discuss! Acklyn Lynch, Sonia Sanchez, Barbara Smith, and myself were the panelists chosen to present papers to the standing room only audience. I had been asked, also, to moderate the proceedings and therefore gave the opening statement, *Where Is the Love?*, which was later published in *Essence* magazine.

2   From phone calls and other kinds of gossip, I knew that the very scheduling of this seminar had managed to divide people into camps prepared for war. Folks were so jumpy, in fact, that when I walked into the theater I ran into several Black feminists and then several Black men who, I suppose, just to be safe, had decided not to speak to anyone outside the immediate circle of supportive friends they had brought with them.

3   The session was going to be hot. Evidently, feminism was being translated into lesbianism, into something interchangeable with lesbianism, and the taboo on feminism, within the Black intellectual community, had long been exceeded in its orthodox severity only by the taboo on the subject of the lesbian. I say within the intellectual Black community, because, minus such terms as *feminist* and *lesbian,* the phenomena of self-directed Black women or the phenomena of Black women loving other women have hardly been uncommon, let alone unbelievable, events to Black people not privy to theoretical strife about correct and incorrect Black experience.

4   This blurring of issues seemed to me incendiary and obnoxious. Once again, the Black woman writer would be lost to view as issues of her sex life claimed public attention at the expense of intellectual and aesthetic focus upon her work. Compared to the intellectual and literary criticism accorded to James Baldwin and Richard Wright, for example, there is damned little attention paid to their bedroom activities. In any case, I do not believe that feminism is a matter, first or last, of sexuality.

5   The seminar was going to be a fight. It was not easy to prepare for this one. From my childhood in Brooklyn I knew that your peers would respect you if you could hurt somebody. Much less obvious was how to elicit respect as somebody who felt and who meant love.

6   I wanted to see if it was possible to say things that people believe they don't want to hear, without having to kick ass and without

looking the fool for holding out your hand. Was there some way to say, to insist on, each, perhaps disagreeable, individual orientation and nonetheless leave the union of Black men and Black women, as a people, intact? I felt that there had to be: If the individual cannot exist then who will be the people?

7   I expected that we, Black panelists and audience, together, would work out a way to deal, even if we didn't want to deal. And that's what happened, at Howard. We did. Nobody walked out. Nobody stopped talking. The session ended because we ran out of time.

* * *

8   As I think about anyone or any thing—whether history or literature or my father or political organizations or a poem or a film—as I seek to evaluate the potentiality, the life-supportive commitment/possibilities of anyone or any thing, the decisive question is, always, *Where is the love?* The energies that flow from hatred, from negative and hateful habits and attitudes and dogma do not promise something good, something I would choose to cherish, to honor with my own life. It is always the love, whether we look to the spirit of Fannie Lou Hamer, or to the spirit of Agostinho Neto, it is always the love that will carry action into positive new places, that will carry your own nights and days beyond demoralization and away from suicide.

9   I am a feminist, and what that means to me is much the same as the meaning of the fact that I am Black: it means that I must undertake to love myself and to respect myself as though my very life depends upon self-love and self-respect. It means that I must everlastingly seek to cleanse myself of the hatred and the contempt that surrounds and permeates my identity, as a woman, and as a Black human being, in this particular world of ours. It means that the achievement of self-love and self-respect will require inordinate, hourly vigilance, and that I am entering my soul into a struggle that will most certainly transform the experience of all the peoples of the earth, as no other movement can, in fact, hope to claim: because the movement into self-love, self-respect, and self-determination is the movement now galvanizing the true, the unarguable majority of human beings everywhere. This movement explicitly demands the testing of the viability of a moral idea: that the health, the legitimacy of any status quo, any governing force, must be measured according to the experiences of those who are, comparatively, powerless. Virtue is not to be discov-

ered in the conduct of the strong vis-à-vis the powerful, but rather it is to be found in our behavior and policies affecting those who are different, those who are weaker, or smaller than we. How do the strong, the powerful, treat children? How do we treat the aged among us? How do the strong and the powerful treat so-called minority members of the body politic? How do the powerful regard women? How do they treat us?

10   Easily you can see that, according to this criterion, the overwhelming reality of power and government and tradition is evil, is diseased, is illegitimate, and deserves nothing from us—no loyalty, no accommodation, no patience, no understanding—except a clear-minded resolve to utterly change this total situation and, thereby, to change our own destiny.

11   As a Black woman, as a Black feminist, I exist, simultaneously, as part of the powerless and as part of the majority peoples of the world in two ways: I am powerless as compared to any man because women, per se, are kept powerless by men/by the powerful; I am powerless as compared to anyone white because Black and Third World peoples are kept powerless by whites/by the powerful. I am the majority because women constitute the majority gender. I am the majority because Black and Third World peoples constitute the majority of life on this planet.

12   And it is here, in this extreme, inviolable coincidence of my status as a Black feminist, my status as someone twice stigmatized, my status as a Black woman who is twice kin to the despised majority of all the human life that there is, it is here, in that extremity, that I stand in a struggle against suicide. And it is here, in this extremity, that I ask, of myself, and of any one who would call me sister, *Where is the love?*

13   The love devolving from my quest for self-love and self-respect and self-determination must be, as I see it, something you can verify in the ways that I present myself to others, and in the ways that I approach people different from myself. How do I reach out to the people I would like to call my sisters and my brothers and my children and my lovers and my friends? If I am a Black feminist serious in the undertaking of self-love, then it seems to me that the legitimate, the morally defensible character of that self-love should be such that I gain and gain and gain in the socio-psychic strength needed so that I may, without fear, be able and willing to love and respect women, for example, who are not like me: women who are not feminists,

women who are not professionals, women who are not as old or as young as I am, women who have neither job nor income, women who are not Black.

14 And it seems to me that the socio-psychic strength that should follow from a morally defensible Black feminism will mean that I become able and willing, without fear, to love and respect all men who are willing and able, without fear, to love and respect me. In short, if the acquirement of my self-determination is part of a worldwide, an inevitable, and a righteous movement, then I should become willing and able to embrace more and more of the whole world, without fear, and also without self-sacrifice.

15 This means that, as a Black feminist, I cannot be expected to respect what somebody else calls self-love if that concept of self-love requires my suicide to any degree. And this will hold true whether that somebody else is male, female, Black, or white. My Black feminism means that you cannot expect me to respect what somebody else identifies as the Good of The People, if that so-called Good (often translated into *manhood* or *family* or *nationalism*) requires the deferral or the diminution of my self-fulfillment. We *are* the people. And, as Black women, we are most of the people, any people, you care to talk about. And, therefore, nothing that is Good for The People is good unless it is good for me, as I determine myself.

16 When I speak of Black feminism, then, I am speaking from an exacerbated consciousness of the truth that we, Black women, huddle together, miserably, on the very lowest levels of the economic pyramid. We, Black women, subsist among the most tenuous and least likely economic conditions for survival.

17 When I speak of Black feminism, then, I am not speaking of sexuality. I am not speaking of heterosexuality or lesbianism or homosexuality or bisexuality; whatever sexuality anyone elects for his or her pursuit is not my business, nor the business of the state. And, furthermore, I cannot be persuaded that one kind of sexuality, as against another, will necessarily provide for the greater happiness of the two people involved. I am not talking about sexuality. I am talking about love, about a steady-state deep caring and respect for every other human being, a love that can only derive from a secure and positive self-love.

18 As a Black woman/feminist, I must look about me, with trembling, and with shocked anger, at the endless waste, the endless suffocation of my sisters: the bitter sufferings of hundreds of thou-

sands of women who are the sole parents, the mothers of hundreds of thousands of children, the desolation and the futility of women trapped by demeaning, lowest-paying occupations, the unemployed, the bullied, the beaten, the battered, the ridiculed, the slandered, the trivialized, the raped, and the sterilized, the lost millions and multimillions of beautiful, creative, and momentous lives turned to ashes on the pyre of gender identity. I must look about me and, as a Black feminist, I must ask myself: *Where is the love?* How is my own lifework serving to end these tyrannies, these corrosions of sacred possibility?

19   As a Black feminist poet and writer I must look behind me with trembling, and with shocked anger, at the fate of Black women writers until now. From the terrible graves of a traditional conspiracy against my sisters in art, I must exhume the works of women writers and poets such as Georgia Douglas Johnson (who?).

20   In the early flush of the Harlem Renaissance, Georgia Johnson accomplished an astonishing, illustrious life experience. Married to Henry Lincoln Johnson, U.S. Recorder of Deeds in Washington, D.C., the poet, in her own right, became no less than Commissioner of Conciliation for the U.S. Department of Labor (*who was that again? Who?*). And she, this poet, furthermore enjoyed the intense, promotional attention of Dean Kelley Miller, here at Howard, and W. E. B. Du Bois, and William Stanley Braithwaite, and Alain Locke. And she published three volumes of her own poetry and I found her work in Countee Cullen's anthology, *Caroling Dusk,* where, Countee Cullen reports, she, Georgia Douglas Johnson, thrived as a kind of Gwendolyn Brooks, holding regular Saturday night get-togethers with the young Black writers of the day.

21   And what did this poet of such acclaim, achievement, connection, and generosity, what did this poet have to say in her poetry, and who among us has ever heard of Georgia Douglas Johnson? And is there anybody in this room who can tell me the name of two or three other women poets from the Harlem Renaissance? And why did she die, and why does the work of all women die with no river carrying forward the record of such grace? How is it the case that whether we have written novels or poetry or whether we have raised our children or cleaned and cooked and washed and ironed, it is all dismissed as "women's work"; it is all, finally, despised as nothing important, and there is no trace, no echo of our days upon the earth?

22   Why is it not surprising that a Black woman as remarkably capable

and gifted and proven as Georgia Douglas Johnson should be the
poet of these pathetic, beggarly lines:

> I'm folding up my little dreams
> within my heart tonight
> And praying I may soon forget
> the torture of their sight
> *"My Little Dreams"*

How long, how long will we let the dreams of women serve merely
to torture and not to ignite, to enflame, and to ennoble the promise
of the years of every lifetime? And here is Georgia Douglas Johnson's
poem "The Heart of a Woman":

> The heart of a woman goes forth with the dawn,
> As a lovebird, softwinging, so restlessly on,
> Afar o'er life's turrets and vales does it roam
> In the wake of those echoes the heart calls home.
>
> The heart of a woman falls back with the night
> And enters some alien cage in its plight,
> And tries to forget it has dreamed of the stars,
> While it breaks, breaks, breaks on the sheltering
>   bars.

23   And it is against such sorrow, and it is against such suicide, and it is
against such deliberated strangulation of the possible lives of women,
of my sisters, and of powerless peoples—men and children—
everywhere, that I work and live, now, as a feminist trusting that I will
learn to love myself well enough to love you (whoever you are), well
enough so that you will love me well enough so that we will know
exactly where is the love: that it is here, between us, and growing
stronger and growing stronger.

I Want a Wife

JUDY BRADY

Judy Brady was born in 1937 in San Francisco. In 1962, she earned a B.F.A. in painting from the University of Iowa. She has been an active supporter of the feminist movement, and she currently writes on social issues for a variety of publications.

"I Want a Wife" appeared in the very first issue of *Ms.* magazine in December 1971. In the essay, Brady takes an imaginative approach to her role as a wife. She presents a persona that speaks with an ironic voice about the duties of any wife. She argues that she too would enjoy having a wife. The premise requires that she classify the roles played by a wife to support a husband and to raise a family. The creative nature of this piece evokes both a humorous response and a serious understanding of the many difficulties faced by women.

1   I belong to that classification of people known as wives. I am A Wife. And, not altogether incidentally, I am a mother.

2   Not too long ago a male friend of mine appeared on the scene fresh from a recent divorce. He had one child, who is, of course, with his ex-wife. He is looking for another wife. As I thought about him while I was ironing one evening, it suddenly occurred to me that I, too, would like to have a wife. Why do I want a wife?

3   I would like to go back to school so that I can become economically independent, support myself, and, if need be, support those dependent on me. I want a wife who will work and send me to

school. And while I am going to school I want a wife to take care of my children. I want a wife to keep track of the children's doctor and dentist appointments. And to keep track of mine, too. I want a wife to make sure my children eat properly and are kept clean. I want a wife who will wash the children's clothes and keep them mended. I want a wife who is a good nurturant attendant to my children, who arranges for their schooling, makes sure that they have an adequate social life with their peers, takes them to the park, the zoo, etc. I want a wife who takes care of the children when they are sick, a wife who arranges to be around when the children need special care, because, of course, I cannot miss classes at school. My wife must arrange to lose time at work and not lose the job. It may mean a small cut in my wife's income from time to time, but I guess I can tolerate that. Needless to say, my wife will arrange and pay for the care of the children while my wife is working.

4   I want a wife who will take care of *my* physical needs. I want a wife who will keep my house clean. A wife who will pick up after my children, a wife who will pick up after me. I want a wife who will keep my clothes clean, ironed, mended, replaced when need be, and who will see to it that my personal things are kept in their proper place so that I can find what I need the minute I need it. I want a wife who cooks the meals, a wife who is a *good* cook. I want a wife who will plan the menus, do the necessary grocery shopping, prepare the meals, serve them pleasantly, and then do the cleaning up while I do my studying. I want a wife who will care for me when I am sick and sympathize with my pain and loss of time from school. I want a wife to go along when our family takes a vacation so that someone can continue to care for me and my children when I need a rest and change of scene.

5   I want a wife who will not bother me with rambling complaints about a wife's duties. But I want a wife who will listen to me when I feel the need to explain a rather difficult point I have come across in my course of studies. And I want a wife who will type my papers for me when I have written them.

6   I want a wife who will take care of the details of my social life. When my wife and I are invited out by my friends, I want a wife who will take care of the baby-sitting arrangements. When I meet people at school that I like and want to entertain, I want a wife who will have the house clean, will prepare a special meal, serve it to me and my friends, and not interrupt when I talk about things that

interest me and my friends. I want a wife who will have arranged that the children are fed and ready for bed before my guests arrive so that the children do not bother us. I want a wife who takes care of the needs of my guests so that they feel comfortable, who makes sure that they have an ashtray, that they are passed the hors d'oeuvres, that they are offered a second helping of the food, that their wine glasses are replenished when necessary, that their coffee is served to them as they like it. And I want a wife who knows that sometimes I need a night out by myself.

7   I want a wife who is sensitive to my sexual needs, a wife who makes love passionately and eagerly when I feel like it, a wife who makes sure that I am satisfied. And, of course, I want a wife who will not demand sexual attention when I am not in the mood for it. I want a wife who assumes the complete responsibility for birth control, because I do not want more children. I want a wife who will remain sexually faithful to me so that I do not have to clutter up my intellectual life with jealousies. And I want a wife who under-stands that *my* sexual needs may entail more than strict adherence to monogamy. I must, after all, be able to relate to people as fully as possible.

8   If, by chance, I find another person more suitable as a wife than the wife I already have, I want the liberty to replace my present wife with another one. Naturally, I will expect a fresh, new life; my wife will take the children and be solely responsible for them so that I am left free.

9   When I am through with school and have a job, I want my wife to quit working and remain at home so that my wife can more fully and completely take care of a wife's duties.

10   My God, who *wouldn't* want a wife?

Where I Come from Is Like This

PAULA GUNN ALLEN

Paula Gunn Allen, who was born in 1939, has roots in the Laguna Pueblo tribe of North America. She serves as professor of Native American and Ethnic Studies at the University of California, Berkeley. She edited *Studies in American Indian Literature* (1983) for the Modern Language Association. She has also won acclaim for several books of poetry, for a novel entitled *The Woman Who Owned the Shadows* (1983), and for numerous essays.

"Where I Come from Is Like This" is a featured essay in Allen's collection, *The Sacred Hoop*. She describes here the redefinition necessary for modern American Indian women, especially the balancing of tribal traditions with the demands of the modern culture. Allen notes that tribes ascribe various roles to women, but "they never portray women as mindless, helpless, simple, or oppressed." Within a tribe, women possess great power and demand respect. But today a "bicultural bind" restricts them; she says, "We vacillate between being dependent and strong, self-reliant and powerless, strongly motivated and hopelessly insecure."

I

1   Modern American Indian women, like their non-Indian sisters, are deeply engaged in the struggle to redefine themselves. In their struggle they must reconcile traditional tribal definitions of women with industrial and postindustrial non-Indian definitions. Yet while these definitions seem to be more or less mutually exclusive, Indian women must somehow harmonize and integrate both in their own lives.

2   An American Indian woman is primarily defined by her tribal identity. In her eyes, her destiny is necessarily that of her people, and her sense of herself as a woman is first and foremost prescribed by her tribe. The definitions of woman's roles are as diverse as tribal cultures in the Americas. In some she is devalued, in others she wields considerable power. In some she is a familial/clan adjunct, in some she is as close to autonomous as her economic circumstances and psychological traits permit. But in no tribal definitions is she perceived in the same way as are women in Western industrial and postindustrial cultures.

3   In the West, few images of women form part of the cultural mythos, and these are largely sexually charged. Among Christians, the Madonna is the female prototype, and she is portrayed as essentially passive: her contribution is simply that of birthing. Little else is attributed to her and she certainly possesses few of the characteristics that are attributed to mythic figures among Indian tribes. This image is countered (rather than balanced) by the witch-goddess/whore characteristics designed to reinforce cultural beliefs about women, as well as Western adversarial and dualistic perceptions of reality.

4   The tribes see women variously, but they do not question the power of femininity. Sometimes they see women as fearful, sometimes peaceful, sometimes omnipotent and omniscient, but they never portray women as mindless, helpless, simple, or oppressed. And while the women in a given tribe, clan, or band may be all these things, the individual woman is provided with a variety of images of women from the interconnected supernatural, natural, and social worlds she lives in.

5   As a half-breed American Indian woman, I cast about in my mind for negative images of Indian women, and I find none that are directed to Indian women alone. The negative images I do have are of Indians in general and in fact are more often of males than of females. All these images come to me from non-Indian sources, and

they are always balanced by a positive image. My ideas of womanhood, passed on largely by my mother and grandmothers, Laguna
Pueblo women, are about practicality, strength, reasonableness, intelligence, wit, and competence. I also remember vividly the women
who came to my father's store, the women who held me and sang
to me, the women at Feast Day, at Grab Days, the women in the
kitchen of my Cubero home, the women I grew up with; none of
them appeared weak or helpless, none of them presented herself
tentatively. I remember a certain reserve on those lovely brown faces;
I remember the direct gaze of eyes framed by bright-colored shawls
draped over their heads and cascading down their backs. I remember
the clean cotton dresses and carefully pressed hand-embroidered
aprons they always wore; I remember laughter and good food, especially the sweet bread and the oven bread they gave us. Nowhere in
my mind is there a foolish woman, a dumb woman, a vain woman,
or a plastic woman, though the Indian women I have known have
shown a wide range of personal style and demeanor.

6   My memory includes the Navajo woman who was badly beaten
by her Sioux husband; but I also remember that my grandmother
abandoned her Sioux husband long ago. I recall the stories about
the Laguna woman beaten regularly by her husband in the presence
of her children so that the children would not believe in the strength
and power of femininity. And I remember the women who drank,
who got into fights with other women and with the men, and who
often won those battles. I have memories of tired women, partying
women, stubborn women, sullen women, amicable women, selfish
women, shy women, and aggressive women. Most of all I remember
the women who laugh and scold and sit uncomplaining in the long
sun on feast days and who cook wonderful food on wood stoves, in
beehive mud ovens, and over open fires outdoors.

7   Among the images of women that come to me from various tribes
as well as my own are White Buffalo Woman, who came to the
Lakota long ago and brought them the religion of the Sacred Pipe
which they still practice; Tinotzin the goddess who came to Juan
Diego to remind him that she still walked the hills of her people and
sent him with her message, her demand, and her proof to the Catholic
bishop in the city nearby. And from Laguna I take the images of
Yellow Woman, Coyote Woman, Grandmother Spider (Spider Old
Woman), who brought the light, who gave us weaving and medicine,
who gave us life. Among the Keres she is known as Thought Woman

who created us all and who keeps us in creation even now. I remember Iyatiku, Earth Woman, Corn Woman, who guides and counsels the people to peace and who welcomes us home when we cast off this coil of flesh as huskers cast off the leaves that wrap the corn. I remember Iyatiku's sister, Sun Woman, who held metals and cattle, pigs and sheep, highways and engines and so many things in her bundle, who went away to the east saying that one day she would return.

II

8   Since the coming of the Anglo-Europeans beginning in the fifteenth century, the fragile web of identity that long held tribal people secure has gradually been weakened and torn. But the oral tradition has prevented the complete destruction of the web, the ultimate disruption of tribal ways. The oral tradition is vital; it heals itself and the tribal web by adapting to the flow of the present while never relinquishing its connection to the past. Its adaptability has always been required, as many generations have experienced. Certainly the modern American Indian woman bears slight resemblance to her forebears—at least on superficial examination—but she is still a tribal woman in her deepest being. Her tribal sense of relationship to all that is continues to flourish. And though she is at times beset by her knowledge of the enormous gap between the life she lives and the life she was raised to live, and while she adapts her mind and being to the circumstances of her present life, she does so in tribal ways, mending the tears in the web of being from which she takes her existence as she goes.

9   My mother told me stories all the time, though I often did not recognize them as that. My mother told me stories about cooking and childbearing; she told me stories about menstruation and pregnancy; she told me stories about gods and heroes, about fairies and elves, about goddesses and spirits; she told me stories about the land and the sky, about cats and dogs, about snakes and spiders; she told me stories about climbing trees and exploring the mesas; she told me stories about going to dances and getting married; she told me stories about dressing and undressing, about sleeping and waking; she told me stories about herself, about her mother, about her grandmother. She told me stories about grieving and laughing, about thinking and doing; she told me stories about school and about

people; about darning and mending; she told me stories about turquoise and about gold; she told me European stories and Laguna stories; she told me Catholic stories and Presbyterian stories; she told me city stories and country stories; she told me political stories and religious stories. She told me stories about living and stories about dying. And in all of those stories she told me who I was, who I was supposed to be, whom I came from, and who would follow me. In this way she taught me the meaning of the words she said, that all life is a circle and everything has a place within it. That's what she said and what she showed me in the things she did and the way she lives.

10   Of course, through my formal, white, Christian education, I discovered that other people had stories of their own—about women, about Indians, about fact, about reality—and I was amazed by a number of startling suppositions that others made about tribal customs and beliefs. According to the un-Indian, non-Indian view, for instance, Indians barred menstruating women from ceremonies and indeed segregated them from the rest of the people, consigning them to some space specially designed for them. This showed that Indians considered menstruating women unclean and not fit to enjoy the company of decent (nonmenstruating) people, that is, men. I was surprised and confused to hear this because my mother had taught me that white people had strange attitudes toward menstruation: they thought something was bad about it, that it meant you were sick, cursed, sinful, and weak and that you had to be very careful during that time. She taught me that menstruation was a normal occurrence, that I could go swimming or hiking or whatever else I wanted to do during my period. She actively scorned women who took to their beds, who were incapacitated by cramps, who "got the blues."

11   As I struggled to reconcile these very contradictory interpretations of American Indians' traditional beliefs concerning menstruation, I realized that the menstrual taboos were about power, not about sin or filth. My conclusion was later borne out by some tribes' own explanations, which, as you may well imagine, came as quite a relief to me.

12   The truth of the matter as many Indians see it is that women who are at the peak of their fecundity are believed to possess power that throws male power totally out of kilter. They emit such force that, in their presence, any male-owned or -dominated ritual or sacred

object cannot do its usual task. For instance, the Lakota say that a menstruating woman anywhere near a yuwipi man, who is a special sort of psychic, spirit-empowered healer, for a day or so before he is to do his ceremony will effectively disempower him. Conversely, among many if not most tribes, important ceremonies cannot be held without the presence of women. Sometimes the ritual woman who empowers the ceremony must be unmarried and virginal so that the power she channels is unalloyed, unweakened by sexual arousal and penetration by a male. Other ceremonies require tumescent women, others the presence of mature women who have borne children, and still others depend for empowerment on postmenopausal women. Women may be segregated from the company of the whole band or village on certain occasions, but on certain occasions men are also segregated. In short, each ritual depends on a certain balance of power, and the positions of women within the phases of womanhood are used by tribal people to empower certain rites. This does not derive from a male-dominant view; it is not a ritual observance imposed on women by men. It derives from a tribal view of reality that distinguishes tribal people from feudal and industrial people.

13   Among the tribes, the occult power of women, inextricably bound to our hormonal life, is thought to be very great; many hold that we possess innately the blood-given power to kill—with a glance, with a step, or with a judicious mixing of menstrual blood into somebody's soup. Medicine women among the Pomo of California cannot practice until they are sufficiently mature; when they are immature, their power is diffuse and is likely to interfere with their practice until time and experience have it under control. So women of the tribes are not especially inclined to see themselves as poor helpless victims of male domination. Even in those tribes where something akin to male domination was present, women are perceived as powerful, socially, physically, and metaphysically. In times past, as in times present, women carried enormous burdens with aplomb. We were far indeed from the "weaker sex," the designation that white aristocratic sisters unhappily earned for us all.

14   I remember my mother moving furniture all over the house when she wanted it changed. She didn't wait for my father to come home and help—she just went ahead and moved the piano, a huge upright from the old days, the couch, the refrigerator. Nobody had told her

she was too weak to do such things. In imitation of her, I would delight in loading trucks at my father's store with cases of pop or fifty-pound sacks of flour. Even when I was quite small I could do it, and it gave me a belief in my own physical strength that advancing middle age can't quite erase. My mother used to tell me about the Acoma Pueblo women she had seen as a child carrying huge ollas (water pots) on their heads as they wound their way up the tortuous stairwell carved into the face of the "Sky City" mesa, a feat I tried to imitate with books and tin buckets. ("Sky City" is the term used by the chamber of commerce for the mother village of Acoma, which is situated atop a high sandstone table mountain.) I was never very successful, but even the attempt reminded me that I was supposed to be strong and balanced to be a proper girl.

15 Of course, my mother's Laguna people are Keres Indian, reputed to be the last extreme mother-right people on earth. So it is no wonder that I got notably nonwhite notions about the natural strength and prowess of women. Indeed, it is only when I am trying to get non-Indian approval, recognition, or acknowledgment that my "weak sister" emotional and intellectual ploys get the better of my tribal woman's good sense. At such times I forget that I just moved the piano or just wrote a competent paper or just completed a financial transaction satisfactorily or have supported myself and my children for most of my adult life.

16 Nor is my contradictory behavior atypical. Most Indian women I know are in the same bicultural bind: we vacillate between being dependent and strong, self-reliant and powerless, strongly motivated and hopelessly insecure. We resolve the dilemma in various ways: some of us party all the time; some of us drink to excess; some of us travel and move around a lot; some of us land good jobs and then quit them; some of us engage in violent exchanges; some of us blow our brains out. We act in these destructive ways because we suffer from the societal conflicts caused by having to identify with two hopelessly opposed cultural definitions of women. Through this destructive dissonance we are unhappy prey to the self-disparagement common to, indeed demanded of, Indians living in the United States today. Our situation is caused by the exigencies of a history of invasion, conquest, and colonization whose searing marks are probably ineradicable. A popular bumper sticker on many Indian cars proclaims: "If You're Indian You're In," to which I always find myself adding under my breath, "Trouble."

III

17 No Indian can grow to any age without being informed that her people were "savages" who interfered with the march of progress pursued by respectable, loving, civilized white people. We are the villains of the scenario when we are mentioned at all. We are absent from much of white history except when we are calmly, rationally, succinctly, and systematically dehumanized. On the few occasions we are noticed in any way other than as howling, bloodthirsty beings, we are acclaimed for our noble quaintness. In this definition, we are exotic curios. Our ancient arts and customs are used to draw tourist money to state coffers, into the pocketbooks and bank accounts of scholars, and into support of the American-in-Disneyland promoters' dream.

18 As a Roman Catholic child I was treated to bloody tales of how the savage Indians martyred the hapless priests and missionaries who went among them in an attempt to lead them to the one true path. By the time I was through high school I had the idea that Indians were people who had benefited mightily from the advanced knowledge and superior morality of the Anglo-Europeans. At least I had, perforce, that idea to lay beside the other one that derived from my daily experience of Indian life, an idea less dehumanizing and more accurate because it came from my mother and the other Indian people who raised me. That idea was that Indians are a people who don't tell lies, who care for their children and their old people. You never see an Indian orphan, they said. You always know when you're old that someone will take care of you—one of your children will. Then they'd list the old folks who were being taken care of by this child or that. No child is ever considered illegitimate among the Indians, they said. If a girl gets pregnant, the baby is still part of the family, and the mother is too. That's what they said, and they showed me real people who lived according to those principles.

19 Of course the ravages of colonization have taken their toll; there are orphans in Indian country now, and abandoned, brutalized old folks; there are even illegitimate children, though the very concept still strikes me as absurd. There are battered children and neglected children, and there are battered wives and women who have been raped by Indian men. Proximity to the "civilizing" effects of white Christians has not improved the moral quality of life in Indian country, though each group, Indian and white, explains the situation differently. Nor is there much yet in the oral tradition that can enable

us to adapt to these inhuman changes. But a force is growing in that direction, and it is helping Indian women reclaim their lives. Their power, their sense of direction and of self will soon be visible. It is the force of the women who speak and work and write, and it is formidable.

20   Through all the centuries of war and death and cultural and psychic destruction have endured the women who raise the children and tend the fires, who pass along the tales and the traditions, who weep and bury the dead, who are the dead, and who never forget. There are always the women, who make pots and weave baskets, who fashion clothes and cheer their children on at powwow, who make fry bread and piki bread, and corn soup and chili stew, who dance and sing and remember and hold within their hearts the dream of their ancient peoples—that one day the woman who thinks will speak to us again, and everywhere there will be peace. Meanwhile we tell the stories of fun and scandal and laugh over all manner of things that happen every day. We watch and we wait.

21   My great-grandmother told my mother: Never forget you are Indian. And my mother told me the same thing. This, then, is how I have gone about remembering, so that my children will remember too.

Pornography

MARGARET ATWOOD

Margaret Atwood was born in Ottawa, Ontario, in 1939. As a novelist, essayist, poet, and playwright, Atwood is recognized as one of Canada's most distinguished writers. Among her novels are *The Edible Woman* (1960), *Surfacing* (1972), *Life Before Man* (1979), *Bodily Harm* (1982), *The Handmaid's Tale* (1986), *Cat's Eye* (1989), and *The Robber Bridegroom* (1993). Her essays have appeared in such magazines as *Ms., The New Republic, The Humanist,* and *Harper's*. Some of her essays were collected in *Second Words* (1982). In both her novels and essays, Atwood addresses the issues that face women, that confront the contemporary world, and that relate to Canadian-American relations.

"Pornography" first appeared in *Chatelaine Magazine,* which circulates principally to women. In it she responds to the various reviews and reactions to her novel *Bodily Harm*. Some reviewers found the book pornographic. In truth, Atwood had tried, after careful research, to show how violent and sadistic pornography had become. Atwood penetrates quickly to the fundamental cultural issues: the human hatred of the body, the male backlash against the feminist movement, the generation of impotent men who can't confront women in person, the intensive promotion of a rich industry. Her key question is this: "Is pornography merely an expression of the sexual confusion of this age or an active contributor to it?" Atwood does not provide an answer, but her investigation should stimulate serious discussion and, perhaps, civic action.

1   When I was in Finland a few years ago for an international writers'
conference, I had occasion to say a few paragraphs in public on the
subject of pornography. The context was a discussion of political
repression, and I was suggesting the possibility of a link between the
two. The immediate result was that a male journalist took several
large bites out of me. Prudery and pornography are two halves of
the same coin, said he, and I was clearly a prude. What could you
expect from an Anglo-Canadian? Afterward, a couple of pleasant
Scandinavian men asked me what I had been so worked up about.
All "pornography" means, they said, is graphic depictions of whores,
and what was the harm in that?

2   Not until then did it strike me that the male journalist and I had
two entirely different things in mind. By "pornography," he meant
naked bodies and sex. I, on the other hand, had recently been doing
the research for my novel *Bodily Harm,* and was still in a state of
shock from some of the material I had seen, including the Ontario
Board of Film Censors' "outtakes." By "pornography," I meant
women getting their nipples snipped off with garden shears, having
meat hooks stuck into their vaginas, being disemboweled; little girls
being raped; men (yes, there are some men) being smashed to a pulp
and forcibly sodomized. The cutting edge of pornography, as far as
I could see, was no longer simple old copulation, hanging from the
chandelier or otherwise: it was death, messy, explicit and highly
sadistic. I explained this to the nice Scandinavian men. "Oh, but
that's just the United States," they said. "Everyone knows they're
sick." In their country, they said, violent "pornography" of that
kind was not permitted on television or in movies; indeed, excessive
violence of any kind was not permitted. They had drawn a clear line
between erotica, which earlier studies had shown did not incite men
to more aggressive and brutal behavior toward women, and violence,
which later studies indicated did.

3   Some time after that I was in Saskatchewan, where, because of
the scenes in *Bodily Harm,* I found myself on an open-line radio
show answering questions about "pornography." Almost no one
who phoned in was in favor of it, but again they weren't talking
about the same stuff I was, because they hadn't seen it. Some of
them were all set to stamp out bathing suits and negligees, and, if
possible, any depictions of the female body whatsoever. God, it was
implied, did not approve of female bodies, and sex of any kind,
including that practised by bumblebees, should be shoved back into

the dark, where it belonged. I had more than a suspicion that *Lady Chatterley's Lover,* Margaret Laurence's *The Diviners,* and indeed most books by most serious modern authors would have ended up as confetti if left in the hands of these callers.

4   For me, these two experiences illustrate the two poles of the emotionally heated debate that is now thundering around this issue. They also underline the desirability and even the necessity of defining the terms. "Pornography" is now one of those catchalls, like "Marxism" and "feminism," that have become so broad they can mean almost anything, ranging from certain verses in the Bible, ads for skin lotion and sex tests for children to the contents of *Penthouse,* Naughty '90s postcards and films with titles containing the word *Nazi* that show vicious scenes of torture and killing. It's easy to say that sensible people can tell the difference. Unfortunately, opinions on what constitutes a sensible person vary.

5   But even sensible people tend to lose their cool when they start talking about this subject. They soon stop talking and start yelling, and the name-calling begins. Those in favor of censorship (which may include groups not noticeably in agreement on other issues, such as some feminists and religious fundamentalists) accuse the others of exploiting women through the use of degrading images, contributing to the corruption of children, and adding to the general climate of violence and threat in which both women and children live in this society; or, though they may not give much of a hoot about actual women and children, they invoke moral standards and God's supposed aversion to "filth," "smut" and deviated *preversion,* which may mean ankles.

6   The camp in favor of total "freedom of expression" often comes out howling as loud as the Romans would have if told they could no longer have innocent fun watching the lions eat up Christians. It too may include segments of the population who are not natural bedfellows: those who proclaim their God-given right to freedom, including the freedom to tote guns, drive when drunk, drool over chicken porn and get off on videotapes of women being raped and beaten, may be waving the same anticensorship banner as responsible liberals who fear the return of Mrs. Grundy, or gay groups for whom sexual emancipation involves the concept of "sexual theatre." *Whatever turns you on* is a handy motto, as is *A man's home is his castle* (and if it includes a dungeon with beautiful maidens strung up in chains and bleeding from every pore, that's his business).

7   Meanwhile, theoreticians theorize and speculators speculate. Is today's pornography yet another indication of the hatred of the body, the deep mind-body split, which is supposed to pervade Western Christian society? Is it a backlash against the women's movement by men who are threatened by uppity female behavior in real life, so like to fantasize about women done up like outsize parcels, being turned into hamburger, kneeling at their feet in slavelike adoration or sucking off guns? Is it a sign of collective impotence, of a generation of men who can't relate to real women at all but have to make do with bits of celluloid and paper? Is the current flood just a result of smart marketing and aggressive promotion by the money men in what has now become a multi-billion-dollar industry? If they were selling movies about men getting their testicles stuck full of knitting needles by women with swastikas on their sleeves, would they do as well, or is this penchant somehow peculiarly male? If so, why? Is pornography a power trip rather than a sex one? Some say that those ropes, chains, muzzles and other restraining devices are an argument for the immense power female sexuality still wields in the male imagination: you don't put these things on dogs unless you're afraid of them. Others, more literary, wonder about the shift from the 19th-century Magic Woman or Femme Fatale image to the lollipop-licker, airhead or turkey-carcass treatment of women in porn today. The proporners don't care much about theory; they merely demand product. The antiporners don't care about it in the final analysis either; there's dirt on the street, and they want it cleaned up, now.

8   It seems to me that this conversation, with its *You're-a-prude/You're-a-pervert* dialectic, will never get anywhere as long as we continue to think of this material as just "entertainment." Possibly we're deluded by the packaging, the format: magazine, book, movie, theatrical presentation. We're used to thinking of these things as part of the "entertainment industry," and we're used to thinking of ourselves as free adult people who ought to be able to see any kind of "entertainment" we want to. That was what the First Choice pay-TV debate was all about. After all, it's only entertainment, right? Entertainment means fun, and only a killjoy would be antifun. What's the harm?

9   This is obviously the central question: *What's the harm?* If there isn't any real harm to any real people, then the antiporners can tsk-

tsk and/or throw up as much as they like, but they can't rightfully expect more legal controls or sanctions. However, the no-harm position is far from being proven.

10   (For instance, there's a clear-cut case for banning—as the federal government has proposed—movies, photos and videos that depict children engaging in sex with adults: real children are used to make the movies, and hardly anybody thinks this is ethical. The possibilities for coercion are too great.)

11   To shift the viewpoint, I'd like to suggest three other models for looking at "pornography"—and here I mean the violent kind.

12   Those who find the idea of regulating pornographic materials repugnant because they think it's Fascist or Communist or otherwise not in accordance with the principles of an open democratic society should consider that Canada has made it illegal to disseminate material that may lead to hatred toward any group because of race or religion. I suggest that if pornography of the violent kind depicted these acts being done predominantly to Chinese, to blacks, to Catholics, it would be off the market immediately, under the present laws. Why is hate literature illegal? Because whoever made the law thought that such material might incite real people to do real awful things to other real people. The human brain is to a certain extent a computer: garbage in, garbage out. We only hear about the extreme cases (like that of American multimurderer Ted Bundy) in which pornography has contributed to the death and/or mutilation of women and/or men. Although pornography is not the only factor involved in the creation of such deviance, it certainly has upped the ante by suggesting both a variety of techniques and the social acceptability of such actions. Nobody knows yet what effect this stuff is having on the less psychotic.

13   Studies have shown that a large part of the market for all kinds of porn, soft and hard, is drawn from the 16-to-21-year-old population of young men. Boys used to learn about sex on the street, or (in Italy, according to Fellini movies) from friendly whores, or, in more genteel surroundings, from girls, their parents, or, once upon a time, in school, more or less. Now porn has been added, and sex education in the schools is rapidly being phased out. The buck has been passed, and boys are being taught that all women secretly like to be raped and that real men get high on scooping out women's digestive tracts.

14   Boys learn their concept of masculinity from other men: is this

what most men want them to be learning? If word gets around that rapists are "normal" and even admirable men, will boys feel that in order to be normal, admirable and masculine they will have to be rapists? Human beings are enormously flexible, and how they turn out depends a lot on how they're educated, by the society in which they're immersed as well as by their teachers. In a society that advertises and glorifies rape or even implicitly condones it, more women get raped. It becomes socially acceptable. And at a time when men and the traditional male role have taken a lot of flak and men are confused and casting around for an acceptable way of being male (and, in some cases, not getting much comfort from women on that score), this must be at times a pleasing thought.

15   It would be naïve to think of violent pornography as just harmless entertainment. It's also an educational tool and a powerful propaganda device. What happens when boy educated on porn meets girl brought up on Harlequin romances? The clash of expectations can be heard around the block. She wants him to get down on his knees with a ring, he wants her to get down on all fours with a ring in her nose. Can this marriage be saved?

16   Pornography has certain things in common with such addictive substances as alcohol and drugs: for some, though by no means for all, it induces chemical changes in the body, which the user finds exciting and pleasurable. It also appears to attract a "hard core" of habitual users and a penumbra of those who use it occasionally but aren't dependent on it in any way. There are also significant numbers of men who aren't much interested in it, not because they're undersexed but because real life is satisfying their needs, which may not require as many appliances as those of users.

17   For the "hard core," pornography may function as alcohol does for the alcoholic: tolerance develops, and a little is no longer enough. This may account for the short viewing time and fast turnover in porn theatres. Mary Brown, chairwoman of the Ontario Board of Film Censors, estimates that for every one mainstream movie requesting entrance to Ontario, there is one porno flick. Not only the quantity consumed but the quality of explicitness must escalate, which may account for the growing violence: once the big deal was breasts, then it was genitals, then copulation, then that was no longer enough and the hard users had to have more. The ultimate kick is death, and after that, as the Marquis de Sade so boringly demonstrated, multiple death.

18   The existence of alcoholism has not led us to ban social drinking. On the other hand, we do have laws about drinking and driving, excessive drunkenness and other abuses of alcohol that may result in injury or death to others.

19   This leads us back to the key question: what's the harm? Nobody knows, but this society should find out fast, before the saturation point is reached. The Scandinavian studies that showed a connection between depictions of sexual violence and increased impulse toward it on the part of male viewers would be a starting point, but many more questions remain to be raised as well as answered. What, for instance, is the crucial difference between men who are users and men who are not? Does using affect a man's relationship with actual women, and, if so, adversely? Is there a clear line between erotica and violent pornography, or are they on an escalating continuum? Is this a "men versus women" issue, with all men secretly siding with the proporners and all women secretly siding against? (I think not; there *are* lots of men who don't think that running their true love through the Cuisinart is the best way they can think of to spend a Saturday night, and they're just as nauseated by films of someone else doing it as women are.) Is pornography merely an expression of the sexual confusion of this age or an active contributor to it?

20   Nobody wants to go back to the age of official repression, when even piano legs were referred to as "limbs" and had to wear pantaloons to be decent. Neither do we want to end up in George Orwell's *1984,* in which pornography is turned out by the State to keep the proles in a state of torpor, sex itself is considered dirty and the approved practise it only for reproduction. But Rome under the emperors isn't such a good model either.

21   If all men and women respected each other, if sex were considered joyful and life-enhancing instead of a wallow in germ-filled glop, if everyone were in love all the time, if, in other words, many people's lives were more satisfactory for them than they appear to be now, pornography might just go away on its own. But since this is obviously not happening, we as a society are going to have to make some informed and responsible decisions about how to deal with it.

You Are What You Say

ROBIN LAKOFF

Robin Lakoff was born in 1942 in Brooklyn, New York. She earned her B.A. at Radcliffe College, an M.A. at Indiana University, and a Ph.D. at Harvard University. She now teaches linguistics at the University of California, Berkeley. Lakoff gained national prominence in 1975 with the publication of *Language and Women's Place*, in which she explains how sexist language reinforces social attitudes toward women. In particular, she examines male language and the manner in which women themselves reveal their own sense of subordination. Lakoff's writing helped launch a multi-fronted attack on sexist language use and its negative effects on modern culture.

"You Are What You Say" first appeared in 1974 in *Ms.* magazine; it became a key ingredient of *Language and Women's Place*. She argues that women are "communicative cripples" who, too often, "are ridiculed for being unable to think clearly, unable to take part in a serious discussion, and therefore unfit to hold a position of power."

1   "Women's language" is that pleasant (dainty?), euphemistic never-aggressive way of talking we learned as little girls. Cultural bias was built into the language we were allowed to speak, the subjects we were allowed to speak about, and the ways we were

spoken of. Having learned our linguistic lesson well, we go out in the world, only to discover that we are communicative cripples—damned if we do, and damned if we don't.

2   If we refuse to talk "like a lady," we are ridiculed and criticized for being unfeminine. ("She thinks like a man" is, at best, a left-handed compliment.) If we do learn all the fuzzy-headed, unassertive language of our sex, we are ridiculed for being unable to think clearly, unable to take part in a serious discussion, and therefore unfit to hold a position of power.

3   It doesn't take much of this for a woman to begin feeling she deserves such treatment because of inadequacies in her own intelligence and education.

4   "Women's language" shows up in all levels of English. For example, women are encouraged and allowed to make far more precise discriminations in naming colors than men do. Words like *mauve, beige, ecru, aquamarine, lavender,* and so on, are unremarkable in a woman's active vocabulary, but largely absent from that of most men. I know of no evidence suggesting that women actually *see* a wider range of colors than men do. It is simply that fine discriminations of this sort are relevant to women's vocabularies, but not to men's; to men, who control most of the interesting affairs of the world, such distinctions are trivial—irrelevant.

5   In the area of syntax, we find similar gender-related peculiarities of speech. There is one construction, in particular, that women use conversationally far more than men: the tag question. A tag is midway between an outright statement and a yes-no question; it is less assertive than the former, but more confident than the latter.

6   A *flat statement* indicates confidence in the speaker's knowledge and is fairly certain to be believed; a *question* indicates a lack of knowledge on some point and implies that the gap in the speaker's knowledge can and will be remedied by an answer. For example, if, at a Little League game, I have had my glasses off, I can legitimately ask someone else: "Was the player out at third?" A *tag question,* being intermediate between statement and question, is used when the speaker is stating a claim, but lacks full confidence in the truth of that claim. So if I say, "Is Joan here?" I will probably not be surprised if my respondent answers "no"; but if I say, "Joan is here, isn't she?" instead, chances are I am already biased in favor of a positive answer, wanting only confirmation. I still want a response, but I have enough knowledge (or think I have) to predict that

response. A tag question, then, might be thought of as a statement that doesn't demand to be believed by anyone but the speaker, a way of giving leeway, of not forcing the addressee to go along with the views of the speaker.

7   Another common use of the tag question is in small talk when the speaker is trying to elicit conversation: "Sure is hot here, isn't it?"

8   But in discussing personal feelings or opinions, only the speaker normally has any way of knowing the correct answer. Sentences such as "I have a headache, don't I?" are clearly ridiculous. But there are other examples where it is the speaker's opinions, rather than perceptions, for which corroboration is sought, as in "The situation in Southeast Asia is terrible, isn't it?"

9   While there are, of course, other possible interpretations of a sentence like this, one possibility is that the speaker has a particular answer in mind—"yes" or "no"—but is reluctant to state it baldly. This sort of tag question is much more apt to be used by women than by men in conversation. Why is this the case?

10   The tag question allows a speaker to avoid commitment, and thereby avoid conflict with the addressee. The problem is that, by so doing, speakers may also give the impression of not really being sure of themselves, or looking to the addressee for confirmation of their views. This uncertainty is reinforced in more subliminal ways, too. There is a peculiar sentence-intonation pattern, used almost exclusively by women, as far as I know, which changes a declarative answer into a question. The effect of using the rising inflection typical of a yes-no question is to imply that the speaker is seeking confirmation, even though the speaker is clearly the only one who has the requisite information, which is why the question was put to her in the first place:

> (Q) When will dinner be ready?
> (A) Oh . . . around six o'clock . . . ?

It is as though the second speaker were saying, "Six o'clock—if that's okay with you, if you agree." The person being addressed is put in the position of having to provide confirmation. One likely consequence of this sort of speech pattern in a woman is that, often unbeknownst to herself, the speaker builds a reputation of tentativeness, and others will refrain from taking her seriously or trusting her with any real responsibilities, since she "can't make up her mind," and "isn't sure of herself."

11   Such idiosyncrasies may explain why women's language sounds much more "polite" than men's. It is polite to leave a decision open, not impose your mind, or views, or claims, on anyone else. So a tag question is a kind of polite statement, in that it does not force agreement or belief on the addressee. In the same way a request is a polite command, in that it does not force obedience on the addressee, but rather suggests something be done as a favor to the speaker. A clearly stated order implies a threat of certain consequences if it is not followed, and—even more impolite—implies that the speaker is in a superior position and able to enforce the order. By couching wishes in the form of a request, on the other hand, a speaker implies that if the request is not carried out, only the speaker will suffer; noncompliance cannot harm the addressee. So the decision is really left up to the addressee. The distinction becomes clear in these examples:

> Close the door.
> Please close the door.
> Will you close the door?
> Will you please close the door?
> Won't you close the door?

12   In the same way as words and speech patterns used *by* women undermine her image, those used *to describe* women make matters even worse. Often a word may be used of both men and women (and perhaps of things as well); but when it is applied to women, it assumes a special meaning that, by implication rather than outright assertion, is derogatory to women as a group.

13   The use of euphemisms has this effect. A euphemism is a substitute for a word that has acquired a bad connotation by association with something unpleasant or embarrassing. But almost as soon as the new word comes into common usage, it takes on the same old bad connotations, since feelings about the things or people referred to are not altered by a change of name; thus new euphemisms must be constantly found.

14   There is one euphemism for *woman* still very much alive. The word, of course, is *lady*. *Lady* has a masculine counterpart, namely *gentleman*, occasionally shortened to *gent*. But for some reason *lady* is very much commoner than *gent(leman)*.

15   The decision to use *lady* rather than *woman*, or vice versa, may considerably alter the sense of a sentence, as the following examples show:

(a) A woman (lady) I know is a dean at Berkeley.
(b) A woman (lady) I know makes amazing things
out of shoelaces and old boxes.

16   The use of *lady* in (a) imparts a frivolous, or nonserious, tone to
the sentence: the matter under discussion is not one of great moment.
Similarly, in (b), using *lady* here would suggest that the speaker
considered the "amazing things" not to be serious art, but merely
a hobby or aberration. If *woman* is used, she might be a serious
sculptor. To say *lady doctor* is very condescending, since no one ever
says *gentleman doctor* or even *man doctor*. For example, mention in
the San Francisco *Chronicle* of January 31, 1972, of Madalyn Murray
O'Hair as the *lady atheist* reduces her position to that of scatter-
brained eccentric. Even *woman atheist* is scarcely defensible: sex is
irrelevant to her philosophical position.

17   Many women argue that, on the other hand, *lady* carries with it
overtones recalling the age of chivalry: conferring exalted stature on
the person so referred to. This makes the term seem polite at first,
but we must also remember that these implications are perilous: they
suggest that a "lady" is helpless, and cannot do things by herself.

18   *Lady* can also be used to infer frivolousness, as in titles of organizations. Those that have a serious purpose (not merely that of enabling
"the ladies" to spend time with one another) cannot use the word *lady*
in their titles, but less serious ones may. Compare the *Ladies' Auxiliary*
of a men's group, or the *Thursday Evening Ladies' Browning and Garden Society* with *Ladies' Liberation* or *Ladies' Strike for Peace*.

19   What is curious about this split is that *lady* is in origin a euphemism—a substitute that puts a better face on something people find
uncomfortable—for *woman*. What kind of euphemism is it that subtly
denigrates the people to whom it refers? Perhaps *lady* functions as
a euphemism for *woman* because it does not contain the sexual
implications present in *woman:* it is not "embarrassing" in that way.
If this is so, we may expect that, in the future, *lady* will replace
woman as the primary word for the human female, since *woman* will
have become too blatantly sexual. That this distinction is already
made in some contexts at least is shown in the following examples,
where you can try replacing *woman* with *lady:*

(a) She's only twelve, but she's already a woman.
(b) After ten years in jail, Harry wanted to find a
woman.

(c) She's my woman, see, so don't mess around
with her.

20 Another common substitute for *woman* is *girl*. One seldom hears a man past the age of adolescence referred to as a boy, save in expressions like "going out with the boys," which are meant to suggest an air of adolescent frivolity and irresponsibility. But women of all ages are "girls": one can have a man—not a boy—Friday, but only a girl—never a woman or even a lady—Friday; women have girlfriends, but men do not—in a nonsexual sense—have boyfriends. It may be that this use of *girl* is euphemistic in the same way the use of *lady* is: in stressing the idea of immaturity, it removes the sexual connotations lurking in *woman*. *Girl* brings to mind irresponsibility: you don't send a girl to do a woman's errand (or even, for that matter, a boy's errand). She is a person who is both too immature and too far from real life to be entrusted with responsibilities or with decisions of any serious or important nature.

21 Now let's take a pair of words which, in terms of the possible relationships in an earlier society, were simple male-female equivalents, analogous to *bull: cow*. Suppose we find that, for independent reasons, society has changed in such a way that the original meanings now are irrelevant. Yet the words have not been discarded, but have acquired new meanings, metaphorically related to their original senses. But suppose these new metaphorical uses are no longer parallel to each other. By seeing where the parallelism breaks down, we discover something about the different roles played by men and women in this culture. One good example of such a divergence through time is found in the pair, *master: mistress*. Once used with reference to one's power over servants, these words have become unusable today in their original master-servant sense as the relationship has become less prevalent in our society. But the words are still common.

22 Unless used with reference to animals, *master* now generally refers to a man who has acquired consummate ability in some field, normally nonsexual. But its feminine counterpart cannot be used this way. It is practically restricted to its sexual sense of "paramour." We start out with two terms, both roughly paraphrasable as "one who has power over another." But the masculine form, once one person is no longer able to have absolute power over another, becomes usable metaphorically in the sense of "having power over *something*." *Master*

requires as its object only the name of some activity, something inanimate and abstract. But *mistress* requires a masculine noun in the possessive to precede it. One cannot say: "Rhonda is a mistress." One must be *someone's* mistress. A man is defined by what he does, a woman by her sexuality, that is, in terms of one particular aspect of her relationship to men. It is one thing to be an *old master* like Hans Holbein, and another to be an *old mistress.*

23   The same is true of the words *spinster* and *bachelor*—gender words for "one who is not married." The resemblance ends with the definition. While *bachelor* is a neuter term, often used as a compliment, *spinster* normally is used pejoratively, with connotations of prissiness, fussiness, and so on. To be a bachelor implies that one has a choice of marrying or not, and this is what makes the idea of a bachelor existence attractive, in the popular literature. He has been pursued and has successfully eluded his pursuers. But a spinster is one who has not been pursued, or at least not seriously. She is old, unwanted goods. The metaphorical connotations of *bachelor* generally suggest sexual freedom; of *spinster,* puritanism or celibacy.

24   These examples could be multiplied. It is generally considered a *faux pas,* in society, to congratulate a woman on her engagement, while it is correct to congratulate her fiancé. Why is this? The reason seems to be that it is impolite to remind people of things that may be uncomfortable to them. To congratulate a woman on her engagement is really to say, "Thank goodness! You had a close call!" For the man, on the other hand, there was no such danger. His choosing to marry is viewed as a good thing, but not something essential.

25   The linguistic double standard holds throughout the life of the relationship. After marriage, bachelor and spinster become man and wife, not man and woman. The woman whose husband dies remains "John's widow;" John, however, is never "Mary's widower."

26   Finally, why is it that salesclerks and others are so quick to call women customers "dear," "honey," and other terms of endearment they really have no business using? A male customer would never put up with it. But women, like children, are supposed to enjoy these endearments, rather than being offended by them.

27   In more ways than one, it's time to speak up.

An American Childhood

ANNIE DILLARD

Annie Dillard was born in 1945 in Pittsburgh. She attended Hollins College in Virginia, where she lived for twelve years. She is the author of ten books, including *An American Childhood* (1987), a memoir; *The Writing Life* (1989), an account; and *Holy the Firm* (1978), a nonfiction narrative. *The Living* (1992), a novel, is the story of four men on the coast of Puget Sound in the second half of the nineteenth century. *Teaching a Stone to Talk* is her sole book of narrative essays. In 1975, *Pilgrim at Tinker Creek*, a narrative, was awarded the Pulitzer Prize in nonfiction.

Dillard's writing appears in *Atlantic, Harper's,* the *New York Times Magazine,* the *Yale Review, Antaeus, American Heritage,* and many anthologies. She has received fellowship grants from the Guggenheim Foundation and the National Endowment for the Arts.

She lived for five years in the Pacific Northwest but has lived for the past fifteen years in Middletown, Connecticut, now with her husband Robert D. Richardson, Jr., a biographer of Thoreau and Emerson.

"An American Childhood" was originally published as part of the memoir with the same title. In it she paints a vivid portrait of her mother, a woman of character and independence, a woman with an inquisitive yet practical mind, and a woman who stood her ground in the world and expected her children to do the same.

1   One Sunday afternoon Mother wandered through our kitchen, where Father was making a sandwich and listening to the ball game. The Pirates were playing the New York Giants at Forbes Field. In those days, the Giants had a utility infielder named Wayne Terwilliger. Just as Mother passed through, the radio announcer cried—with undue drama—"Terwilliger bunts one!"

2   "Terwilliger bunts one?" Mother cried back, stopped short. She turned. "Is that English?"

3   "The player's name is Terwilliger," Father said. "He bunted."

4   "That's marvelous," Mother said. " 'Terwilliger bunts one.' No wonder you listen to baseball. 'Terwilliger bunts one.' "

5   For the next seven or eight years, Mother made this surprising string of syllables her own. Testing a microphone, she repeated, "Terwilliger bunts one"; testing a pen or a typewriter, she wrote it. If, as happened surprisingly often in the course of various improvised gags, she pretended to whisper something else in my ear, she actually whispered, "Terwilliger bunts one." Whenever someone used a French phrase, or a Latin one, she answered solemnly, "Terwilliger bunts one." If Mother had had, like Andrew Carnegie, the opportunity to cook up a motto for a coat of arms, hers would have read simply and tellingly, "Terwilliger bunts one." (Carnegie's was "Death to Privilege.")

6   She served us with other words and phrases. On a Florida trip, she repeated tremulously, "That . . . is a royal poinciana." I don't remember the tree; I remember the thrill in her voice. She pronounced it carefully, and spelled it. She also liked to say "portulaca."

7   The drama of the words "Tamiami Trail" stirred her, we learned on the same Florida trip. People built Tampa on one coast, and they built Miami on another. Then—the height of visionary ambition and folly—they piled a slow, tremendous road through the terrible Everglades to connect them. To build the road, men stood sunk in muck to their armpits. They fought off cottonmouth moccasins and six-foot alligators. They slept in boats, wet. They blasted muck with dynamite, cut jungle with machetes; they laid logs, dragged drilling machines, hauled dredges, heaped limestone. The road took fourteen years to build up by the shovelful, a Panama Canal in reverse, and cost hundreds of lives from tropical, mosquito-carried diseases. Then, capping it all, some genius thought of the word Tamiami: they called the road from Tampa to Miami, this very road under our spinning wheels, the Tamiami Trail. Some

called it Alligator Alley. Anyone could drive over this road without a thought.

8   Hearing this, moved, I thought all the suffering of road building was worth it (it wasn't my suffering), now that we had this new thing to hang these new words on—Alligator Alley for those who liked things cute, and, for connoisseurs like Mother, for lovers of the human drama in all its boldness and terror, the Tamiami Trail.

9   Back home, Mother cut clips from reels of talk, as it were, and played them back at leisure. She noticed that many Pittsburghers confuse "leave" and "let." One kind relative brightened our morning by mentioning why she'd brought her son to visit: "He wanted to come with me, so I left him." Mother filled in Amy and me on locutions we missed. "I can't do it on Friday," her pretty sister told a crowded dinner party, "because Friday's the day I lay in the stores."

10   (All unconsciously, though, we ourselves used some pure Pittsburghisms. We said "tele pole," pronounced "telly pole," for that splintery sidewalk post I loved to climb. We said "slippy"—the sidewalks are "slippy." We said, "That's all the farther I could go." And we said, as Pittsburghers do say, "This glass needs washed," or "The dog needs walked"—a usage our father eschewed; he knew it was not standard English, nor even comprehensible English, but he never let on.)

11   "Spell 'poinsettia,' " Mother would throw out at me, smiling with pleasure. "Spell 'sherbet.' " The idea was not to make us whizzes, but, quite the contrary, to remind us—and I, especially, needed reminding—that we didn't know it all just yet.

12   "There's a deer standing in the front hall," she told me one quiet evening in the country.

13   "Really?"

14   "No. I just wanted to tell you something once without your saying, 'I know.' "

15   Supermarkets in the middle 1950s began luring, or bothering, customers by giving out Top Value Stamps or Green Stamps. When, shopping with Mother, we got to the head of the checkout line, the checker, always a young man, asked, "Save stamps?"

16   "No," Mother replied genially, week after week, "I build model airplanes." I believe she originated this line. It took me years to determine where the joke lay.

17   Anyone who met her verbal challenges she adored. She had surgery on one of her eyes. On the operating table, just before she conked

out, she appealed feelingly to the surgeon, saying, as she had been planning to say for weeks, "Will I be able to play the piano?" "Not on me," the surgeon said. "You won't pull that old one on me."

18   It was, indeed, an old one. The surgeon was supposed to answer, "Yes, my dear, brave woman, you will be able to play the piano after this operation," to which Mother intended to reply, "Oh, good, I've always wanted to play the piano." This pat scenario bored her; she loved having it interrupted. It must have galled her that usually her acquaintances were so predictably unalert; it must have galled her that, for the length of her life, she could surprise everyone so continually, so easily, when she had been the same all along. At any rate, she loved anyone who, as she put it, saw it coming, and called her on it.

19   She regarded the instructions on bureaucratic forms as straight lines. "Do you advocate the overthrow of the United States government by force or violence?" After some thought she wrote, "Force." She regarded children, even babies, as straight men. When Molly learned to crawl, Mother delighted in buying her gowns with drawstrings at the bottom, like Swee'pea's, because, as she explained energetically, you could easily step on the drawstring without the baby's noticing, so that she crawled and crawled and crawled and never got anywhere except into a small ball at the gown's top.

20   When we children were young, she mothered us tenderly and dependably; as we got older, she resumed her career of anarchism. She collared us into her gags. If she answered the phone on a wrong number, she told the caller, "Just a minute," and dragged the receiver to Amy or me, saying, "Here, take this, your name is Cecile," or, worse, just, "It's for you." You had to think on your feet. But did you want to perform well as Cecile, or did you want to take pity on the wretched caller?

21   During a family trip to the Highland Park Zoo, Mother and I were alone for a minute. She approached a young couple holding hands on a bench by the seals, and addressed the young man in dripping tones: "Where have you been? Still got those baby-blue eyes; always did slay me. And this"—a swift nod at the dumbstruck young woman, who had removed her hand from the man's—"must be the one you were telling me about. She's not so bad, really, as you used to make out. But listen, you know how I miss you, you

know where to reach me, same old place. And there's Ann over there—see how she's grown? See the blue eyes?"

22   And off she sashayed, taking me firmly by the hand, and leading us around briskly past the monkey house and away. She cocked an ear back, and both of us heard the desperate man begin, in a high-pitched wail, "I swear, I never saw her before in my life . . ."

23   On a long, sloping beach by the ocean, she lay stretched out sunning with Father and friends, until the conversation gradually grew tedious, when without forethought she gave a little push with her heel and rolled away. People were stunned. She rolled deadpan and apparently effortlessly, arms and legs extended and tidy, down the beach to the distant water's edge, where she lay at ease just as she had been, but half in the surf, and well out of earshot.

24   She dearly loved to fluster people by throwing out a game's rules at whim—when she was getting bored, losing in a dull sort of way, and when everybody else was taking it too seriously. If you turned your back, she moved the checkers around on the board. When you got them all straightened out, she denied she'd touched them; the next time you turned your back, she lined them up on the rug or hid them under your chair. In a betting rummy game called Michigan, she routinely played out of turn, or called out a card she didn't hold, or counted backward, simply to amuse herself by causing an uproar and watching the rest of us do double takes and have fits. (Much later, when serious suitors came to call, Mother subjected them to this fast card game as a trial by ordeal; she used it as an intelligence test and a measure of spirit. If the poor man could stay a round without breaking down or running out, he got to marry one of us, if he still wanted to.)

25   She excelled at bridge, playing fast and boldly, but when the stakes were low and the hands dull, she bid slams for the devilment of it, or raised her opponents' suit to bug them, or showed her hand, or tossed her cards in a handful behind her back in a characteristic swift motion accompanied by a vibrantly innocent look. It drove our stolid father crazy. The hand was over before it began, and the guests were appalled. How do you score it, who deals now, what do you do with a crazy person who is having so much fun? Or they were down seven, and the guests were appalled. "Pam!" "Dammit, Pam!" He groaned. What ails such people? What on earth possesses them? He rubbed his face.

26   She was an unstoppable force; she never let go. When we moved across town, she persuaded the U.S. Post Office to let her keep her old address—forever—because she'd had stationery printed. I don't know how she did it. Every new post office worker, over decades, needed to learn that although the Doaks' mail is addressed to here, it is delivered to there.

27   Mother's energy and intelligence suited her for a greater role in a larger arena—mayor of New York, say—than the one she had. She followed American politics closely; she had been known to vote for Democrats. She saw how things should be run, but she had nothing to run but our household. Even there, small minds bugged her; she was smarter than the people who designed the things she had to use all day for the length of her life.

28   "Look," she said. "Whoever designed this corkscrew never used one. Why would anyone sell it without trying it out?" So she invented a better one. She showed me a drawing of it. The spirit of American enterprise never faded in Mother. If capitalizing and tooling up had been as interesting as theorizing and thinking up, she would have fired up a new factory every week, and chaired several hundred corporations.

29   "It grieves me," she would say, "it grieves my heart," that the company that made one superior product packaged it poorly, or took the wrong tack in its advertising. She knew, as she held the thing mournfully in her two hands, that she'd never find another. She was right. We children wholly sympathized, and so did Father; what could she do, what could anyone do, about it? She was Samson in chains. She paced.

30   She didn't like the taste of stamps so she didn't lick stamps; she licked the corner of the envelope instead. She glued sandpaper to the sides of kitchen drawers, and under kitchen cabinets, so she always had a handy place to strike a match. She designed, and hounded workmen to build against all norms, doubly wide kitchen counters and elevated bathroom sinks. To splint a finger, she stuck it in a lightweight cigar tube. Conversely, to protect a pack of cigarettes, she carried it in a Band-Aid box. She drew plans for an over-the-finger toothbrush for babies, an oven rack that slid up and down, and—the family favorite—Lendalarm. Lendalarm was a beeper you attached to books (or tools) you loaned friends. After ten days, the beeper sounded. Only the rightful owner could silence it.

31   She repeatedly reminded us of P. T. Barnum's dictum: You could

sell anything to anybody if you marketed it right. The adman who thought of making Americans believe they needed underarm deodorant was a visionary. So, too, was the hero who made a success of a new product, Ivory soap. The executives were horrified, Mother told me, that a cake of this stuff floated. Soap wasn't supposed to float. Anyone would be able to tell it was mostly whipped-up air. Then some inspired adman made a leap: Advertise that it floats. Flaunt it. The rest is history.

32   She respected the rare few who broke through to new ways. "Look," she'd say, "here's an intelligent apron." She called upon us to admire intelligent control knobs and intelligent pan handles, intelligent andirons and picture frames and knife sharpeners. She questioned everything, every pair of scissors, every knitting needle, gardening glove, tape dispenser. Hers was a restless mental vigor that just about ignited the dumb household objects with its force.

33   Torpid conformity was a kind of sin; it was stupidity itself, the mighty stream against which Mother would never cease to struggle. If you held no minority opinions, or if you failed to risk total ostracism for them daily, the world would be a better place without you.

34   Always I heard Mother's emotional voice asking Amy and me the same few questions: "Is that your own idea? Or somebody else's?" "*Giant* is a good movie," I pronounced to the family at dinner. "Oh, really?" Mother warmed to these occasions. She all but rolled up her sleeves. She knew I had't seen it. "Is that your considered opinion?"

35   She herself held many unpopular, even fantastic, positions. She was scathingly sarcastic about the McCarthy hearings while they took place, right on our living-room television; she frantically opposed Father's wait-and-see calm. "We don't know enough about it," he said. "I do," she said. "I know all I need to know."

36   She asserted, against all opposition, that people who lived in trailer parks were not bad but simply poor, and had as much right to settle on beautiful land, such as rural Ligonier, Pennsylvania, as did the oldest of families in the finest of hidden houses. Therefore, the people who owned trailer parks, and sought zoning changes to permit trailer parks, needed our help. Her profound belief that the country-club pool sweeper was a person, and that the department-store saleslady, the bus driver, telephone operator, and house-painter were people, and even in groups the steelworkers who carried pickets and the

Christmas shoppers who clogged intersections were people—this was a conviction common enough in democratic Pittsburgh, but not altogether common among our friends' parents, or even, perhaps, among our parents' friends.

37   Opposition emboldened Mother, and she would take on anybody on any issue—the chairman of the board, at a cocktail party, on the current strike; she would fly at him in a flurry of passion, as a songbird selflessly attacks a big hawk.

38   "Eisenhower's going to win," I announced after school. She lowered her magazine and looked me in the eyes: "How do you know?" I was doomed. It was fatal to say, "Everyone says so." We all knew well what happened. "Do you consult this Everyone before you make your decisions? What if Everyone decided to round up all the Jews?" Mother knew there was no danger of cowing me. She simply tried to keep us all awake. And in fact it was always clear to Amy and me, and to Molly when she grew old enough to listen, that if our classmates came to cruelty, just as much as if the neighborhood or the nation came to madness, we were expected to take, and would be each separately capable of taking, a stand.

Memory and Imagination

PATRICIA HAMPL

Patricia Hampl was born in 1946 in St. Paul, Minnesota. She earned a B.A. in 1968 at the University of Minnesota and an M.F.A. in 1970 at the University of Iowa. She now teaches writing at the University of Minnesota. She writes poetry, short fiction, and nonfiction. She has published two books of poetry: *Women before an Aquarium* (1978) and *Resort and Other Poems* (1983). Her autobiography, *A Romantic Education* (1981), won the Houghton Mifflin Literary Fellowship.

"Memory and Imagination" is taken from *A Romantic Education* and serves as Hampl's definition of her role as a memoirist. She opens with a description of her first piano lesson, but then questions her own memory of the events. She admits that she has distorted the truth and asks why we remember what we do and why our memories are distorted. She argues that we invent rather than transcribe the truth about what really happened in our past. She then explains her primary thesis: "I write in order to find out what I know." For her, then, a memoir is "the intersection of narration and reflection, of storytelling and essay-writing." So she writes autobiography because of "the radiance of the past—it draws me back and back to it."

1   When I was seven, my father, who played the violin on Sundays
with a nicely tortured flair which we considered artistic, led me by
the hand down a long, unlit corridor in St. Luke's School basement,
a sort of tunnel that ended in a room full of pianos. There many
little girls and a single sad boy were playing truly tortured scales and
arpeggios in a mash of troubled sound. My father gave me over to
Sister Olive Marie, who did look remarkably like an olive.

2   Her oily face gleamed as if it had just been rolled out of a can
and laid on the white plate of her broad, spotless wimple. She was
a small, plump woman; her body and the small window of her face
seemed to interpret the entire alphabet of olive: her face was a sallow
green olive placed upon the jumbo ripe olive of her black habit. I
trusted her instantly and smiled, glad to have my hand placed in the
hand of a woman who made sense, who provided the satisfaction of
being what she was: an Olive who looked like an olive.

3   My father left me to discover the piano with Sister Olive Marie
so that one day I would join him in mutually tortured piano-violin
duets for the edification of my mother and brother who sat at the
table meditatively spooning in the last of their pineapple sherbet
until their part was called for: they put down their spoons and clapped
while we bowed, while the sweet ice in their bowls melted, while
the music melted, and we all melted a little into each other for a
moment.

4   But first Sister Olive must do her work. I was shown middle C,
which Sister seemed to think terribly important. I stared at middle
C and then glanced away for a second. When my eye returned,
middle C was gone, its slim finger lost in the complicated grasp of
the keyboard. Sister Olive struck it again, finding it with laughable
ease. She emphasized the importance of middle C, its central position,
a sort of North Star of sound. I remember thinking, "Middle C is
the belly button of the piano," an insight whose originality and
accuracy stunned me with pride. For the first time in my life I was
astonished by metaphor. I hesitated to tell the kindly Olive for some
reason; apparently I understood a true metaphor is a risky business,
revealing of the self. In fact, I have never, until this moment of
writing it down, told my first metaphor to anyone.

5   Sunlight flooded the room; the pianos, all black, gleamed. Sister
Olive, dressed in the colors of the keyboard, gleamed; middle C
shimmered with meaning and I resolved never—never—to forget its
location: it was the center of the world.

6   Then Sister Olive, who had had to show me middle C twice but who seemed to have drawn no bad conclusions about me anyway, got up and went to the windows on the opposite wall. She pulled the shades down, one after the other. The sun was too bright, she said. She sneezed as she stood at the windows with the sun shedding its glare over her. She sneezed and sneezed, crazy little convulsive sneezes, one after another, as helpless as if she had the hiccups.

7   "The sun makes me sneeze," she said when the fit was over and she was back at the piano. This was odd, too odd to grasp in the mind. I associated sneezing with colds, and colds with rain, fog, snow and bad weather. The sun, however, had caused Sister Olive to sneeze in this wild way, Sister Olive who gleamed benignly and who was so certain of the location of the center of the world. The universe wobbled a bit and became unreliable. Things were not, after all, necessarily what they seemed. Appearance deceived: here was the sun acting totally out of character, hurling this woman into sneezes, a woman so mild that she was named, so it seemed, for a bland object on a relish tray.

8   I was given a red book, the first Thompson book, and told to play the first piece over and over at one of the black pianos where the other children were crashing away. This, I was told, was called practicing. It sounded alluringly adult, practicing. The piece itself consisted mainly of middle C, and I excelled, thrilled by my savvy at being able to locate that central note amidst the cunning camouflage of all the other white keys before me. Thrilled too by the shiny red book that gleamed, as the pianos did, as Sister Olive did, as my eager eyes probably did. I sat at the formidable machine of the piano and got to know middle C intimately, preparing to be as tortured as I could manage one day soon with my father's violin at my side.

9   But at the moment Mary Katherine Reilly was at my side, playing something at least two or three lessons more sophisticated than my piece. I believe she even struck a chord. I glanced at her from the peasantry of single notes, shy, ready to pay homage. She turned toward me, stopped playing, and sized me up.

10 Sized me up and found a person ready to be dominated. Without introduction she said, "'My grandfather invented the collapsible opera hat."

11 I nodded, I acquiesced, I was hers. With that little stroke it was decided between us—that she should be the leader, and I the sidekick. My job was admiration. Even when she added, "But he didn't make

a penny from it. He didn't have a patent"—even then, I knew and
she knew that this was not an admission of powerlessness, but the
easy candor of a master, of one who can afford a weakness or two.

12   With the clairvoyance of all fated relationships based on dominance
and submission, it was decided in advance: that when the time came
for us to play duets, I should always play second piano, that I should
spend my allowance to buy her the Twinkies she craved but was not
allowed to have, that finally, I should let her copy from my test
paper, and when confronted by our teacher, confess with convincing
hysteria that it was I, I who had cheated, who had reached above
myself to steal what clearly belonged to the rightful heir of the
inventor of the collapsible opera hat. . . .

13   There must be a reason I remember that little story about my first
piano lesson. In fact, it isn't a story, just a moment, the beginning
of what could perhaps become a story. For the memoirist, more
than for the fiction writer, the story seems already *there,* already
accomplished and fully achieved in history ("in reality," as we naively
say). For the memoirist, the writing of the story is a matter of transcription.

14   That, anyway, is the myth. But no memoirist writes for long
without experiencing an unsettling disbelief about the reliability of
memory, a hunch that memory is not, after all, *just* memory. I don't
know why I remembered this fragment about my first piano lesson.
I don't, for instance, have a single recollection of my first arithmetic
lesson, the first time I studied Latin, the first time my grandmother
tried to teach me to knit. Yet these things occurred too, and must
have their stories.

15   It is the piano lesson that has trudged forward, clearing the haze
of forgetfulness, showing itself bright with detail more than thirty
years after the event. I did not choose to remember the piano lesson.
It was simply there, like a book that has always been on the shelf,
whether I ever read it or not, the binding and title showing as I skim
across the contents of my life. On the day I wrote this fragment I
happened to take that memory, not some other, from the shelf and
paged through it. I found more detail, more event, perhaps a little
more entertainment than I had expected, but the memory itself was
there from the start. Waiting for me.

16   Or was it? When I reread what I had written just after I finished
it, I realized that I had told a number of lies. I *think* it was my father

who took me the first time for my piano lesson—but maybe he only took me to meet my teacher and there was no actual lesson that day. And did I even know then that he played the violin—didn't he take up his violin again much later, as a result of my piano playing, and not the reverse? And is it even remotely accurate to describe as "tortured" the musicianship of a man who began every day by belting out "Oh What a Beautiful Morning" as he shaved?

17   More: Sister Olive Marie did sneeze in the sun, but was her name Olive? As for her skin tone—I would have sworn in was olive-like; I would have been willing to spend the better part of an afternoon trying to write the exact description of imported Italian or Greek olive her face suggested: I wanted to get it right. But now, were I to write that passage over, it is her intense black eyebrows I would see, for suddenly they seem the central fact of that face, some indicative mark of her serious and patient nature. But the truth is, I don't remember the woman at all. She's a sneeze in the sun and a finger touching middle C. That, at least, is steady and clear.

18   Worse: I didn't have the Thompson book as my piano text. I'm sure of that because I remember envying children who did have this wonderful book with its pictures of children and animals printed on the pages of music.

19   As for Mary Katherine Reilly. She didn't even go to grade school with me (and her name isn't Mary Katherine Reilly—but I made that change on purpose). I met her in Girl Scouts and only went to school with her later, in high school. Our relationship was not really one of leader and follower; I played first piano most of the time in duets. She certainly never copied anything from a test paper of mine: she was a better student, and cheating just wasn't a possibility with her. Though her grandfather (or someone in her family) did invent the collapsible opera hat and I remember that she was proud of that fact, she didn't tell me this news as a deft move in a childish power play.

20   So, what was I doing in this brief memoir? Is it simply an example of the curious relation a fiction writer has to the material of her own life? Maybe. That may have some value in itself. But to tell the truth (if anyone still believes me capable of telling the truth), I wasn't writing fiction. I was writing memoir—or was trying to. My desire was to be accurate. I wished to embody the myth of memoir: to write as an act of dutiful transcription.

21   Yet clearly the work of writing narrative caused me to do some-

thing very different from transcription. I am forced to admit that memoir is not a matter of transcription, that memory itself is not a warehouse of finished stories, not a static gallery of framed pictures. I must admit that I invented. But why?

22   Two whys: why did I invent, and then, if a memoirist must inevitably invent rather than transcribe, why do I—why should anybody—write memoir at all?

23   I must respond to these impertinent questions because they, like the bumper sticker I saw the other day commanding all who read it to QUESTION AUTHORITY, challenge my authority as a memoirist and as a witness.

24   It still comes as a shock to realize that I don't write about what I know: I write in order to find out what I know. Is it possible to convey to a reader the enormous degree of blankness, confusion, hunch and uncertainty lurking in the act of writing? When I am the reader, not the writer, I too fall into the lovely illusion that the words before me (in a story by Mavis Gallant, an essay by Carol Bly, a memoir by M. F. K. Fisher), which *read* so inevitably, must also have been *written* exactly as they appear, rhythm and cadence, language and syntax, the powerful waves of the sentences laying themselves on the smooth beach of the page one after another faultlessly.

25   But here I sit before a yellow legal pad, and the long page of the preceding two paragraphs is a jumble of crossed-out lines, false starts, confused order. A mess. The mess of my mind trying to find out what it wants to say. This is a writer's frantic, grabby mind, not the poised mind of a reader ready to be edified or entertained.

26   I sometimes think of the reader as a cat, endlessly fastidious, capable, by turns, of mordant indifference and riveted attention, luxurious, recumbent, and ever poised. Whereas the writer is absolutely a dog, panting and moping, too eager for an affectionate scratch behind the ears, lunging frantically after any old stick thrown in the distance.

27   The blankness of a new page never fails to intrigue and terrify me. Sometimes, in fact, I think my habit of writing on long yellow sheets comes from an atavistic fear of the writer's stereotypic "blank white page." At least when I begin writing, my page isn't utterly blank; at least it has a wash of color on it, even if the absence of words must finally be faced on a yellow sheet as truly as on a blank white one. Well, we all have our ways of whistling in the dark.

28   If I approach writing from memory with the assumption that I

know what I wish to say, I assume that intentionality is running the show. Things are not that simple. Or perhaps writing is even more profoundly simple, more telegraphic and immediate in its choices than the grating wheels and chugging engine of logic and rational intention. The heart, the guardian of intuition with its secret, often fearful intentions, is the boss. Its commands are what a writer obeys—often without knowing it. Or, I do.

29   That's why I'm a strong adherent of the first draft. And why it's worth pausing for a moment to consider what a first draft really is. By my lights, the piano lesson memoir is a first draft. That doesn't mean it exists here exactly as I first wrote it. I like to think I've cleaned it up from the first time I put it down on paper. I've cut some adjectives here, toned down the hyperbole there, smoothed a transition, cut a repetition—that sort of housekeeperly tidying-up. But the piece remains a first draft because I haven't yet gotten to know it, haven't given it a chance to tell me anything. For me, writing a first draft is a little like meeting someone for the first time. I come away with a wary acquaintanceship, but the real friendship (if any) and genuine intimacy—that's all down the road. Intimacy with a piece of writing, as with a person, comes from paying attention to the revelations it is capable of giving, not by imposing my own preconceived notions, no matter how well-intentioned they might be.

30   I try to let pretty much anything happen in a first draft. A careful first draft is a failed first draft. That may be why there are so many inaccuracies in the piano lesson memoir: I didn't censor, I didn't judge. I kept moving. But I would not publish this piece as a memoir on its own in its present state. It isn't the "lies" in the piece that give me pause, though a reader has a right to expect a memoir to be as accurate as the writer's memory can make it. No, it isn't the lies themselves that make the piano lesson memoir a first draft and therefore "unpublishable."

31   The real trouble: the piece hasn't yet found its subject; it isn't yet about what it wants to be about. Note: what *it* wants, not what I want. The difference has to do with the relation a memoirist—any writer, in fact—has to unconscious or half-known intentions and impulses in composition.

32   Now that I have the fragment down on paper, I can read this little piece as a mystery which drops clues to the riddle of my feelings, like a culprit who wishes to be apprehended. My narrative self (the

culprit who has invented) wishes to be discovered by my reflective self, the self who wants to understand and make sense of a half-remembered story about a nun sneezing in the sun. . . .

33   We only store in memory images of value. The value may be lost over the passage of time (I was baffled about why I remembered that sneezing nun, for example), but that's the implacable judgment of feeling: *this,* we say somewhere deep within us, is something I'm hanging on to. And of course, often we cleave to things because they possess heavy negative charges. Pain likes to be vivid.

34   Over time, the value (the feeling) and the stored memory (the image) may become estranged. Memoir seeks a permanent home for feeling and image, a habitation where they can live together in harmony. Naturally, I've had a lot of experiences since I packed away that one from the basement of St. Luke's School; that piano lesson has been effaced by waves of feeling for other moments and episodes. I persist in believing the event has value—after all, I remember it—but in writing the memoir I did not simply relive the experience. Rather, I explored the mysterious relationship between all the images I could round up and the even more impacted feelings that caused me to store the images safely away in memory. Stalking the relationship, seeking the congruence between stored image and hidden emotion—that's the real job of memoir.

35   By writing about that first piano lesson, I've come to know things I could not know otherwise. But I only know these things as a result of reading this first draft. While I was writing, I was following the images, letting the details fill the room of the page and use the furniture as they wished. I was their dutiful servant—or thought I was. In fact, I was the faithful retainer of my hidden feelings which were giving the commands.

36   I really did feel, for instance, that Mary Katherine Reilly was far superior to me. She was smarter, funnier, more wonderful in every way—that's how I saw it. Our friendship (or she herself) did not require that I become her vassal, yet perhaps in my heart that was something I wanted; I wanted a way to express my feeling of admiration. I suppose I waited until this memoir to begin to find the way.

37   Just as, in the memoir, I finally possess that red Thompson book with the barking dogs and bleating lambs and winsome children. I couldn't (and still can't) remember what my own music book was, so I grabbed the name and image of the one book I could remember.

It was only in reviewing the piece after writing it that I saw my inaccuracy. In pondering this "lie," I came to see what I was up to: I was getting what I wanted. At last.

38 The truth of many circumstances and episodes in the past emerges for the memoirist through details (the red music book, the fascination with a nun's name and gleaming face), but these details are not merely information, not flat facts. Such details are not allowed to lounge. They must work. Their work is the creation of symbol. But it's more accurate to call it the *recognition* of symbol. For meaning is not "attached" to the detail by the memoirist; meaning is revealed. That's why a first draft is important. Just as the first meeting (good or bad) with someone who later becomes the beloved is important and is often reviewed for signals, meanings, omens, and indications.

39 Now I can look at that music book and see it not only as "a detail," but for what it is, how it *acts*. See it as the small red door leading straight into the dark room of my childhood longing and disappointment. That red book *becomes* the palpable evidence of that longing. In other words, it becomes symbol. There is no symbol, no life-of-the-spirit in the general or the abstract. Yet a writer wishes—indeed all of us wish—to speak about profound matters that are, like it or not, general and abstract. We wish to talk to each other about life and death, about love, despair, loss, and innocence. We sense that in order to live together we must learn to speak of peace, of history, of meaning and values. Those are a few.

40 We seek a means of exchange, a language which will renew these ancient concerns and make them wholly and pulsingly ours. Instinctively, we go to our store of private images and associations for our authority to speak of these weighty issues. We find, in our details and broken and obscured images, the language of symbol. Here memory impulsively reaches out its arms and embraces imagination. That is the resort to invention. It isn't a lie, but an act of necessity, as the innate urge to locate personal truth always is.

41 All right. Invention is inevitable. But why write memoir? Why not call it fiction and be done with all the hashing about, wondering where memory stops and imagination begins? And if memoir seeks to talk about "the big issues," about history and peace, death and love—why not leave these reflections to those with expert and scholarly knowledge? Why let the common or garden variety memoirist

into the club? I'm thinking again of that bumper sticker: why Question Authority?

42   My answer, of course, is a memoirist's answer. Memoir must be written because each of us must have a created version of the past. Created: that is, real, tangible, made of the stuff of a life lived in place and in history. And the down side of any created thing as well: we must live with a version that attaches us to our limitations, to the inevitable subjectivity of our points of view. We must acquiesce to our experience and our gift to transform experience into meaning and value. You tell me your story, I'll tell you my story.

43   If we refuse to do the work of creating this personal version of the past, someone else will do it for us. That is a scary political fact. "The struggle of man against power," a character in Milan Kundera's novel *The Book of Laughter and Forgetting* says, "is the struggle of memory against forgetting." He refers to willful political forgetting, the habit of nations and those in power (Question Authority!) to deny the truth of memory in order to disarm moral and ethical power. It's an efficient way of controlling masses of people. It doesn't even require much bloodshed, as long as people are entirely willing to give over their personal memories. Whole histories can be rewritten. As Czeslaw Milosz said in his 1980 Nobel Prize lecture, the number of books published that seek to deny the existence of the Nazi death camps now exceeds one hundred.

44   What is remembered is what *becomes* reality. If we "forget" Auschwitz, if we "forget" My Lai, what then do we remember? And what is the purpose of our remembering? If we think of memory naively, as a simple story, logged like a documentary in the archive of the mind, we miss its beauty but also its function. The beauty of memory rests in its talent for rendering detail, for paying homage to the senses, its capacity to love the particles of life, the richness and idiosyncrasy of our existence. The function of memory, on the other hand, is intensely personal and surprisingly political.

45   Our capacity to move forward as developing beings rests on a healthy relation with the past. Psychotherapy, that widespread method of mental health, relies heavily on memory and on the ability to retrieve and organize images and events from the personal past. We carry our wounds and perhaps even worse, our capacity to wound, forward with us. If we learn not only to tell our stories but to listen to what our stories tell us—to write the first draft and then return for the second draft—we are doing the work of memoir.

46   Memoir is the intersection of narration and reflection, of storytelling and essay-writing. It can present its story *and* reflect and consider the meaning of the story. It is a peculiarly open form, inviting broken and incomplete images, half-recollected fragments, all the mass (and mess) of detail. It offers to shape this confusion—and in shaping, of course it necessarily creates a work of art, not a legal document. But then, even legal documents are only valiant attempts to consign the truth, the whole truth and nothing but the truth to paper. Even they remain versions.

47   Locating touchstones—the red music book, the olive Olive, my father's violin playing—is deeply satisfying. Who knows why? Perhaps we all sense that we can't grasp the whole truth and nothing but the truth of our experience. Just can't be done. What can be achieved, however, is a version of its swirling, changing wholeness. A memoirist must acquiesce to selectivity, like any artist. The version we dare to write is the only truth, the only relationship we can have with the past. Refuse to write your life and you have no life. At least, that is the stern view of the memoirist.

48   Personal history, logged in memory, is a sort of slide projector flashing images on the wall of the mind. And there's precious little order to the slides in the rotating carousel. Beyond that confusion, who knows who is running the projector? A memoirist steps into this darkened room of flashing, unorganized images and stands blinking for a while. Maybe for a long while. But eventually, as with any attempt to tell a story, it is necessary to put something first, then something else. And so on, to the end. That's a first draft. Not necessarily the truth, not even *a* truth sometimes, but the first attempt to create a shape.

49   The first thing I usually notice at this stage of composition is the appalling inaccuracy of the piece. Witness my first piano lesson draft. Invention is screamingly evident in what I intended to be transcription. But here's the further truth: I feel no shame. In fact, it's only now that my interest in the piece truly quickens. For I can see what isn't there, what is shyly hugging the walls, hoping not to be seen. I see the filmy shape of the next draft. I see a more acute version of the episode or—this is more likely—an entirely new piece rising from the ashes of the first attempt.

50   The next draft of the piece would have to be a true re-vision, a new seeing of the materials of the first draft. Nothing merely cosmetic will do—no rouge buffing up the opening sentence, no glossy adjec-

tive to lift a sagging line, nothing to attempt covering a patch of gray writing. None of that. I can't say for sure, but my hunch is the revision would lead me to more writing about my father (why was I so impressed by that ancestral inventor of the collapsible opera hat? Did I feel I had nothing as remarkable in my own background? Did this make me feel inadequate?). I begin to think perhaps Sister Olive is less central to this business than she is in this draft. She is meant to be a moment, not a character.

51   And so I might proceed, if I were to undertake a new draft of the memoir. I begin to feel a relationship developing between a former self and me.

52   And, even more compelling, a relationship between an old world and me. Some people think of autobiographical writing as the precious occupation of a particularly self-absorbed person. Maybe, but I don't buy that. True memoir is written in an attempt to find not only a self but a world.

53   The self-absorption that seems to be the impetus and embarrassment of autobiography turns into (or perhaps always was) a hunger for the world. Actually, it begins as hunger for *a* world, one gone or lost, effaced by time or a more sudden brutality. But in the act of remembering, the personal environment expands, resonates beyond itself, beyond its "subject," into the endless and tragic recollection that is history.

54   We look at old family photographs in which we stand next to black, boxy Fords and are wearing period costumes, and we do not gaze fascinated because there we are young again, or there we are standing, as we never will again in life, next to our mother. We stare and drift because there we are . . . historical. It is the dress, the black car that dazzle us now and draw us beyond our mother's bright arms which once caught us. We reach into the attractive impersonality of something more significant than ourselves. We write memoir, in other words. We accept the humble position of writing a version rather than "the whole truth."

55   I suppose I write memoir because of the radiance of the past—it draws me back and back to it. Not that the past is beautiful. In our communal memoir, in history, the death camps *are* back there. In intimate life too, the record is usually pretty mixed. "I could tell you stories . . ." people say and drift off, meaning terrible things have happened to them.

56   But the past is radiant. It has the light of lived life. A memoirist

wishes to touch it. No one owns the past, though typically the first act of new political regimes, whether of the left or the right, is to attempt to re-write history, to grab the past and make it over so the end comes out right. So their power looks inevitable.

57　No one owns the past, but it is a grave error (another age would have said a grave sin) not to inhabit memory. Sometimes I think it is all we really have. But that may be a trifle melodramatic. At any rate, memory possesses authority for the fearful self in a world where it is necessary to have authority in order to Question Authority.

58　There may be no more pressing intellectual need in our culture than for people to become sophisticated about the function of memory. The political implications of the loss of memory are obvious. The authority of memory is a personal confirmation of selfhood. To write one's life is to live it twice, and the second living is both spiritual and historical, for a memoir reaches deep within the personality as it seeks its narrative form and also grasps the life-of-the-times as no political treatise can.

59　Our most ancient metaphor says life is a journey. Memoir is travel writing, then, notes taken along the way, telling how things looked and what thoughts occurred. But I cannot think of the memoirist as a tourist. This is the traveller who goes on foot, living the journey, taking on mountains, enduring deserts, marveling at the lush green places. Moving through it all faithfully, not so much a survivor with a harrowing tale to tell as a pilgrim, seeking, wondering.

Wounded Chevy
at Wounded Knee

DIANA
HUME GEORGE

Diana Hume George (b. 1948) grew up in New York near the Cattaraugus Seneca Indian Reservation. As a rebellious teenager, she says, "I . . . shifted my social and sexual arena entirely to the Indian world." She married an Indian carnival worker, bore him a son, and lived with Native Americans for five years. After leaving the reservation, she entered the academic world to write extensively in American studies and feminist theory. Her special interest has been the life and poetry of Anne Sexton, which has resulted in *Oedipus Anne: The Poetry of Anne Sexton* (1987). In addition, George has published two volumes of her own poetry, a book on Blake and Freud, and *Epitaph and Icon: A Field Guide to the Old Burying Grounds of Cape Cod, Martha's Vineyard, and Nantucket* (1983, coauthored with Malcolm A. Nelson).

"Wounded Chevy at Wounded Knee" appeared in *The Missouri Review* in 1990. It is part of her larger work, *The Lonely Other: A Woman Watching America,* a group of essays that blend her social analysis with her personal experiences. In this essay, she travels with a fellow historian in search of answers at Wounded Knee, the sight of an Indian massacre in 1890. She admits that her "position has been very strange perhaps, given that I was married to an American Indian for five years, lived on a reservation, and am the mother of a half-Indian son." What she communicates in the essay is a grim forecast: "Any culture in its death throes is a grim spectacle, and there can be no grimmer reality than that endured by people on their way to annihilation." Her experiences among the Lakota Indians only confirmed her vision.

-Pine Ridge Sioux Reservation, July 1989

1   "If you break down on that reservation, your car belongs to the Indians. They don't like white people out there." This was our amiable motel proprietor in Custer, South Dakota, who asked where we were headed and then propped a conspiratorial white elbow on the counter and said we'd better make sure our vehicle was in good shape. To get to Wounded Knee, site of the last cavalry massacre of the Lakota in 1890 and of more recent confrontations between the FBI and the American Indian Movement, you take a road out of Pine Ridge on the Lakota Reservation and go about eight miles. If you weren't watching for it you could miss it, because nothing is there but a hill, a painted board explaining what happened, a tiny church, and a cemetery.

2   The motel man told us stories about his trucking times, when by day his gas stops were friendly, but by night groups of Indian men who'd been drinking used to circle his truck looking for something to steal—or so he assumed. He began carrying a .357 Magnum with him "just in case." Once he took his wife out to Pine Ridge. "She broke out in hives before we even got there." And when they were stopped on the roadside and a reservation policeman asked if they needed help, she was sure he was going to order her out of the car, steal it, and, I suppose, rape and scalp her while he was at it. As he told us these contradictory stories, he seemed to be unaware of the irony of warning us that the Indians would steal our car if they got a chance, and following with a story about an Indian who tried to help them just in case they might be having trouble.

3   He did make a distinction between the reservation toughs and the police. He wasn't a racist creep, but rather a basically decent fellow whose view of the world was narrowly white. I briefly entertained the notion of staying a while, pouring another cup of coffee, and asking

him a few questions that would make him address the assumptions behind his little sermon, but I really wanted to get on my way, and I knew he wasn't going to change his mind about Indians here in the middle of his life in the middle of the Black Hills.

4   Mac and I exchanged a few rueful remarks about it while we drove. But we both knew that the real resistance to dealing with Indian culture on these trips that have taken us through both Pueblo and Plains Indian territories hasn't come from outside of our car or our minds, but rather from within them. More specifically, from within me. For years Mac has read about the Plains Indians with real attentiveness, and with an openness to learning what he can about the indigenous peoples of North America. He reads histories, biographies, novels, and essays, thinks carefully about the issues involved, remembers what he has read, informs himself with curiosity and respect about tribes that have occupied the areas we visit. For a couple of years he urged me toward these materials, many of which have been visible around our home for years: *Black Elk Speaks, In a Sacred Manner We Live, Bury My Heart at Wounded Knee,* studies of Indian spiritual and cultural life. While we were in Lakota country this time, he was reading Mari Sandoz' biography of Crazy Horse. But he has long since given up on getting me to pay sustained attention to these rich materials, because my resistance has been firm and long-standing. I am probably better informed about Indian life than most Americans ever thought of being, but not informed enough for a thoughtful reader and writer. My resistance has taken the form of a mixture of pride and contempt: pride that I already know more than these books can tell me, and contempt for the white liberal-intellectual's romance with all things Indian. But my position has been very strange perhaps, given that I was married to an American Indian for five years, lived on a reservation, and am the mother of a half-Indian son.

5   I've been mostly wrong in my attitudes, but it's taken me years to understand that. Wounded Knee is where I came to terms with my confusion, rejection, and ambivalence, and it happened in a direct confrontation with past events that are now twenty years old. My resistance broke down because of an encounter with a young Lakota named Mark, who is just about my own son's age.

6   I grew up in the 1950s and 1960s in a small white community on the edge of the Cattaraugus Seneca Indian Reservation in western New York State. Relations between Indians and whites in my world

were bitter, and in many respects replicated the dynamics between whites and blacks in the South, with many exceptions due to the very different functions and circumstances of these two groups of people of color in white America. The school system had recently been integrated after the closing of the Thomas Indian School on the reservation. The middle class whites wanted nothing to do with the Indians, whom they saw as drunkards and degenerates, in many cases subhuman. When I rebelled against the restraints of my white upbringing, the medium for asserting myself against my parents and my world was ready-made, and I grabbed it.

7   I began hanging out on the reserve with young Indians and shifted my social and sexual arena entirely to the Indian world. I fell in love with an idea of noble darkness in the form of an Indian carnival worker, got pregnant by him, married him, left the white world completely, and moved into his. Despite the fact that this was the sixties, my actions weren't politically motivated; or, rather, my politics were entirely personal at that point. While my more aware counterparts might have done some of the same things as conscious political and spiritual statements, I was fifteen when I started my romance with Indians, and I only knew that I was in love with life outside the constricting white mainstream, and with all the energy that vibrates on the outer reaches of cultural stability. My heart, and what would later become my politics, were definitely in the right place, and I have never regretted where I went or what I came to know. But for twenty years that knowledge spoiled me for another kind of knowing.

8   Whatever my romantic notions were about the ideal forms of American Indian wisdom—closeness to the land, respect for other living creatures, a sense of harmony with natural cycles, a way of walking lightly in the world, a manner of living that could make the ordinary and profane into the sacred—I learned that on the reservation I was inhabiting a world that was contrary to all these values. American Indian culture at the end of the road has virtually none of these qualities. White America has destroyed them. Any culture in its death throes is a grim spectacle, and there can be no grimmer reality than that endured by people on their way to annihilation.

9   I did not live among the scattered wise people or political activists of the Seneca Nation. I did not marry a nominal American Indian from a middle-class family. I married an illiterate man who dropped out of school in the seventh grade and was in school only intermit-

tently before that. He traveled around the east with carnivals running a ferris wheel during the summer months, and logged wood on the reservation during the winter—when he could get work. Home base was an old trailer without plumbing, in the woods, where his mother lived. He drank sporadically but heavily, and his weekends, often his weekdays, were full of pool tables, bar brawls, the endlessness of hanging out with little to do. He didn't talk much. How I built this dismal life into a romanticized myth about still waters running deep gives me an enduring respect for the mythopoeic, self-deluding power of desire, wish, will.

10   When I was married to him my world was a blur of old cars driven by drunk men in the middle of the night, of honky-tonk bars, country music, late night fights with furniture flying, food stamps and welfare lines, stories of injury and death. The smell of beer still sickens me slightly. I was sober as a saint through all of this, so I didn't have the insulation of liquor, only of love. I lived the contrary of every white myth about Indian life, both the myths of the small town white racists and those of the smitten hippies. When I finally left that life behind, extricating myself and my child in the certain knowledge that to stay would mean something very like death for both of us, I removed myself in every respect. I knew how stupid white prejudice was, understood the real story about why Indians drank and wasted their lives, felt the complexities so keenly that I couldn't even try to explain them to anyone white. But similarly, I knew how bird-brained the lovechild generation's romance with Indian culture was.

11   My husband went on to a career of raping white women that had begun during—or maybe before—our marriage. When he was finally caught, convicted and sent to Attica, I was long since done with that part of my life. My son pulled me back toward it with his own love for his father, and I still keep in touch with my husband's mother on the reservation, sometimes helping her to handle white bureaucracy, but that's all. I heard at a remove of miles, of eons, it seemed, about the early deaths of young men I'd known well—deaths due to diabetes, to lost limbs, or to car wrecks at high speed—and I felt something, but I didn't have to deal with it. When I tried to think about that past life in order to put it into some kind of perspective, no whole picture emerged. When I tried to write about it, no words would come. And when I tried to be open to learning something new about Indians in America on my trips, my heart closed up tight, and with it my mind. When I went to Wounded Knee, the wounds

of these other Indians half a continent and half a lifetime away were a part of the landscape.

12 We pull off the side of the road to read the billboard that tells what happened here. "MASSACRE OF WOUNDED KNEE" is the header, but upon close inspection you see that "Massacre" is a new addition, painted over something else. "Battle," perhaps? What did it used to say, I wonder, and hope I'll run into a local who can tell me. While I'm puzzling over this, an old Chevy sputters into the pull-off and shakes to a stop. It's loaded with dark faces, a young man and an older woman with many small children. The man gets out and walks slowly to the front of the car, rolling up his T-shirt over his stomach to get air on his skin. As he raises the hood, a Comanche truck pulls in beside him with one woman inside. It's very hot, and I weave a little in the glare of sun. Suddenly I see the past, superimposed on this hot moment. I've seen it before, again and again, cars full of little Indian kids in the heat of summer on the sides of roads. I glance again, see the woman in the front seat, know that she's their mother or their aunt. She looks weary and resigned, not really sad. She expects this.

13 And then in another blink it's not only that I have seen this woman; I have *been* this woman, my old car or someone else's packed with little kids who are almost preternaturally quiet, wide-eyed and dark skinned and already knowing that this is a big part of what life is about, sitting in boiling back seats, their arms jammed against the arms of their brother, their sister, their cousin. There is no use asking when they'll get there, wherever "there" is. It will happen when it happens, when the adults as helpless as they figure out what to do. In the meantime they sweat and stare. But I am not this woman any more, not responsible for these children, some of whose intelligent faces will blank into a permanent sheen of resignation before they're five. I am a tourist in a new Plymouth Voyager, my luggage rack packed with fine camping equipment, my Minolta in my hand to snap pictures of the places I can afford to go.

14 When Mac suggests that we offer to help them, I am not surprised at my flat negative feeling. He doesn't know what that means, I surmise, and I don't have any way to tell him. Help them? Do you want to get anywhere today, do you have the whole afternoon? The young man's shoulders bend over the motor. He is fit and beautiful, his good torso moves knowingly but powerlessly over the heat rising

from beneath the hood. I recognize him, as well as the woman. He has no job. He talks about getting off the reservation, finding work, living the dreams he still has. He'll talk this way for a few more years, then give up entirely. He drinks too much. He has nothing to do. Drinking is the only thing that makes him really laugh, and his only way to release rage. I also know that whatever else is wrong with it the car is out of gas, and that these people have no money. Okay, sure, I say to Mac, standing to one side while he asks how we can help. Close to the car now, I see that the woman is the young man's mother. These kids are his brothers and sisters.

15   The car is out of gas and it needs a jump. The battery is bad. The woman in the other car is the young man's aunt, who can give him a jump but has no money to give him for gas—or so she says. I know her, too. She is more prosperous than her relatives, and has learned the hard way never to give them any money, because she needs it herself and if she gives it to them she'll never see it again. She made her policy years ago, and makes it stick no matter what. She has to.

16   Well, then, we'll take them to the nearest gas station. Do they have a gas can? No, just a plastic washer fluid jug with no top. Okay, that will have to do. How far is the nearest gas? Just up the road a couple of miles. But they don't have any money because they were on their way to cash his mother's unemployment check when they ran out of gas, and the town where they can do that is many miles away. So can we loan them some money for gas? We can. He gets in the front seat. I get in the back, and as we pull away from the windy parking area, I look at the woman and the kids who will be sitting in the car waiting until we return. She knows she can't figure out how soon that will be. She stares straight ahead. I don't want to catch her eye, nor will she catch mine.

17   Right here up this road. Mark is in his early twenties. Mac asks him questions. He is careful and restrained in his answers at first, then begins to open up. No, there's no work around here. Sometimes he does a little horse-breaking or fence-mending for the ranchers. All the ranches here are run by whites who had the money to make the grim land yield a living. They lease it from the Lakota. Mark went away to a Job Corps camp last year, but he had to come back because his twenty-one year old brother died last winter, leaving his mother alone with the little ones. He froze to death. He was drinking at a party, and went outside to take a leak. Mark said they figured he must have just stopped for a minute to rest, and then he fell

asleep. They found him frozen in the morning. Mark had to come back home to bury his brother and help his mother with the kids.

18   As we bounce over the dirt road, I stare at the back of Mark's head and at his good Indian profile when he turns toward Mac to speak. He is so familiar to me that I could almost reach out to touch his black straight hair, his brown shoulder. He is my husband, he is my son. I want to give him hope. He speaks about getting out of here, going to "Rapid"—Lakota shorthand for Rapid City—and making a life. He is sick of having nothing to do, he wants work, wants an apartment. But he can't leave yet; he has to stay to help his mother. But things are going to be okay, because he has just won a hundred thousand dollars and is waiting for them to send the check.

19   What?

20   "You know the Baja Sweepstakes?" He pronounces it Bay-jah. "Well, I won it, I think I won it, I got a letter. My little brother sent in the entry form we got with my CD club and he put my name on it, and it came back saying that I'm one of a select few chosen people who've won a hundred thousand dollars. That's what it said, it said that, and I had to scratch out the letters and if three of them matched it means I win, and they matched, and so I sent it back in and now I'm just waiting for my money. It should come pretty soon and then everything will be okay." He repeats it over and over again in the next few minutes: he's one of a select few chosen people.

21   As he speaks of this, his flat voice becomes animated. Slowly I begin to believe that he believes this. Whatever part of him knows better is firmly shelved for now. This hope, this belief that hundreds of thousands of dollars are on the way is what keeps him going, what keeps him from walking out into the sky—or to the outhouse in the winter to take a leak and a nap in the snow. What will you do with the money, I ask. Well, first he is going to buy his mother and the kids a house.

22   The first gas stop is a little shack that's closed when we finally get there. Sandy wind and no sign of life. Miles on down the road is a small Lakota grocery store with only a few items on the shelves and a sign that reads "Stealing is not the Lakota way." Mac hands Mark a five-dollar bill. You can kiss that five bucks good-bye, I say to Mac. I know, he nods. When Mark comes back out he has the gas, and also a big cup of Seven-Up and a bag of Nachos. You want some, he asks me? He hands Mac a buck fifty in change. On the way back

I hold the gas can in the back seat, placing my hand over the opening. Despite the open windows, the van fills with fumes. My head begins to ache. I am riding in a dream of flatness, ranch fences, Mark's dark head in front of me wishing away his life, waiting for the break that takes him to Rapid. Later I learn that we are in Manderson, and this is the road where Black Elk lived.

23   Mark is talking about white people now. Yes, they get along okay. For "yes" he has an expression of affirmation that sounds sort of like "huh." Mari Sandoz spells it "hou" in her books on the Lakota. The Lakota are infiltrated in every way by whites, according to Mark. Lots of people in charge are white, the ranchers are white. And there's a place in Rapid called Lakota Hills, fancy houses meant for Lakotas, but whites live in them. Later it occurs to us that this is probably a development named Lakota Hills that has nothing at all to do with the Indians, but it has their name and so Mark thinks it belongs to them. I am angry for him that we borrow their name this way and paste it on our air-conditioned prosperity. I don't have anything to say to him. I lean back and close my eyes. It would be easy to be one of them again. I remember now how it's done. You just let everything flatten inside.

24   And when we return to Wounded Knee, the pull-off is empty. Mother, children, car, aunt, all are gone. There's nothing but wind and dust. This doesn't surprise me. Mark's mother knows better than to wait for her son's return if other help comes along. Mark means well, but maybe she has learned that sometimes it's hours before he gets back with gas—hours and a couple of six-packs if he has the chance. Now we face the prospect of driving Mark around the reservation until we can find them. I have just resigned myself to this when his aunt pulls back in and says they're broken down again a couple of miles up. We can leave now. Mark thanks us, smiles, and shyly allows us the liberty of having his aunt take a picture of all three of us. I am feeling a strange kind of shame, as though I had seen him naked, because he told us his secret and I knew it was a lie.

25   Unemployment, high rates of suicide and infant mortality, fetal alcohol syndrome, death by accident and drinking-related diseases such as diabetes: these are now the ways that American Indians are approaching their collective demise. Over a century ago, American whites began this destruction by displacing and killing the *pte*, the Indian name for the buffalo the plains Indians depended upon. We

herded them together in far crueler ways than they had herded the bison, whose sacredness the Indians respected even as they killed them for food and shelter. The history of our genocide is available in many historical and imaginative sources. What is still elusive, still amazingly misunderstood, is how and why the Indians seem to have participated in their own destruction by their failure to adapt to changed circumstances.

26   Whites can point to the phenomenal adjustments of other non-Caucasian groups in America, most recently the Asians, who were badly mistreated and who have nevertheless not only adapted but excelled. Indians even come off badly in comparison to the group in some respects most parallel to them, American blacks, whose slowness in adapting seems at first glance to have more justification. Blacks were, after all, our slaves, brought here against their will, without close cultural ties to keep them bound together in a tradition of strength; and on the whole blacks are doing better than Indians. However slowly, a black middle class is emerging in America. What's the matter with Indians? Why haven't they adjusted better as a group?

27   The American Indian Movement is of course strong in some areas, and Indians have articulate, tough leaders and savvy representatives of their cause who are fighting hard against the tide of despair gripping the heart of their race. But they're still losing, and they know it. Estimates of unemployment on the Pine Ridge and Rosebud reservations run as high as 85%. Health officials at Pine Ridge estimate that as many as 25% of babies born on the reservation now have fetal alcohol syndrome. This culturally lethal condition cannot be overemphasized, since it means that the next generation of Lakota are genetically as well as socioeconomically crippled; one of the consequences of fetal alcohol syndrome is not only physical disability, but mental retardation. The prospects are phenomenally depressing for Lakota leaders whose traditional values are associated with mental acuity and imaginative wisdom. Mark is vastly ignorant and gullible, but he is intelligent enough. Many of his younger brothers and sisters are not only underprivileged and without educational advantages, but also—let the word be spoken—stupid. When the light of inquiry, curiosity, mental energy, dies out in the eyes of young Indians early in their stunted lives because they have nowhere to go and nothing to do, it is one kind of tragedy. When it is never present to die out in the first place, the magnitude of the waste and devastation is exponentially increased. Indian leaders who are now concentrating

on anti-alcohol campaigns among their people are doing so for good reasons.

28   Indian leaders disagree about culpability at this point. Essentially the arguments become theories of genocide or suicide. On one end of the spectrum of blame is the theory that it is all the fault of white America. The evidence that can be marshalled for this point of view is massive: broken treaties, complete destruction of the Indian ways of life, welfare dependency established as the cheapest and easiest form of guilt payment, continued undermining of Indian autonomy and rights. The problem with this perspective, say others, is that it perpetuates Indian desperation and permits the easy way out—spend your life complaining that white America put you here, and drink yourself into the oblivion of martyrdom instead of taking responsibility for your own life. Some Indians say they've heard enough about white America's culpability, and prefer to transfer responsibility—not blame, but responsibility—to the shoulders of their own people. "White people aren't doing this to us—we're doing it to ourselves," said one Pine Ridge health official on National Public Radio's Morning Edition recently. She sees the victim stance as the lethal enemy now.

29   The situation is as nearly hopeless as it is possible to be. Assimilation failed the first time and would fail if tried concertedly again, because Indian culture is rural and tribal, and tied to open land, not urban airlessness. The Indian model is the encampment or village—the latter more recently and under duress—and not the city. Even the more stationary pueblo model is by definition not urban. The only real hope for Indian prosperity would be connected to vast tracts of land—not wasteland, but rich land. Nor are most Indians farmers in the sense that white America defines the farm. Though they might be, and have been, successful farmers under pressure, this is not their traditional milieu. Supposing that many tribes could adapt to the farming model over hunting and gathering, they would need large tracts of fine land to farm—and there are none left to grant them.

30   When the American government gave the Lakota 160 acres apiece and said "Farm this," they misunderstood the Indians completely; and even if Indians had been able to adapt readily—a change approximately as difficult as asking an urban yuppie to become a nomad moving from encampment to encampment—the land they were given was inadequate to the purpose. Grubbing a living out of the land

we have given them—in what John Wesley Powell called "the arid region" west of the one hundredth meridian—takes a kind of know-how developed and perfected by white Americans, and it also takes capital. It is no coincidence that the large ranches on Pine Ridge are almost entirely leased by whites who had the initial wherewithal to make the land yield.

31   The Sioux were a people whose lives were shaped by a sense of seeking and vision that white America could barely understand, even if we were to try—and we do not try. The life of a Sioux of a century and a half ago was framed by the Vision Quest, a search for goals, identity, purpose. One primary means of fulfillment was self-sacrifice. Now, as Royal Hassrick has written, "No longer is there anything which they can deny themselves, and so they have sacrificed themselves in pity." Whereas they were once people whose idea of being human was bound to creative self-expression, their faces now reflect what Hassrick calls "apathy and psychic emaciation." Collectively and individually they have become a people without a vision.

32   Why do they drink themselves into obliteration and erasure? Why not? When white America approaches the problem from within our own ethnocentric biases, we can't see why people would allow themselves to be wasted in this way, why they would not take the initiative to better themselves, to save themselves through the capitalist individuality that says "*I* will make it out of this." But in fact part of their problem is that they have tried to do this, as have most Indian peoples. They've bought the American dream in part, and become greedy for money and material goods. Life on an Indian reservation—almost any reservation—is a despairing imitation of white middle-class values. In this respect Indians are like all other minority groups in ghettos in America, and this explains why Mark has a CD player instead of the more modest possessions we would not have begrudged him. If he is anything like the Indians I lived with, he also has a color TV, though he may well live in a shack or trailer without plumbing and without siding.

33   Their own dreams have evaded them, and so have ours. Mark and his brothers and sisters have been nourished on memories of a culture that vanished long before they were born, and on the promises of a different one, from whose advantages they are forever excluded. Does Mark really believe he has won the sweepstakes? What he received was obviously one of those computer letters that invites the recipient to believe that he has won something. Without the education that

could teach him to read its language critically—or to read it adequately at all—he has been deceived into believing that a *deus ex machina* in the form of the Baja Sweepstakes will take him out of his despair.

34   In 1890, the year of the final defeat of the Sioux at Wounded Knee, the Ghost Dance was sweeping the plains. Begun by a few leaders, especially the Paiute seer Wovoka, the Ghost Dance promised its practitioners among the warriors that the buffalo would return and the white man would be defeated. Ghost Dancers believed that their ceremonial dancing and the shirts they wore would make them proof against the white man's bullets. Among the Sioux Warriors at Wounded Knee, the willing suspension of disbelief was complete. It made the warriors reckless and abandoned, throwing normal caution and survival strategy to the wind.

35   A tragically inverted form of the self-delusion embodied in the Ghost Dance is practiced today on Pine Ridge and other Sioux reservations. The original Ghost Dance has beauty and vitality, as well as desperation, as its sources. Now many Sioux men who would have been warriors in another time behave as though liquor and passivity will not kill them. Mark chooses to suspend his disbelief in white promises, and to wait for a hundred thousand dollars to arrive in the mail.

36   Hank Doctor was my husband's best friend on the Seneca reservation. He was raunchy, hard-drinking, outrageous in behavior and looks. His hair was long and scraggly, his nearly black eyes were genuinely wild, and his blue jeans were always caked with dust and falling down his hips. His wit was wicked, his laugh raucous, dangerous, infectious. Hank was merciless toward me, always making white-girl jokes, telling me maybe I better go home to my mama where I'd be safe from all these dark men. He wanted me to feel a little afraid in his world, told me horrible stories about ghost-dogs that would get me on the reservation if I ventured out at night—and then he'd laugh in a way that said hey, white girl, just joking, but not entirely. He alternated his affection toward me with edgy threats; made fun of the too-white way I talked or walked; took every opportunity to make me feel foolish and out of place. He was suspicious that I was just slumming it as a temporary rebellion—maybe taking notes in my head—and that I'd probably run for home when the going got too tough. Of course he was right, even though I didn't know it at the time. I liked him a lot.

37   A few years ago, my son Bernie went through a period when he chose to remove himself from my world and go live in his father's, from which I'd taken him when he was three. I didn't try to stop him, even though I knew he was hanging out with people who lived dangerously. I used to lie in bed unable to go to sleep because I was wondering what tree he'd end up wrapped around with his dad. He was a minor, but I was essentially helpless to prevent this. If I'd forced the issue, it would only have made his desire to know a forbidden world more intense. He lived there for months, and I slowly learned to get to sleep at night. Mothers can't save their children. And he had a right.

38   The day I knew he'd ultimately be okay was when he came home and told me about Hank. He wondered if I'd known Hank? He'd never met him before because Hank had been out west for years. Now he was back home, living in a shack way out in the country, terribly crippled with diabetes and other ailments from drinking, barely able to walk. Hank would have been in his midforties at this time. Bernie and his dad took rabbits to Hank when they went hunting so that Hank would have something to eat. During these visits, Hank talked non-stop about the old days, reminding big Bernard of all their bar brawls, crowing to young Bernie that the two of them could beat anyone then they fought as a team, recounting the times they'd dismantled the insides of buildings at four in the morning. He told his stories in vivid, loving detail. His gift for metaphor was precise and fine, his memory perfect even if hyperbolic. He recalled the conversations leading up to fights; the way a person had leaned over the bar; and who had said what to whom just before the furniture flew.

39   Bernie was impressed with him, but mostly he thought it was pathetic, this not-yet-old man, who looked like he was in his seventies, with nothing to remember but brawls. I told Bernie to value Hank for the way he remembered, the way he could make a night from twenty years ago intensely present again, his gift for swagger and characterization, his poetry, his laughter. In another time Hank would have been a tribal narrator, a story-catcher with better exploits to recount. He would have occupied a special place in Seneca life because of his gifts.

40   My son left the reservation valuing and understanding important things about his father's world, but not interested in living in its grip. He lives in Florida where he's a chef in a resort, and he's going

to college. A month ago his daughter, my granddaughter, was born. She is named Sequoia, after the Cherokee chief who gave his people an alphabet and a written language. Bernie took her to the reservation on his recent visit north and introduced the infant Sequoia to her great-grandmother. My husband's mother says that big Bernard is drinking again, using up her money, and she doesn't know how much more she can take. I know she'll take as much as she has to. I hope I'll see Bernard some day soon to say hello, and maybe we can bend together over our granddaughter, for whom I know we both have many hopes.

41   Just before we leave Wounded Knee, I walk over to Aunt Lena's Comanche and point to the tribal sign that tells the story. "It says 'Massacre' there, but it used to say something else." I ask her if she knows what it said before. She looks over my shoulder and laughs. "That's funny," she says, "I've lived here all my life, but you know, I never did read that sign." We're miles down the road before I realize that I never finished reading it myself.

A Question of Language

GLORIA NAYLOR

Gloria Naylor was born in 1950 in New York City, where she earned a B.A. at Brooklyn College. She earned an M.A. at Yale University in 1983. She has taught writing at several universities, including George Washington University, Princeton University, and the University of Pennsylvania. Her 1982 novel, *The Women of Brewster Place,* which explores the world of seven black women, won the American Book Award for best first novel. She followed it with *Linden Hills* (1985), *Mama Day* (1988), and *Bailey's Cafe* (1992). One critic, Deirdre Donahue, says, "Naylor is not afraid to grapple with life's big subjects: sex, birth, love, death, grief. Her women feel deeply, and she unflinchingly transcribes their emotions."

"A Question of Language" examines the role of one word in the experience of the African American—*nigger.* Naylor examines its usage by blacks and explains that, in the singular, it shows distinguished accomplishment, expresses endearment, and praises the "essence of manhood." In the plural, however, it tends to be used as a term of condemnation, and its usage by whites always has negative connotations.

1 Language is the subject. It is the written form with which I've managed to keep the wolf away from the door and, in diaries, to

keep my sanity. In spite of this, I consider the written word inferior to the spoken, and much of the frustration experienced by novelists is the awareness that whatever we manage to capture in even the most transcendent passages falls far short of the richness of life. Dialogue achieves its power in the dynamics of a fleeting moment of sight, sound, smell, and touch.

2   I'm not going to enter the debate here about whether it is language that shapes reality or vice versa. That battle is doomed to be waged whenever we seek intermittent reprieve from the chicken and egg dispute. I will simply take the position that the spoken word, like the written word, amounts to a nonsensical arrangement of sounds or letters without a consensus that assigns "meaning." And building from the meanings of what we hear, we order reality. Words themselves are innocuous; it is the consensus that gives them true power.

3   I remember the first time I heard the word *nigger*. In my third-grade class, our math tests were being passed down the rows, and as I handed the papers to a little boy in back of me, I remarked that once again he had received a much lower mark than I did. He snatched his test from me and spit out that word. Had he called me a nymphomaniac or a necrophiliac, I couldn't have been more puzzled. I didn't know what a nigger was, but I knew that whatever it meant, it was something he shouldn't have called me. This was verified when I raised my hand, and in a loud voice repeated what he had said and watched the teacher scold him for using a "bad" word. I was later to go home and ask the inevitable question that every black parent must face—"Mommy, what does 'nigger' mean?"

4   And what exactly did it mean? Thinking back, I realize that this could not have been the first time the word was used in my presence. I was part of a large extended family that had migrated from the rural South after World War II and formed a close-knit network that gravitated around my maternal grandparents. Their ground-floor apartment in one of the buildings they owned in Harlem was a weekend mecca for my immediate family, along with countless aunts, uncles, and cousins who brought along assorted friends. It was a bustling and open house with assorted neighbors and tenants popping in and out to exchange bits of gossip, pick up an old quarrel or referee the ongoing checkers game in which my grandmother cheated shamelessly. They were all there to let down their hair and

put up their feet after a week of labor in the factories, laundries, and shipyards of New York.

5   Amid the clamor, which could reach deafening proportions—two or three conversations going on simultaneously, punctuated by the sound of a baby's crying somewhere in the back rooms or out on the street—there was still a rigid set of rules about what was said and how. Older children were sent out of the living room when it was time to get into the juicy details about "you-know-who" up on the third floor who had gone and gotten herself "p-r-e-g-n-a-n-t!" But my parents, knowing that I could spell well beyond my years, always demanded that I follow the others out to play. Beyond sexual misconduct and death, everything else was considered harmless for our young ears. And so among the anecdotes of the triumphs and disappointments in the various workings of their lives, the word *nigger* was used in my presence, but it was set within contexts and inflections that caused it to register in my mind as something else.

6   In the singular, the word was always applied to a man who had distinguished himself in some situation that brought their approval for his strength, intelligence, or drive:

7   "Did Johnny really do that?"

8   "I'm telling you, that nigger pulled in $6,000 of overtime last year. Said he got enough for a down payment on a house."

9   When used with a possessive adjective by a woman—"my nigger"—it became a term of endearment for husband or boyfriend. But it could be more than just a term applied to a man. In their mouths it became the pure essence of manhood—a disembodied force that channeled their past history of struggle and present survival against the odds into a victorious statement of being: "Yeah, that old foreman found out quick enough—you don't mess with a nigger."

10   In the plural, it became a description of some group within the community that had overstepped the bounds of decency as my family defined it: Parents who neglected their children, a drunken couple who fought in public, people who simply refused to look for work, those with excessively dirty mouths or unkempt households were all "trifling niggers." This particular circle could forgive hard times, unemployment, the occasional bout of depression—they had gone through all of that themselves—but the unforgivable sin was lack of self-respect.

11   A woman could never be a *nigger* in the singular, with its connotation of confirming worth. The noun *girl* was its closest equivalent

in that sense, but only when used in direct address and regardless of the gender doing the addressing. *Girl* was a token of respect for a woman. The one-syllable word was drawn out to sound like three in recognition of the extra ounce of wit, nerve or daring that the woman had shown in the situation under discussion.

12   "G-i-r-l, stop. You mean you said that to his face?"

13   But if the word was used in a third-person reference or shortened so that it almost snapped out of the mouth, it always involved some element of communal disapproval. And age became an important factor in these exchanges. It was only between individuals of the same generation, or from an older person to a younger (but never the other way around), that "girl" would be considered a compliment.

14   I don't agree with the argument that use of the word *nigger* at this social stratum of the black community was an internalization of racism. The dynamics were the exact opposite: the people in my grandmother's living room took a word that whites used to signify worthlessness or degradation and rendered it impotent. Gathering there together, they transformed *nigger* to signify the varied and complex human beings they knew themselves to be. If the word was to disappear totally from the mouths of even the most liberal of white society, no one in that room was naïve enough to believe it would disappear from white minds. Meeting the word head-on, they proved it had absolutely nothing to do with the way they were determined to live their lives.

15   So there must have been dozens of times that the word *nigger* was spoken in front of me before I reached the third grade. But I didn't "hear" it until it was said by a small pair of lips that had already learned it could be a way to humiliate me. That was the word I went home and asked my mother about. And since she knew that I had to grow up in America, she took me in her lap and explained.

Reflections on Race and Sex

BELL HOOKS

bell hooks, born in 1952, contributes a regular column, "Sisters of the Yam," to *Z Magazine* and is an English professor at City University of New York. She has published several books, including *Ain't I a Woman: Black Women and Feminism* (1981), *Feminist Theory from Margin to Center* (1984), *Talking Back: Thinking Feminist, Thinking Black* (1989), and *Yearning: Race, Gender, and Cultural Politics* (1990).

"Reflections on Race and Sex," which appeared in *Yearning*, serves as her reminder that race and sex intermingle in the power play of civilizations. Racial dominance also brings with it sexual dominance, as dominating men demonstrate to dominated men that they have lost control and power over their women. Thus, rape of the women becomes "a gesture of symbolic castration." She argues that one cannot separate sexism and racism, and she suggests re-visioning the black liberation movement from "a feminist standpoint."

1   Race and sex have always been overlapping discourses in the United States. That discourse began in slavery. The talk then was not about black men wanting to be free so that they would have access to the bodies of white women—that would come later. Then, black women's bodies were the discursive terrain, the playing fields

where racism and sexuality converged. Rape as both right and rite of the white male dominating group was a cultural norm. Rape was also an apt metaphor for European imperialist colonization of Africa and North America.

2   Sexuality has always provided gendered metaphors for colonization. Free countries equated with free men, domination with castration, the loss of manhood, and rape—the terrorist act re-enacting the drama of conquest, as men of the dominating group sexually violate the bodies of women who are among the dominated. The intent of this act was to continually remind dominated men of their loss of power; rape was a gesture of symbolic castration. Dominated men are made powerless (i.e., impotent) over and over again as the women they would have had the right to possess, to control, to assert power over, to dominate, to fuck, are fucked and fucked over by the dominating victorious male group.

3   There is no psychosexual history of slavery that explores the meaning of white male sexual exploitation of black women or the politics of sexuality, no work that lays out all the available information. There is no discussion of sexual sado-masochism, of the master who forced his wife to sleep on the floor as he nightly raped a black woman in bed. There is no discussion of sexual voyeurism. And what were the sexual lives of white men like who were legally declared "insane" because they wanted to marry black slave women with whom they were sexually and romantically involved? Under what conditions did sexuality serve as a force subverting and disrupting power relations, unsettling the oppressor/oppressed paradigm? No one seems to know how to tell this story, where to begin. As historical narrative it was long ago supplanted by the creation of another story (pornographic sexual project, fantasy, fear, the origin has yet to be traced). That story, invented by white men, is about the overwhelming desperate longing black men have to sexually violate the bodies of white women. The central character in this story is the black male rapist. Black men are constructed, as Michael Dyson puts it, as "peripatetic phalluses with unrequited desire for their denied object—white women." As the story goes, this desire is not based on longing for sexual pleasure. It is a story of revenge, rape as the weapon by which black men, the dominated, reverse their circumstance, regain power over white men.

4   Oppressed black men and women have rarely challenged the use of gendered metaphors to describe the impact of racist domination and/or black liberation struggle. The discourse of black resistance

has almost always equated freedom with manhood, the economic and material domination of black men with castration emasculation. Accepting these sexual metaphors forged a bond between oppressed black men and their white male oppressors. They shared the patriarchal belief that revolutionary struggle was really about the erect phallus, the ability of men to establish political dominance that could correspond to sexual dominance. Careful critical examination of black power literature in the sixties and early seventies exposes the extent to which black women and men were using sexualized metaphors to talk about the effort to resist racist domination. Many of us have never forgotten that moment in *Soul on Ice* when Eldridge Cleaver, writing about the need to "redeem my conquered manhood," described raping black women as practice for the eventual rape of white women. Remember that readers were not shocked or horrified by this glamorization of rape as a weapon of terrorism men might use to express rage about other forms of domination, about their struggle for power with other men. Given the sexist context of the culture, it made sense. Cleaver was able to deflect attention away from the misogynist sexism of his assertions by poignantly justifying these acts as a "natural" response to racial domination. He wanted to force readers to confront the agony and suffering black men experience in a white supremacist society. Again, freedom from racial domination was expressed in terms of redeeming black masculinity. And gaining the right to assert one's manhood was always about sexuality.

5   During slavery, there was perhaps a white male who created his own version of *Soul on Ice,* one who confessed how good it felt to assert racial dominance over black people, and particularly black men, by raping black women with impunity, or how sexually stimulating it was to use the sexual exploitation of black women to humiliate and degrade white women, to assert phallocentric domination in one's household. Sexism has always been a political stance mediating racial domination, enabling white men and black men to share a common sensibility about sex roles and the importance of male domination. Clearly both groups have equated freedom with manhood, and manhood with the right of men to have indiscriminate access to the bodies of women. Both groups have been socialized to condone patriarchal affirmation of rape as an acceptable way to maintain male domination. It is this merging of sexuality with male domination within patriarchy that informs the construction of masculinity for

men of all races and classes. Robin Morgan's book, *The Demon Lover: On the Sexuality of Terrorism,* begins with rape. She analyses the way men are bonded across class, race, and nationalities through shared notions of manhood which make masculinity synonymous with the ability to assert power-over through acts of violence and terrorism. Since terrorist acts are most often committed by men, Morgan sees the terrorist as "the logical incarnation of patriarchal politics in a technological world." She is not concerned with the overlapping discourses of race and sex, with the interconnectedness of racism and sexism. Like many radical feminists, she believes that male commitment to maintaining patriarchy and male domination diminishes or erases difference.

6   Much of my work within feminist theory has stressed the importance of understanding difference, of the ways race and class status determine the degree to which one can assert male domination and privilege and most importantly the ways racism and sexism are interlocking systems of domination which uphold and sustain one another. Many feminists continue to see them as completely separate issues, believing that sexism can be abolished while racism remains intact, or that women who work to resist racism are not supporting feminist movement. Since black liberation struggle is so often framed in terms that affirm and support sexism, it is not surprising that white women are uncertain about whether women's rights struggle will be diminished if there is too much focus on resisting racism, or that many black women continue to fear that they will be betraying black men if they support feminist movement. Both these fears are responses to the equation of black liberation with manhood. This continues to be a central way black people frame our efforts to resist racist domination; it must be critiqued. We must reject the sexualization of black liberation in ways that support and perpetuate sexism, phallocentrism, and male domination. Even though Michele Wallace tried to expose the fallacy of equating black liberation with the assertion of oppressive manhood in *Black Macho and the Myth of the Superwoman,* few black people got the message. Continuing this critique in *Ain't I a Woman: Black Women and Feminism,* I found that more and more black women were rejecting this paradigm. It has yet to be rejected by most black men, and especially black male political figures. As long as black people hold on to the idea that the trauma of racist domination is really the loss of black manhood, then we invest in the racist narratives that perpetuate the idea that all black

men are rapists, eager to use sexual terrorism to express their rage about racial domination.

7   Currently we are witnessing a resurgence of such narratives. They are resurfacing at a historical moment when black people are bearing the brunt of more overt and blatant racist assaults, when black men and especially young black men are increasingly disenfranchised by society. Mainstream white supremacist media make it appear that a black menace to societal safety is at large, that control, repression, and violent domination are the only effective ways to address the problem. Witness the use of the Willie Horton case to discredit Dukakis in the 1988 Presidential election. Susan Estrich in her post-campaign articles has done a useful job of showing how racist stereotypes were evoked to turn voters against Dukakis, and how Bush in no way denounced this strategy. In all her articles she recounts the experience of being raped by a black man fifteen years ago, describing the way racism determined how the police responded to the crime, and her response. Though her intent is to urge societal commitment to antiracist struggle, every article I have read has carried captions in bold print emphasizing the rape. The subversive content of her work is undermined and the stereotype that all black men are rapists is reinscribed and reinforced. Most people in this society do not realize that the vast majority of rapes are not interracial, that all groups of men are more likely to rape women who are the same race as themselves.

8   Within popular culture, Madonna's video "Like a Prayer" also makes use of imagery which links black men with rape, reinforcing this representation in the minds of millions of viewers—even though she has said that her intention is to be antiracist, and certainly the video suggests that not all black men who are accused of raping white women are guilty. Once again, however, this subversive message is undermined by the overall focus on sexually charged imagery of white female sexuality and black male lust. The most subversive message in the video has nothing to do with antiracism; it has to do with the construction of white females as desiring subjects who can freely assert sexual agency. Of course the taboo expression of that agency is choosing to be sexual with black men. Unfortunately this is a continuation of the notion that ending racist domination is really about issues of interracial sexual access, a myth that must be critiqued so that this society can confront the actual material, economic, and moral consequences of perpetuating white supremacy and its traumatic genocidal impact on black people.

9   Images of black men as rapists, as dangerous menaces to society, have been sensational cultural currency for some time. The obsessive media focus on these representations is political. The role it plays in the maintenance of racist domination is to convince the public that black men are a dangerous threat who must be controlled by any means necessary, including annihilation. This is the cultural backdrop shaping media response to the Central Park rape case, and the media has played a major role in shaping public response. Many people are using this case to perpetuate racial stereotypes and racism. Ironically, the very people who claim to be shocked by the brutality of this case have no qualms about suggesting that the suspects should be castrated or killed. They see no link between this support of violence as a means of social control and the suspects' use of violence to exercise control. Public response to this case highlights the lack of understanding about the interconnectedness of racism and sexism.

10   Many black people, especially black men, using the sexist paradigm that suggests rape of white women by black men is a reaction to racist domination, view the Central Park case as an indictment of the racist system. They do not see sexism as informing the nature of the crime, the choice of victim. Many white women have responded to the case by focusing solely on the brutal assault as an act of gender domination, of male violence against women. A piece in the *Village Voice* written by white female Andrea Kannapell carried captions in bold print which began with the statement in all capitals for greater emphasis, "THE CRIME WAS MORE SEXIST THAN RACIST! . . ." Black women responding to the same issue all focused on the sexist nature of the crime, often giving examples of black male sexism. Given the work black women have done within feminist writing to call attention to the reality of black male sexism, work that often receives little or no attention or is accused of attacking black men, it is ironic that the brutal rape of a white woman by a group of young black males serves as the catalyst for admission that sexism is a serious problem in black communities. Lisa Kennedy's piece, "Body Double: The Anatomy of a Crime," also published in the *Village Voice,* acknowledges the convergence of racism and sexism as politics of domination that inform this assault. Kennedy writes:

> If I accept the premise of the coverage, that this rape is more heartbreaking than all the rapes that happen to women of color, then what happens to

the value of my body? What happens to the quality
of my blackness?

These questions remain unanswered, though she closes with "a call
for a sophisticated feminist offensive." Such an offensive should begin
with cultivating critical awareness of the way racism and sexism are
interlocking systems of domination.

11   Public response to the Central Park case reveals the extent to
which the culture invests in the kind of dualistic thinking that helps
reinforce and maintain all forms of domination. Why must people
decide whether this crime is more sexist than racist, as if these are
competing oppressions? Why do white people, and especially feminist
white women, feel better when black people, especially black women,
disassociate themselves from the plight of black men in white supremacist capitalist patriarchy to emphasize opposition to black male
sexism? Cannot black women remain seriously concerned about the
brutal effect of racist domination on black men and also denounce
black male sexism? And why is black male sexism evoked as though
it is a special brand of this social disorder, more dangerous, more
abhorrent and life-threatening than the sexism that pervades the
culture as a whole, or the sexism that informs white male domination
of women? These questions call attention to the either/or ways
of thinking that are the philosophical underpinning of systems of
domination. Progressive folks must then insist, wherever we engage
in discussions of this crime or of issues of race and gender, on the
complexity of our experience in a racist sexist society.

12   The Central Park crime involves aspects of sexism, male domination, misogyny, and the use of rape as an instrument of terror. It
also involves race and racism; it is unlikely that young black males
growing up in this society, attacking a white woman, would see her
as "just a woman"—her race would be foremost in their consciousness as well as her sex, in the same way that masses of people hearing
about this crime were concerned with identifying first her race. In a
white supremacist sexist society all women's bodies are devalued, but
white women's bodies are more valued than those of women of
color. Given the context of white supremacy, the historical narratives
about black male rapists, the racial identities of both victim and
victimizers enable this tragedy to be sensationalized.

13   To fully understand the multiple meanings of this incident, it must
be approached from an analytical standpoint that considers the impact

of sexism and racism. Beginning there enables many of us to empathize with both the victim and the victimizers. If one reads *The Demon Lover* and thinks again about this crime, one can see it as part of a continuum of male violence against women, of rape and terror as weapons of male domination—yet another horrific and brutal expression of patriarchal socialization. And if one considers this case by combining a feminist analysis of race and masculinity, one sees that since male power within patriarchy is relative, men from poorer groups and men of color are not able to reap the material and social rewards for their participation in patriarchy. In fact they often suffer from blindly and passively acting out a myth of masculinity that is life-threatening. Sexist thinking blinds them to this reality. They become victims of the patriarchy. No one can truly believe that the young black males involved in the Central Park incident were not engaged in a suicidal ritual enactment of a dangerous masculinity that will ultimately threaten their lives, their well-being.

14   If one reads again Michael Dyson's piece "The Plight of Black Men," focusing especially on the part where he describes the reason many young black men form gangs—"the sense of absolute belonging and unsurpassed love"—it is easy to understand why young black males are despairing and nihilistic. And it is rather naive to think that if they do not value their own lives, they will value the lives of others. Is it really so difficult for folks to see the connection between the constant pornographic glorification of male violence against women that is represented, enacted, and condoned daily in the culture and the Central Park crime? Does racism create and maintain this blind spot or does it allow black people and particularly black men to become the scapegoats, embodying society's evils?

15   If we are to live in a less violent and more just society, then we must engage in antisexist and antiracist work. We desperately need to explore and understand the connections between racism and sexism. And we need to teach everyone about those connections so that they can be critically aware and socially active. Much education for critical consciousness can take place in everyday conversations. Black women and men must participate in the construction of feminist thinking, creating models for feminist struggle that address the particular circumstances of black people. Still, the most visionary task of all remains that of reconceptualizing masculinity so that alternative, transformative models are there in the culture, in our daily lives, to help boys and men who are working to construct a self, to build

new identities. Black liberation struggle must be re-visioned so that it is no longer equated with maleness. We need a revolutionary vision of black liberation, one that emerges from a feminist standpoint and addresses the collective plight of black people.

16 Any individual committed to resisting politics of domination, to eradicating sexism and racism, understands the importance of not promoting an either/or competition between the oppressive systems. We can empathize with the victim and the victimizers in the Central Park case, allowing that feeling to serve as a catalyst for renewed commitment to antisexist and antiracist work. Yesterday I heard this story. A black woman friend called to say that she had been attacked on the street by a black man. He took her purse, her house keys, her car keys. She lives in one of the poorest cities in the United States. We talked about poverty, sexism, and racial domination to place what had happened in a perspective that will enable both individual healing and political understanding of this crime. Today I heard this story. A white woman friend called to say that she had been attacked in her doorway by a black man. She screamed and he ran away. Neighbors coming to her aid invoked racism. She refused to engage in this discussion even though she was shocked by the intensity and degree of racism expressed. Even in the midst of her own fear and pain, she remained politically aware, so as not to be complicit in perpetuating the white supremacy that is the root of so much suffering. Both of these women feel rage at their victimizers; they do not absolve them even as they seek to understand and to respond in ways that will enrich the struggle to end domination—so that sexism, sexist violence, racism, and racist violence will cease to be an everyday happening.

Selected Bibliography

Cleaver, Eldridge. *Soul on Ice.* New York: McGraw-Hill, 1967.

Dyson, Michael. "The Plight of Black Men," *Z Magazine,* February, 1989.

Morgan, Robin. *The Demon Lover: On the Sexuality of Terrorism.* New York: Norton, 1988.

Wallace, Michele. *Black Macho and the Myth of the Superwoman.* New York: Dial Press, 1979.

Anatomy and Destiny

PERRI KLASS

Perri Klass is an American who was born in Tuna-puna, Trinidad, in 1958. Her father was an anthropologist and her mother a writer and professor. She earned her B.A. at Harvard in 1979 and an M.D. in 1986. Most of her career has been spent at Boston's Children's Hospital as a pediatrician, but her second love is writing. She has written for numerous newspapers and magazines, including *Self, Esquire,* and the *New York Times.* She has also written two novels, *Recombinations* (1985) and *Other Women's Children* (1990); a collection of short stories, *I Am Having an Adventure* (1986); and an autobiography, *A Not Entirely Benign Procedure: Four Years as a Medical Student* (1987).

"Anatomy and Destiny" originally appeared in *Ms.* magazine in 1987. In this essay, she examines the term *feminism* in relation to the medical sciences. She says that in medical school, "one of the courses everyone gets, like it or not, is an introduction to sexual politics. Many of the men, of course, don't quite realize it's going on." In part, the essay recognizes that she and others succeeded in medical school because of the strength of previous women who "battered down the doors."

1   When I was a medical student, writing about being a medical student, I had two different editors ask me whether professors had

taught anatomy with *Playboy* pinups instead of diagrams, or lecturers had made offensive jokes about women. There seemed to be a sort of common knowledge about the medical school experience that my articles didn't incorporate. In fact, I went through medical school without encountering that sort of nonsense, and if a lecturer did occasionally try a would-be witty, would-be provocative remark about women, he got roundly hissed for his trouble—it's very satisfying to hiss a lecturer, and few of them keep their composure well during the process.

2   There were, however, other, more subtle, ways in which medical school made me aware that I and my kind were newcomers. There was, above all, the unending parade of male lecturers. There was the pervasive (and almost unconscious) practice of using the generic *he* for the doctor in any clinical anecdote, and the generic *she* for the patient (provided it wasn't prostate trouble, of course). I can still remember a day when one of our rare female lecturers said to us something on the order of, "So one day someone will come in with these symptoms, and you'll get an orthopedist to look at the patient with you, and she'll tell you such and such," and the women in the audience burst into applause.

3   So we hissed sexist jokes and we applauded the use of the female pronoun. Did that mean that the women with whom I went to medical school considered themselves feminists? I can't say, but I do know this: many of us felt poised, as women entering a traditionally (and sometimes militantly) male profession, between gratitude to the women who had fought their way through before us on the one hand, and a desire to identify with our new brotherhood on the other.

4   Most people who go to medical school want very badly to be doctors. It takes a great deal of effort to get to medical school, let alone to get through. Wanting to be a doctor means identifying with the people up ahead of you, the group you are trying to join, and up until very recently, that group has been a brotherhood, in every sense of the word. For some women, the word *feminist* may have been unwelcome, a reminder that they might never be fully accepted into that brotherhood, an awkward and public attempt to make an ideology out of a fact of life. And yet, I think my class was still close enough to the pioneers who had gone before for us to understand that we owed our opportunity, our comparatively easy path, entirely to those resolute embattled pioneers. The graffiti in the women's

bathroom in the dormitory at my medical school read, "Every time you sit down here, thank the women who have come before you."

5   I have taken for granted that I was a feminist ever since I was in junior high school, but I have never seen myself as a banner-carrier. Certainly in college and in graduate school there were women who would have considered me a fellow traveler at best: because I did not live a truly politically correct life, because I was not more active in women's causes. I never minded this and it never kept me from considering myself a feminist; others could carry the banners but I would march; I would acknowledge the debt I owed to other women and to the Women's Movement. I was a feminist, but I was not The Feminist.

6   When I got to medical school, I discovered that I was a radical feminist. By medical school standards I was in fact The Feminist, or one of them. It didn't take much; there was almost no one person, and certainly no group, to carry the banner or smile patronizingly at my lack of seriousness. I found myself running the medical school women's association, along with a friend. Our activities were far short of revolutionary; we used to invite speakers to come and talk once a week. We covered topics of obvious relevance to women—battered women, midwifery—and also medical topics that we thought might be relevant—alcoholism, child abuse—and we also invited a number of women physicians to come talk about their training and their lives. The talks were generally very well attended, by both female and male students, and they were fun, but not particularly radical. Still, one day when I and a couple of other women from our class were talking to the women who had directed the organization before us about possible speakers and other activities (develop a women's medical directory of the area? get involved with a study that was being done of the medical school's failure to give tenure to women?), one of my classmates said abruptly that she didn't want to help run the organization since it was clear that the group was going to be headed by some radical people. It wasn't that I minded the label. I was vaguely thrilled to find myself finally something other than a weak-minded fellow traveler. But it was disconcerting not to know when I was doing something "extreme."

7   I was once called to the office of the director of medical school admissions along with the heads of some other student groups to discuss his concern because the women's organization was writing to female applicants, offering encouragement and information, even

offering to put them up when they came for interviews. He pointed out that the Hispanic and black student groups were making similar offers to their constituents, and he wanted to put a stop to all these separate letters. Among other things, he said, it just wasn't fair—no one was writing to the white men. There was a pause, and then I said, in unison with one of the other students present, "And yet, somehow they keep coming!" The lesson, in the end, was that medicine is fundamentally a conservative world, that medical students as a group are a far more conservative context for any kind of political thinking than college students or graduate students.

8   Most female medical students, as I remember, were highly aware of the sex ratios on the hospital teams on which they worked. And I remember a sense of betrayal when a female resident or attending physician proved ineffective, unpleasant, uninspiring. I also remember how different it felt the first time I was ever in an operating room with an all-female group: the orthopedic resident, the surgical intern, the medical student (me), the scrub nurse, *and* the patient. And in fact it was nothing like the usual operating room drama; there was less yelling, more courtesy, more collegiality and less strict hierarchy. That distinction has held up in a fair number of operating rooms since then.

9   You can't help feeling these differences, whatever the association you choose to claim with feminism. However wary you may be of the word, medical school is an educational experience, and one of the courses everyone gets, like it or not, is an introduction to sexual politics. Many of the men, of course, don't quite realize it's going on.

10   Now I am doing a residency in pediatrics, a field that has traditionally had a relatively high percentage of women. In my own program there are many female residents. When the list of interns came out for next year, several of us reviewed with fascination the list of the people who would take over our position at the very bottom of the totem pole. Only later did we realize that none of us had thought to count how many of the new interns were male and how many female—the most striking evidence, we all agreed, that we are in a situation where that really isn't an issue. When half or more of the residents are female, a female resident doesn't feel she is by definition on probation. Polarizations of male and female doctor styles are acknowledged; residents are regularly twitted for being macho.

11   Many of the young female doctors I work with today would call

themselves feminists. Their feminism involves a sense of entitlement, and that is also valuable. In a way the victory is the sense of entitlement, the feeling that you belong. You need both—you need a balance of a rock-hard confidence that you belong in medicine, and also an awareness that you only got there because the women ahead of you battered down the doors. With that confidence and that awareness, the hope is you can enjoy your position, preserve it for those who will come next, and also preserve the challenge to the traditional style that is one of the greatest contributions women bring to medicine.

Acknowledgments

Allen, Paula Gunn, "Where I come From is Like This." From THE SACRED HOOP by Paula Gunn Allen. Copyright © 1986, 1992 by Paula Gunn Allen. Reprinted by permission of Beacon Press.

Angelou, Maya, Excerpt here titled "Graduation" from I KNOW WHY THE CAGED BIRD SINGS by Maya Angelou. Copyright © 1969 by Maya Angelou. Reprinted by permission of Random House, Inc.

Atwood, Margaret, "Pornography" which originally appeared in CHATELAINE MAGAZINE, 1983. © Margaret Atwood, 1983. Reprinted by permission of the author.

Brady, Judy, "I Want a Wife," as appeared in MS Magazine, December 13, 1971. Reprinted by permission of the author.

Brownmiller, Susan, "Prologue" from FEMININITY, by Susan Brownmiller. COPYRIGHT © 1983 by Susan Brownmiller. Reprinted by permission of Simon & Schuster, Inc.

Didion, Joan, "On Self Respect" from SLOUCHING TOWARDS BETHLEHEM by Joan Didion. Copyright © 1961, 1967, 1968 by Joan Didion. Reprinted by permission of Farrar, Straus & Giroux, Inc.

Dillard, Annie, "An American Childhood" from AN AMERICAN CHILDHOOD by Annie Dillard. Copyright © 1987 by Annie Dillard. Reprinted by permission of HarperCollins Publishers, Inc.

George, Diana Hume, "Wounded Chevy at Wounded Knee." Originally appeared in THE MISSOURI REVIEW. Reprinted by permission of 1990 by Diana Hume George. Reprinted by permission of the author.

Hampl, Patricia, "Memory and Imagination." Copyright © 1985 by Patricia Hampl. Originally published in THE DOLPHIN READER. Permission to reprint granted by The Rhoda Weyr Agency, New York.

Heilbrun, Carolyn G., "Writing a Woman's Life." Reprinted from WRITING A WOMAN'S LIFE by Carolyn G. Heilbrun, by permission of W. W. Norton & Company, Inc. Copyright © 1988 by Carolyn G. Heilbrun.

hooks, bell, "Reflections on Race and Sex" from YEARNING by bell hooks. Reprinted by permission of South End Press.

Hurston, Zora Neale, "How It Feels to Be Colored Me" from THE WORLD TOMORROW, May 11, 1928. Reprinted by permission of the Estate of Zora Neale Hurston.

Jordan, June, "Where is the Love?" from CIVIL WARS by June Jordan. Copyright © 1980 by June Jordan. Reprinted by permission of the author.

Keller, Helen. Materials from "Three Days to See" by Helen Keller have been reprinted with permission from American Foundation for the Blind, 15 W. 16th Street, New York, NY 10011.

Klass, Perri, "Anatomy and Destiny," as appeared in MS. Magazine, July/August 1987. Reprinted by permission of Ms. Magazine, © 1987.

Lakoff, Robin, "You Are What You Say," originally appeared in MS. Magazine. Reprinted by permission of Robin Lakoff.

Levertov, Denise, "Relearning the Alphabet" (excerpt) from POEMS 1968–1972. Copyright © 1970 by Denise Levertov. Reprinted by permission of New Directions Publishing Corporation.

Mead, Margaret, "Women: A House Divided." From MARGARET MEAD Some Personal Views Edited by Rhoda Metraux. Copyright © 1979 by Mary Catherine Bateson and Rhoda Metraux. Reprinted by permission of Walker and Company, 435 Hudson Street, New York, New York 10014, 1-800-289-2553. All Rights Reserved.

Index of Authors and Titles

Instructor's Manual

Daughters of the Revolution

Classic Essays by Women

James D. Lester
Austin Peay State University

Prepared by Violet Smith

NTC Publishing Group
Lincolnwood, Illinois USA

Contents

Essays by Women of the Late 20th Century: Breaking Free   IM-18

Preface

༄

NTC's Library of Classic Essays was developed to provide students with in-depth yet inexpensive collections of classic essays. While the scope of each book is necessarily limited (by design and by practicalities), we hope that, individually and as a whole, this series illuminates this diverse genre for your students.

This Instructor's Manual is intended to help you introduce the essays in the student text to your students. For each essay, there is a brief paragraph outlining possible approaches to classroom discussion, along with suggested discussion questions and writing assignments. While these materials are no replacement for your insight into the essays, we hope that they might help you to arouse your students' interest in and responsiveness to these classic essays.

ESSAYS BY WOMEN OF THE 18TH AND 19TH CENTURIES: JOINING THE FRAY

from A Vindication of the Rights of Woman

MARY WOLLSTONECRAFT

Begin your discussion by focusing on the importance Wollstonecraft gives to women's development of themselves "as rational creatures" and by noting how unusual this would have been in her time. Then note that she presents mothering as the second duty of women, as though it was not the usual practice for a woman to raise her own children. Next, examine the importance Wollstonecraft places on women having meaningful work to do. Notice how this fits with her earlier statement regarding women's development of the self: meaningful use of women's time is needed "to keep their faculties from rusting." Examine Wollstonecraft's analysis of what happens to women who are barred from meaningful work and, more importantly, what happens to a society when this is the norm. Examine her analysis of what would happen if women could earn their own living. Notice that again she points out how this would benefit *society*, not just women. Note how this leads to her examination of the need for women to be better educated so that they might be capable of performing meaningful work and be better, more useful citizens. Finally, consider her statement that emancipation would make a woman "a helpmeet" for her husband. This is an allusion to the Bible and its statement that woman was created for man to be a "helpmeet for him" (Genesis 2:18). This reference would not have gone unnoticed by Wollstonecraft's audience. Notice how it gives a kind of "divine sanction" to her words, thereby strengthening her argument.

Discussion Questions

1. What does Wollstonecraft consider to be the first duty of women? Why is this an unusual statement for a woman to make, especially in Wollstonecraft's time?
2. What does Wollstonecraft state is the next most important duty for women? How does this differ from more recent feminist writing? What does it say about the society in which Wollstonecraft lived?
3. Why does Wollstonecraft consider meaningful work so important for women? What happens to women who don't have this? What happens to a society where women are barred from important work? How does Wollstonecraft view idleness, as among the idle rich?
4. What reasons does Wollstonecraft give for why women should be able to earn their own living? What reasons does she give to show that this would benefit society as a whole?
5. What provision does Wollstonecraft's argument make for women of different degrees of intelligence or scholarly interest? How might this distinction be applied to today's society?
6. According to Wollstonecraft, what would be the benefits, both to women and to society, if women "were educated in a more orderly manner"? What changes did Wollstonecraft think must take place in terms of society's attitude toward women's employment before women could realize the benefits of that education?

Writing Assignments

1. Consider Wollstonecraft's essay in the light of when it was written and write an essay comparing it to what you know of feminist thought today. How much of Wollstonecraft's message is as

appropriate now as when it was written? How many of the issues she raises have been resolved?

2. Consider Wollstonecraft's position that women in "rational fellowship" with men rather than "slavish obedience" would have better relationships with their families and be better citizens. Write an essay supporting or refuting Wollstonecraft's stand.

3. Consider Wollstonecraft's position that an educated, emancipated women makes a better "helpmeet" for her husband. Write an essay supporting or refuting this stand, using many examples to back up your thesis.

Declaration of Sentiments and Resolutions: Adopted by the Seneca Falls Convention, July 19–20, 1848

ELIZABETH CADY STANTON

Begin your discussion by comparing Stanton's "Declaration" to the Declaration of Independence. Note the parallels in the structure of the two documents and explore how this parallelism enhances

Stanton's argument by using a document "sacred" to the men who would have been Stanton's audience. Next, study the listing of Stanton's grievances and look for any patterns and any significance to their order. Then study each one of the "rights" Stanton asks for individually. Note which ones have been granted to women and which ones women are still fighting for. Point out that some of these rights might not fit neatly into an either/or categorization; for example, "to administer chastisement" might not be *legal* today, but some men still consider it their right, and the law is not quick to punish. Note that there are rights that are still the subject of much debate. Next, point out places where Stanton uses men's logic and rationale against them; for example, if women are superior morally, and the expectations placed on women imply that, then it is logical for women to be the spiritual leaders of society, yet they are barred from the ministry in many denominations. Finally, examine the rational tone of Stanton's essay and how that tone, together with the logic of her argument, makes her points sound reasonable and eliminates any potential accusation of emotional hysteria.

Discussion Questions

1. Which specific passages in this essay do you recognize as being the same as in the Declaration of Independence? How does Stanton's style of writing in a form parallel to the Declaration of Independence enhance her argument?
2. How are Stanton's grievances organized? How could they be categorized? Is there a pattern to how they are presented?
3. Which of the rights of women that Stanton lists have been granted to women? Which are still denied? Which have been granted legally but are still denied in most women's everyday life? Which of these rights are still the subject of much debate?
4. In what places does Stanton use logic to find fallacies in men's rationalization for keeping women in their place? How does this enhance her argument?
5. How does Stanton employ religious belief and faith in God to enhance her argument? Why would this inclusion be important, especially in Stanton's time?
6. What is the tone of Stanton's essay? How does it enhance her argument?

Writing Assignments

1. Consider Stanton's resolution concerning the need to "enlighten" women, so that they will not be "declaring themselves satisfied with their present position" or "asserting that they have all the rights they want." Write an essay examining this concept in the light of today's feminist thought. Are there women today who oppose the women's movement by claiming they don't need it? Would "enlightening" them violate their rights? Write an essay exploring the basis for this difference of opinion.

2. Consider Stanton's resolution where she challenges "a perverted application of the Scriptures." What is she talking about? Is this "perverted application" still going on in the church? Write an essay examining the role of religious institutions in blocking equal rights to women. What is the rationale for this and is there any justification for it?

3. Write an essay comparing Stanton's "Declaration" to Mary Wollstonecraft's "A Vindication of the Rights of Women." In what ways is "Declaration," written in 1848, an answer to the plea of "Vindication," written in 1792?

Only Temper

GEORGE ELIOT

Begin your discussion by examining the character Touchwood. Note how Eliot describes his behavior and his attitude; use this analysis to understand Eliot's view of a bad-tempered man. Note that Eliot's criticism is of irrational temper and its justification by those who have it; she does not criticize the healthy expression of anger in response to a real stimulus. Point out the parallel she makes between Touchwood and the woman who effects a "mysterious inability to be pleased." Both are individuals no one wants around for long.

Contrast Touchwood's characteristics with those of the persons with "healthy mental habits," and note how this reveals Eliot's definition of a person with "high character." Finally, examine the tone of this essay: note its satirical voice with its contrasts between words of passionate appeal and biting humor.

Discussion Questions

1. How would you describe Touchwood; what characteristics does he possess? What is his attitude toward other people? What specific behaviors reveal his attitude?
2. How effective is Eliot's use of the character Touchwood to present her argument?
3. How does Eliot view a person's passionate adherence to an opinion in the face of facts? How does Eliot link this characteristic to bad temper?
4. How does Eliot define "healthy mental habits"? Why does she see a person of bad temper as being incapable of having them?
5. What is the thesis of Eliot's essay? Is her message as appropriate today as when she wrote this essay?

Writing Assignments

1. Do you know a person like Touchwood? Write an essay describing him or her. How much do you feel you must tolerate his or her temper? Are there positive characteristics that are sufficient to outweigh the person's bad temper?
2. Examine the concept of temper as it relates to gender. Is the type of overt temper Eliot describes more common in men? If so, in what other, perhaps more subtle, ways does temper manifest itself in women?
3. Has the gender differential noted by Eliot changed since Eliot's time?

ESSAYS BY WOMEN OF THE EARLY 20TH CENTURY: EXPLORING BOUNDARIES

Three Days to See

HELEN KELLER

Begin your discussion by looking at the opening paragraph of Keller's essay, noting how it establishes her thesis and gets the reader's attention. Next, divide the essay into its three sections—the three days—and categorize what she envisions doing on each day. Examine the order of the days' activities and determine if there is significance in that order (such as values revealed). Explore her choices and ask the class members if anything important was left out. Note the clues to Keller's questioning intellect (her view of books) and her interest in her fellow human beings (a whole day to study history and art). Examine her admonishment to the reader at the end and ask the students for their thoughts on the subject. Is Keller's point valid? Should we take care to use our senses more acutely than we do, or has Keller missed something? Are there things we had rather *not* be so aware of? Finally, examine what Keller's essay implies about her attitude toward her blindness. Is she focused on the value of sight simply because she cannot see? Is this a reflection of the tendency of most people to value what they do not have above what they do have?

Discussion Questions

1. Keller opens her essay by saying that if she were president of a university, she would "establish a compulsory course in 'How to Use Your Eyes.' " Why would she do this? How does this statement provide an effective opening to Keller's essay?

2. How does Keller divide her imaginary visual experiences into the three days? Is there a category you could assign to each day? How does this structure serve Keller's essay?

3. What substitute does Keller use for vision? What are the limitations of her method of "seeing"? Are there any advantages? What kinds of knowledge and experience has Keller been able to acquire?

4. Why does Keller refer to books as "a great shining lighthouse"? What does this statement reveal to us about her?

5. Why would Keller value spending part of the second day studying art? What does this tell us about her?

6. What does Keller admonish the reader to do? How does her writing style allow her to lead up to this without preaching? How does this paragraph provide an effective ending to Keller's essay?

7. There are many places in this essay where Keller uses the word *should* where we might use *would*. What choice about English usage is revealed by this?

Writing Assignments

1. Imagine that you have been told that you will lose your sight in three days, and write an essay revealing what would you do in those three days. Give your essay an organized structure, such as the one Keller gives to hers.

2. Write an essay examining the assumptions Keller makes in her vision of what she would see on her last day of sight. Is her vision realistic, or is she too optimistic and too focused on the beauty of the world? From the impression you get of her in her

essay, how do you see her reacting to a ghetto, a homeless
person, or a crack baby?

3. Research Keller's life and perhaps read a biography or autobiog-
    raphy of another handicapped person. Write an essay describing
    the obstacles that must be overcome.

Professions
for Women

VIRGINIA WOOLF

Begin your discussion by examining Woolf's analysis of the woman
writer's life. Examine why she feels that writing is a profession
that many women choose, why it appeals to women, and why it
is not resisted by the women's families. Then examine the obstacles
that appear later to women writers and how these problems are
unique to women. Explore particularly the image of the Angel of
the House, especially how the Angel reflects the values of Woolf's
time, and why the writer, or any professional woman, must destroy
the Angel's influence in order to survive. Next, examine Woolf's
explanation of how to awaken and release the spirit of imagination.
Examine the problems that are unique to women when the
imagination dashes "itself against something hard." Note how she
relates this struggle with her "many ghosts" to that of women
in other professions in order to create a bridge between all women
of all professions. Finally, examine Woolf's conclusions that there
is still much work to do, that "the room is your own, but it is
still bare." This could lead into a discussion of what progress has
been made since Woolf's time and to what extent women's rooms
still have "to be furnished."

Discussion Questions

1. What are the reasons Woolf gives for why "writing was a reputable and harmless occupation" for women? What do these reasons say about a woman's place in Woolf's society?

2. How might the cat that Woolf buys with her first paycheck be functioning in her essay as a symbol, especially since it "very soon involved me in bitter disputes with my neighbors"?

3. What does the Angel of the House admonish Woolf to do? How is the Angel an effective device in Woolf's essay? Why "angel" and not "devil" or "dragon"?

4. Woolf writes, "Now that she had rid herself of falsehood, that young woman had only to be herself." Why is ridding oneself of falsehood a difficult task?

5. What does Woolf mean when she says, "a novelist's chief desire is to be as unconscious as possible"? Why is this a necessary part of the writing process?

6. What does Woolf mean by the statement that the woman writer still has "many ghosts to fight"? How does she relate this concept to women of other professions? How does she say that women can support each other?

Writing Assignments

1. Consider Woolf's statement concerning the Angel of the House: "Had I not killed her she would have killed me." Write an essay exploring the forms in which this "angel" is still with us and why a woman must kill her to survive, both personally and professionally.

2. Consider Woolf's statement that "it is far harder to kill a phantom than a reality." Why is this so? Write an essay examining the power of "phantoms" to hold us to a pattern of thought and behavior. You may examine this question from a psychological perspective (internal, personal phantoms) or a sociological perspective (exterior, societal, or culture-induced phantoms).

3. Woolf says, "the room is your own, but it is bare." How would you furnish a room of your life? Write an essay exploring your dreams and aspirations, using the metaphor of furnishing a room to illustrate your vision.

How It Feels to Be Colored Me

ZORA NEALE HURSTON

Begin your discussion by looking at Hurston's opening paragraphs in which she describes herself, her background, and her early feelings about herself. Contrast this with her later life experiences and how she reacts to them: what does all this say about Hurston's character and self-image? Explore how this serves her and keeps her self-esteem intact. Note how this strong self-image keeps her from being defeated by either life's circumstances or whatever discrimination she encounters. Next, explore Hurston's feeling that her race is a *part* of her and not the whole of her, and how she experiences moments when she feels her race strongly and other times when she is just herself. Try relating this to other self-identifiers, such as gender or national origin; broaden the concept to explore how we are all individuals as well as conformists within groups. Explore the reasons why we judge each other by the groups we are part of rather than trying to see the individual. Finally, examine Hurston's final paragraph and her use of the metaphor that people are different colored bags filled with much of the same thing. Examine how this illustrates the greater message of her essay and how the description of the Creator as the "Great Stuffer of Bags" shows Hurston's laughing and joyous spirit.

Discussion Questions

1. What does Hurston mean by the statement that she is "the only Negro . . . whose grandfather on the mother's side was *not* an Indian chief"? What does this statement tell us about her attitude about herself and about her race?
2. Hurston describes in detail greeting the white tourists who

passed through her town as she watched them from her front porch. What does this scene tell us about her character, her personality, and her self-image? How does this add to the essay as a whole?

3. What events in Hurston's life made her aware of being "a little colored girl"? Did this change her view of herself or of the world? If so, how?

4. What does Hurston mean by the statement, "I am not tragically colored"? What does she mean by the last line in that paragraph: "I am too busy sharpening my oyster knife"? In a later paragraph she says that discrimination does not make her angry, but merely astonished: "How *can* any deny themselves the pleasure of my company?" What do these statements tell us about Hurston's character and personality?

5. Hurston gives us several examples of circumstances when her "color comes." What do these times have in common? Why do they make her aware of her race?

6. How does Hurston's calling the Creator the "Great Stuffer of Bags" reflect her religious views, as we have come to know them from her essay? How does this line serve as an effective ending to her essay?

7. Hurston uses many variations of sentence length and structure, even fragments, in her essay. How do these variations enhance her essay's message? How do they give it sound and rhythm?

Writing Assignments

1. Consider Hurston's statements about feeling her race at certain times, while at other times she is just herself. Write an essay relating this concept to aspects of yourself. Are there times when you feel your race as a dominant part of your being? What about your gender? Your religion? Your ethnic or regional background? Your socioeconomic class? What are the circumstances that trigger those feelings? How do those feelings differ from times when you are just yourself?

2. Examine the last paragraph of Hurston's essay, where she describes people as bags of different colors. Study the metaphors in this paragraph—those of the bags themselves and of the contents of her bag, which she pours out. Write an essay exploring

what each of these metaphors could mean. Consider how many of these same things are in your bag and what this says about the common bond of being human.

3. Using the last paragraph of Hurston's essay as a model, describe what items within the bag are a part of you, and write an essay analyzing what this says about you.

Women: A House Divided

MARGARET MEAD

Begin your discussion by focusing on the question that Mead raises in the opening. Explore how this question works as an effective beginning to Mead's essay. Establish who Mead is addressing and how women are both those being addressed and those referred to as the "daughters." Next, begin to examine Mead's points, beginning with her statement that "most women put their families first." Examine how this serves to point out the major problem society has with giving women "career jobs." Then examine Mead's next point—that women do not support the progress of other women, that they do not seek female mentors, and that they do not look to other women for companionship. Point out Mead's statement regarding the importance of women treating each other as full human beings. At this point, you may wish to begin to consider to what extent this essay is dated. How much have things changed in the twenty-five years since this essay was written? Next, examine Mead's statements that women downgrade their role as homemakers yet won't allow another woman to come into the home and serve as homemaker. How does Mead see this situation as growing out of past concepts of home and women's role as "chief executive" of the home? Consider Mead's statement that women have "a special responsibility to accord dignity to women's work." Finally, return to

Mead's idea that change is something that will take place over time, that women must understand their connection to the past, and that women must look beyond their present generation in order to prepare their children to be part of a new society.

Discussion Questions

1. What does Mead see as the basic issue of women's lives that is likely to be obscured by more immediate concerns? What does she see as the limit of change in our own time?

2. According to Mead, what do most women put first in their lives? How does this create a conflict in women's lives that is unlike any male experience? How does our society reinforce this conflict?

3. How do women's priorities and society's perceptions about these priorities serve to keep women out of career jobs? How do women's perceptions of other women serve this same end? How do women's perceptions of their traditional roles "as homemakers and caretakers of people" affect women's rights?

4. Why does Mead believe that "women as a group do not easily achieve working solidarity? How does this serve to keep women from becoming "full human beings"?

5. What does Mead see as the different contributions that men and women can make to "multiple problems of public life"? How does she see these as coming together to create a better society?

6. What, according to Mead, does the outcome of the changes in women's roles depend on? How does this view differ from that of other writers on this subject?

7. How is Mead's background as an anthropologist reflected in the views that are expressed in her essay? Why is the title of this essay particularly appropriate?

Writing Assignments

1. Consider Mead's thesis that women are the ones who downgrade the role of homemaker as one of low status. Do you agree? Is the status of housewives the result of women's values or society's? Write an essay exploring the status of the homemaker. Support your assertions with plenty of examples.

2. Consider Mead's suggestion that working wives employ another woman to serve as "homemaker" in their homes. Write an essay exploring the results of such a situation. Is the concept of the home as "a very private place" a trap for women, as Mead contends, or are there valid reasons for maintaining this privacy? How would the presence of a professional homemaker change the dynamics of a home? What advantages and disadvantages do you see to such a set-up? How would this change the status of homemaker? Why?

3. Consider Mead's statement that a homemaker is "chief executive" in her home. Is this true, or is she a simply glorified servant? Write an essay supporting or challenging Mead's viewpoint, perhaps contrasting it with that of Judy Brady in "I Want a Wife."

To Dispel Fears of Live Burial

JESSICA MITFORD

Begin your discussion by examining the basic facts of embalming as presented by Mitford in this essay. Consider her statement that a relative used to be present when this was done but that this is no longer the case. Note how this fact sets up her essay for the examination of present-day funeral home procedures. Examine the steps in the procedure of preparing a corpse for viewing and then consider how Mitford breaks the steps down into categories: Embalming, cosmetic attention, and "casketing." Next, examine Mitford's ironic tone and how she uses specific stylistic devices to achieve and sustain that tone. Note her use of understatement ("once the blood is removed, chances of live burial are indeed remote"), specific word choices ("to have at Mr. Jones," "returns to the attack"), use of euphemisms ("Mr. Jones is reposing in the preparation room"), and use of coined words and phrases ("to casket," "lipdrift"). Consider how language can be used to alter perceptions in the mind in the same way a mortician's cosmetics can alter the physical appearance of a body. Look at Mitford's use of quotations; consider how they enhance her ironic style even though they are intended by the speakers to be factual and serious ("a favorite injection and drainage point"). Note how Mitford picks the phrase "intestinal fortitude" from the quote by Mayer and uses it in other places in her essay with humorous results. Finally, examine the purpose of Mitford's essay in order to evaluate the effectiveness of her ironic tone in achieving that purpose.

Discussion Questions

1. What is the complete reversal regarding the subject of embalming that Mitford refers to in the second paragraph? What does this reversal say about the profession of the undertaker? What does it say about changes in society's attitudes toward embalming?

2. What are the steps of embalming that Mitford relates for us in her essay? How does the order in which the steps are presented give them a special significance?

3. What is the tone of this essay? How does Mitford achieve that tone? Pick out specific places where her word choice affects her tone. How would her tone be lost if a different word were used in these places? How does Mitford use understatement to sustain her tone? Find specific examples of its use.

4. Notice how Mitford employs euphemisms in paragraph four. Are there other places in her essay where she does this? What is Mitford saying about the power of language?

5. How does Mitford use quotations to enhance her essay? Are the quotations intended to be serious? How does she use the language of these quotations to sustain her ironic tone?

6. What is the purpose of Mitford's essay? Is she effective in achieving this purpose?

Writing Assignments

1. Consider the reality of the picture Mitford gives us about the process of making a corpse "presentable for viewing in an attitude of *healthy* repose" (emphasis added). What does this

say about our attitude toward death? Write an essay on how our society avoids confronting death and to what degree this is a reflection of an overall desire to avoid facing life's harshness.

2. Examine Mitford's treatment of euphemisms and write an essay exploring euphemisms for other taboo subjects. Do we use language in the same way a mortician uses cosmetics, to make more attractive what we don't want to hear? To what extent is the use of euphemisms necessary and at what point do they become absurd?

3. Consider Mitford's statement that funeral directors might fear that "public information about embalming might lead patrons to wonder if they really want this service." Do you think this is a possibility, or is our desire to avoid facing death so strong we would want it anyway? Do you think that public knowledge would lead to any sort of "reform" in the mortuary business? Write a brief essay exploring these issues.

ESSAYS BY WOMEN OF THE LATE 20TH CENTURY: BREAKING FREE

Writing a Woman's Life

CAROLYN HEILBRUN

Begin your discussion by examining Heilbrun's thoughts on a writer's use of a pen name and why this is something women writers do so much more than men. Look at the examples she gives of female writers in the past who have published under pen names; examine what kinds of protection a pen name gives to a writer and what kinds of freedom it gives to Heilbrun's own writing and to her creation of characters. Examine her belief that "secrecy is power," and explore what this could mean even beyond protecting a writer from an audience's censure. Explore the reasons women have needed (and still need) a means of recreating the self and expanding the self beyond gender, and discuss with the students how writing is a particularly effective tool for accomplishing this goal. Examine the components of these fantasy characters, and explore what they tell us about women's aspirations and dreams. Finally, explore the concept of writer as creator—both other-creator and self-creator—and how the process of self-creation involves the writer's craft as a writer as well as the personal exposure of self. Consider Heilbrun's statements concerning how she changed as a writer and how she found Kate Fansler changing as a character.

Discussion Questions

1. Why did Heilbrun feel it necessary to write under a pen name? How does she later see this as a particularly significant action for a woman in a way it would not be for a man? What does Heilbrun mean by the statement "secrecy is power"?

2. How did using a pen name free Charlotte Brontë as a writer? In what ways was Heilbrun's situation the same, despite the fact that she was writing decades later?

3. Why have women, in particular, "sought an escape from gender?" How does writing provide a particularly effective way of doing this? What does Heilbrun mean by the statement, "women come to writing . . . simultaneously with self-creation"?

4. What characteristics did Kate Fansler have that made her a fantasy? How did these characteristics change from the time Heilbrun first created Kate to when Heilbrun wrote this essay?

5. In what ways did Heilbrun's writing change in reaction to the women's movement?

6. Note the passages where Heilbrun refers to herself in the third person. Why does she do this? What meaning does it carry in the overall context of the essay?

Writing Assignments

1. Recall the female protagonist of a work or works by a woman writer you have read (for example, Charlotte Brontë, Willa Cather, Agatha Christie, or others). Using these characters as your examples, write an essay defending or refuting Heilbrun's definition of the components of the writer's fantasy character or alter-ego.

2. Consider the concept of writing to recreate the self, and then write a story creating a character who embodies the lifestyle and characteristics you would like for yourself. Let the story reveal those fantasies through your character.

3. Consider Heilbrun's statements about Kate Fansler taking on a life of her own, and write an essay comparing those ideas to Patricia Hampl's statements in "Memory and Imagination" on the concept of a piece of writing taking on a life of its own. Are these two writers saying the same thing? What do these state-

ments say about the source of writing and the craft of writing? What is the role of writing in the psychological development of the writer?

Graduation

MAYA ANGELOU

Begin your discussion by looking at Maya Angelou as a character and as the persona of this narrative, examining what we know about her and what specific incidents in the story reveal these traits. Examine how the aspects of her character in the early sections make her reactions to the negative events at the graduation ceremony predictable. Briefly examine her relationships with the people around her, particularly the close relationship she has with her brother, Bailey, and how this functions within the narrative. Next, examine the character Henry Reed: what does Angelou tell us about him, and what do his actions reveal about him? How does his action at the graduation ceremony serve to alter the possible outcome for Angelou and end the essay on an inspirational note? Examine how his action joins with Angelou's perception to illustrate the thesis of the essay. Define the word *commencement,* and note how the events serve to make this graduation ceremony a true commencement for Angelou.

Discussion Questions

1. In what specific ways were the members of Angelou's class made to feel special by their fellow students? How was this reinforced by the community? How does this sense of bonding function within the essay to build toward the climax?
2. What was Angelou's relationship with her brother, Bailey? What specific events illustrate this?
3. How does Angelou foreshadow the negative events at the graduation ceremony?

4. What does Henry Reed do after his speech that raises the spirits of the graduating class? How does this provide a strong climax to Angelou's essay?
5. How does Angelou effectively use language to show her rising anger throughout Donleavy's speech and the rest of the graduation ceremony? How does her continued use of overstatement in the first section contribute to the essay's impact?
6. What is the thesis of Angelou's essay? Does the narrative's structure (the change in her feelings from positive to negative to positive again) support this thesis? If so, how?

Writing Assignments

1. Examine the last sentence of Angelou's essay. How is she defining the term *poet*, considering that she includes preachers, musicians, and blues singers? In a brief essay, examine how the poets of any society contribute to its survival.
2. Write an essay examining the use of the poem "Annabelle Lee" within the context of Angelou's essay. How does the use of this particular poem contribute to the overall message of Angelou's essay? To what extent does the poem echo Angelou's essay in meaning? In tone? In the immaturity of the speaker?
3. Find a copy of the poem that Angelou read at Bill Clinton's inauguration and compare its message with the message of "Graduation."

On Self-Respect

JOAN DIDION

Begin your discussion by focusing on Didion's definition of self-respect and the specific attributes of the person who has self-respect.

Contrast this with her definition of the person who lacks self-respect, and note how she equates the compulsion to please others with a lack of self-respect. Next, explore the cause-and-effect relationships she sets up. Discuss the differences between the attitude and behavior of individuals who have self-respect and those persons without it. Examine the personal event Didion relates in the beginning of the essay and the concept of passive virtues she brought from childhood into adult life. Discuss how this event marked a turning point in her life. Finally, examine the ending to the essay in comparison with the beginning, noting that the last sentence uses the concept of the return to the self, providing a kind of frame to the essay's structure and reflecting its meaning.

Discussion Questions

1. What effect did not being elected to Phi Beta Kappa have on Didion? In what way did this event mark a change in Didion's view of life? How did this experience cause Didion to begin to acquire true self-respect?

2. What does Didion mean when she says that "people with self-respect have the courage of their mistakes"?

3. What does Didion define as "the source from which self-respect springs"? What are some of the possible indicators that an individual has this respect for himself or herself?

4. What is the paradox, according to Didion, that individuals without self-respect experience? How does she see this manifesting itself in an individual's life? How is an individual who has self-respect different from one who does not?

5. Examine the rhetorical techniques that Didion uses in her essay. How does she use definition in her essay? Comparison-contrast? Cause-effect? Narration?

Writing Assignments

1. Write an essay examining Didion's belief that the desire to please others is counter to self-respect. Do you agree with her? Are there situations where it is important to please others? Compare the results of pleasing oneself and of pleasing others. Is one

ultimately healthier for the individual? For a society as a whole? If the two must be balanced, how is that balance achieved?

2. Write an essay examining the following phrases: "those rather passive virtues which had won me approval as a child" and "faith in the totem power of good manners, clean hair, and proven competence on the Stanford-Benet scale." What are the "passive virtues," and how do they differ from "active virtues"? Are these qualities a stumbling block to success and happiness as an adult, and, if so, why are they taught to children? Are girls more apt to win approval with them, and, if so, is this treatment part of the problem women face in gaining equal status with men?

3. Are you a passive person? Are you an active person? Write an essay detailing the virtues of your type of personality.

Ruth's Song (Because She Could Not Sing It)

GLORIA STEINEM

Begin your discussion by focusing on Ruth and on what we learn about her both before and after her breakdown. Examine what effect that breakdown had on Steinem. Note how the details of Ruth's life are revealed to us gradually, in imitation of the gradual way that Steinem herself learned about Ruth. Consider the parallel drawn between Ruth and Uncle Ed and how he functions as a figure for comparing and contrasting. Explore Steinem's conclusions as to why her mother never received effective treatment for her mental illness, her criticism of the doctor's prescribing tranquilizers, and her mother's perhaps justified terror of hospitals. Most important, examine

Steinem's beliefs as to why her mother became mentally ill; consider
her statement to the doctor that her mother's spirit had been broken.
Note how Steinem's awareness of this breaking of spirit would affect
her own beliefs as a feminist, and examine what other effects
Steinem's mother may have had on her, both personally and professionally. Finally, examine Steinem's style in this essay. Note her use
of the question format in her treatment of Uncle Ed, the family
mystery. Note her use of fragments to reveal broken bits of memory.
Note her use of irony, such as when she describes how she and her
mother listened to the coverage of a royal wedding while the man
downstairs beat his wife. Note how many of her descriptive passages
also function as symbols.

Discussion Questions

1. How does the story of Uncle Ed provide an effective opening
   to Steinem's essay? In what ways does Uncle Ed's story parallel
   Ruth's? What purpose does its telling provide for the essay?

2. What kind of person was Ruth as a young woman? How is this
   information gradually unfolded for us? How does this method
   of gradual revelation serve Steinem's purpose?

3. What kind of a person was Ruth after her breakdown? How did
   she change in later years, after Steinem's sister was able to find
   effective medical treatment for her? How did she change as she
   grew old?

4. What is Steinem's conclusion as to why her mother never received
   good medical care for her illness when she was a young woman?
   Is Steinem's criticism valid, or was good medical treatment for
   mental illness just not available at this time?

5. What does Steinem believe are the reasons why her mother
   became mentally ill? What was the critical incident that Steinem
   feels broke her mother's spirit? What was the initial symptom in
   Ruth after this incident that indicated she was a changed woman?

6. In what way do we see the influence of Steinem's mother on
   her as a writer? As a woman? As a feminist?

7. What stylistic devices does Steinem use in her essay? Where does
   she use a question format? Where does she use irony? Symbol?
   Fragments? How do each of these devices enhance her essay?

8. How does the title enhance Steinem's essay? Why does she use "Ruth" instead of "Mother"? How is this essay a song?

Writing Assignments

1. Consider the statement Steinem makes in the opening paragraph: "families are all mysterious." Do you have any mysteries in your family's past, such as a strange relative—something that you have always wondered about but have never had answered? Write an essay discussing this mystery and exploring why the answers to it have never been revealed and whether you believe your questions concerning it will ever be answered.

2. Write an essay comparing and contrasting Steinem's mother to Annie Dillard's mother as portrayed in "An American Childhood." In what ways are these two women alike? In what ways was their impact on their daughters alike or different? What do you think enabled Dillard's mother to cope with life's limitations in a way that Ruth could not?

3. Write an essay applying Virginia Woolf's concept of the Angel of the House, who had to be killed in order for Woolf to survive, to Ruth's mental breakdown. To what extent was the Angel present in Ruth's life and in what ways was it the cause of her breakdown? In what ways is Ruth a testimony to the need to destroy the Angel of the House?

Femininity

SUSAN BROWNMILLER

Begin your discussion by examining Brownmiller's perceptions of how society has defined femininity and how these perceptions changed as she grew from childhood to adolescence to adulthood.

Note how secure she felt in being feminine when she was a child, and how femininity later became "an exasperation." Examine why the loss of femininity was such a frightening possibility to Brownmiller as she grew older and how this led to her concept of femininity as "a romantic sentiment." Note Brownmiller's distinction between "biological femaleness," which every woman has as a part of her physical make-up, and "femininity," which is a state defined largely by men. Examine Brownmiller's concept of how adhering to the male definition of femininity forces a woman to make "a grand collection of compromises." Note how she defines the masculine principle and the feminine principle as opposites and how this leads to her conclusion: that femininity exists as an ideal to make men feel stronger. Finally, examine the last sentence of Brownmiller's essay; what is her final position on the value of "trivial feminine activities"?

Discussion Questions

1. What did femininity mean to Brownmiller when she was a child? How did this change when she reached adolescence?
2. How does Brownmiller distinguish between "biological femaleness" and "femininity"? How is this distinction important to her position?
3. What does Brownmiller see as the price of being "insufficiently feminine"?
4. According to Brownmiller, what is the irony contained within the "competitive edge" that femininity seems to promise?
5. In what ways does femininity give men "an unchallenged space in which to breathe freely"?

Writing Assignments

1. Write an essay examining Brownmiller's position in light of women's lives today. Do you think there is more acceptance of strength in women today? What evidence exists to support your position?
2. Write an essay exploring the impact of gender definitions in our society. Have the challenges to traditional sex roles raised by

feminist writers like Brownmiller ultimately hurt or benefited women as individuals? Have they benefited society? In what ways?

3. Write an essay examining "the male and his masculinity" or on "the childlike and childish person."

Where Is the Love?

JUNE JORDAN

Begin your discussion by examining the controversy that Jordan remembers from the writer's conference. Define the specifics of the controversy and then examine how Jordan's explanation of the terms involved leads us into the central issue of her essay. Examine the title of the essay, its repeated use throughout the essay, and how it expresses the central idea of her essay. Next, examine her focus on self-love and how she sees this as the only path to loving others. Explore how this runs counter to many of our traditional concepts of love, concepts that require self-sacrifice and focus on other's needs, especially from women. Look at Jordan's perception of other terms, such as *virtue, evil,* and *suicide,* all of which she defines in ways different from traditional thought. Examine how all these definitions add to the understanding of what she means by love and how that love is realized. Finally, look at the stylistic techniques of Jordan's essay. What tone does Jordan use? What is the function of the two poems she includes? How does the closing paragraph provide a powerful ending?

Discussion Questions

1. What was the controversy at the Black Writer's Conference that Jordan relates in the opening paragraphs of her essay? Why was

feminism such a hot topic? Why was this controversy so "incendiary and obnoxious" to Jordan? How does this controversy fit into the larger context of Jordan's essay?

2. What was the problem in separating feminism from women's sexuality? Why were these terms so blurred together that they were made inseparable issues?

3. Why does "Where Is the Love?" serve as an appropriate title for this essay? How does the repeated use of this question enhance the essay as a whole?

4. Why is Jordan concerned about the individual as well as the "union of Black men and Black women"? What does individual strength have to do with love? Why is self-love and self-respect so important to Jordan?

5. How does Jordan define *virtue*? How does this definition lead to her conclusion that the "reality of power and government and tradition is evil"? What does Jordan feel we owe these power structures?

6. What does Jordan see as the "morally defensible character of . . . self-love"? What does she see as the result of the "socio-psychic strength"? How does she define *suicide*? How are the definitions of all these terms important to her argument?

7. How does Jordan's use of the two poems add to the message of her essay? How does it add to the tone of her essay?

Writing Assignments

1. Consider Jordan's definition of love as something that is realized only when one loves oneself and her idea that self-love does not allow suicide for the sake of another. Write an essay contrasting this model with that of the traditional belief that love requires the denial of self in order to serve another, perhaps using Judy Brady's definition of a wife ("I Want a Wife") as a model.

2. Study the poem "The Heart of a Woman" by Georgia Douglas Johnson and write an essay discussing how it captures the pain in the lives of women. What are the many forms the "alien cage" takes in the lives of women?

3. Jordan says, "We, Black women, huddle together, miserably on
    the very lowest levels of the economic pyramid," and she speaks
    of being able in the *future* "to love and respect women . . . who
    are not Black." Contrast this view of race as self-identity with
    that of Zora Neale Hurston in "How It Feels to Be Colored
    Me." How do these two women view the world and relationships
    with others? What views do they share?

I Want a Wife

JUDY BRADY

Begin your discussion by asking the class to react to the content
of Brady's essay: In what ways does the essay reveal a true picture
of the expectations placed on wives, and in what ways is it
exaggerated? Is it unfair to men and, if so, how? Ask the class
how relevant they feel the essay is today (it was first published
in 1971). Are the same expectations placed on women today, or
have things changed? Next, begin to focus on the structure of
the essay by examining each individual paragraph. Ask the class
to examine the duties of a wife described within a given paragraph
and what these duties have in common; is there a category that
could be assigned to each paragraph? Look at the order in which
these categories are arranged, and ask if this order serves a purpose.
Look for the common element in all these subcategories and note
how it reveals Brady's definition of a wife as one who serves the
needs of others. Next, examine the tone of the essay. Point out
the repeated use of the phrase "I want a wife who," and ask the
class how this functions in the essay and what it does to help
create the ironic tone of the essay. Ask what is meant by the
capitalization of "a wife" in the second sentence and how this
device helps to set the tone of the essay. Point out that Brady

never uses the pronouns *he* or *she* to refer to the wife she wants, and examine how this contributes to the tone of the piece. Finally, ask the class what the thesis of the essay is. Since the thesis is implied rather than directly stated, this essay provides an excellent example of how meaning is conveyed by the manner in which an essay is *structured*, rather than simply by what it says.

Discussion Questions

1. Examine the duties of a wife that Brady describes in each paragraph. What could a possible heading for each paragraph be?
2. What is the common element of all the duties described? Does this reflect the purpose of the essay?
3. How does Brady use irony to enhance her essay? Find specific words and phrases that create her ironic tone. Would another approach work better?
4. How does Brady use repetition of key words and phrases in her essay? How does this device enhance the essay's effectiveness?
5. What opinions about a wife's role are conveyed in this essay but not directly stated? Does this technique make the essay stronger?

Writing Assignments

1. Write an essay examining the message of Brady's essay in light of today's society. To what extent is it dated and to what extent does it apply to women's lives today? What aspects of the ideal wife are women still expected to take on? What aspects have changed, and what do you believe has caused them to change?
2. Write an essay examining another role in our society that has unrealistic expectations placed on it. What are these expectations, where do they come from, and why do they persist? What impact do these expectations have on an individual who takes on the role and can't live up to the expectations? (Or on the individual who can?)
3. Write an essay comparing Brady's message to that of Brownmiller in "Femininity." In what ways do these essays support each other? Are there any differences in the point of view of each? Which essay's style is stronger?

Where I Come from Is Like This

PAULA GUNN ALLEN

Begin your discussion of Allen's essay by establishing an understanding of her thesis: that Indian and white cultures define women in opposite ways and that Indian women experience an inner conflict between these two self-definitions—a conflict she describes as a "bicultural bind." Next, explore the cultural, mythic, and religious images that might give rise to these definitions, what specifically Allen tells us about Indian beliefs, how these beliefs differ from white culture's beliefs, and what specific memories Allen uses to reinforce her different view of what women are. Examine Allen's treatment of feminine power and how she sees this as a uniquely Indian viewpoint. Ask students if they agree with Allen that white culture's definitions of women are really as polarized as she says; ask them if they see Allen as being guilty of her own form of bias, as when she expresses admiration for her mother's moving furniture on her own and relates her mother's scorn for menstruating women who were "incapacitated by cramps." This could lead to a more general discussion about freedom and personal power and how much any cultural system will inevitably limit an individual's right to be who he or she is.

Discussion Questions

1. According to Allen, what does the Indian woman see as her primary identity? How does this view differ from that of non-Indians?
2. How does Allen define white culture's perceptions of women? How do these perceptions differ from those of Indian cultures?

3. What is the "bicultural bind" that Allen describes? How does
   she see it manifested in the lives of Indian women?
4. How do mythic images and religious beliefs play a part in both
   Indian and non-Indian perceptions of women?
5. How does Indian culture perceive or define feminine power?
   Do you see any contradictions in Allen's argument that Indian
   culture perceives women as strong and white culture does not?
6. How does Allen balance the personal, autobiographical details
   with the persuasive message of the essay?

Writing Assignments

1. Write an essay examining the impact of culture in the development of our self-concepts. To what extent are we shaped by our
   culture's definitions of us and to what extent are we free to
   define ourselves?
2. Do cultural imagines truly have the power to bind us into a role
   or to confuse us so much with conflicting signals that our self-
   worth is deeply affected? Write an essay exploring this question.

Pornography

MARGARET ATWOOD

Begin your discussion by establishing an understanding of Atwood's
definition of pornography, especially how this definition makes a
distinction between erotica and sexual violence. Note how the fusing
of these two elements causes the pornography debate to be polarized,
with each side composed of groups "not noticeably in agreement
on other issues." Discuss the theories on pornography's popularity

today and examine whether it is necessary to understand why it is popular before taking action against it. Raise the question, as Atwood does, "Is there in fact a clear distinction between erotica and violence, or is erotica a continuum that will ultimately result in violent expression?" Finally, examine the question "who does it harm?" in light of Atwood's essay, your own findings, and the class's viewpoint.

Discussion Questions

1. What is the difference between the Scandinavian journalists' and Atwood's definitions of pornography?
2. What are the two main sides in the pornography debate? How do they perpetuate the controversy and insure that there will be no resolution to the debate?
3. What are the theories as to why pornography continues to flourish?
4. According to Atwood, what is the central question of the pornography debate?
5. How important is the *definition* of pornography to Atwood's argument?

Writing Assignments

1. Write an essay examining the concept of the availability of pornographic materials in a free society. In what ways is pornography an unavoidable part of a free society? In what ways is pornography a counterforce in a free society?
2. In a brief essay, examine the role of the women's movement in the pornography issue. To what extent has the women's movement and the subsequent blurring of gender roles contributed to the popularity of pornography? To what extent has the women's movement acted instead as a challenge to the proliferation of pornography, making it less acceptable?
3. Write an essay exploring the role of technology in the pornography issue. Is the real problem the ease with which pornographic materials are produced and made available to the public today rather than any particular change in society?

You Are What You Say

ROBIN LAKOFF

Begin your discussion by examining Lakoff's use of the term *women's language* as she describes it in her opening paragraphs. Establish an understanding of why Lakoff sees women's language as less effectual than men's, why it makes women "communicative cripples," and why it contributes to women's low self-esteem. Next, explore the differences in the vocabulary of women's language and the use of the tag question. Establish why Lakoff sees the use of both of these patterns as a linguistic weakness that "allows a speaker to avoid commitment . . . and conflict." Next, examine her study of the use of euphemisms for the word *woman*, starting with her thoughts on why we use euphemisms and how they function in the language. Examine her study of the word *lady* and why it has changed in ways that *gentleman* has not. Ask the class if they feel that Lakoff's analysis still holds true today, or whether some changes in meaning and usage have taken place. In the same way, explore Lakoff's study of the use of *girl* and her analysis of the changes in meaning of *master* and *mistress,* *bachelor* and *spinster,* and how these usages reflect attitudes toward women in our society. Finally, examine the structure of Lakoff's essay. Look at the order of her examples of women's language and how they represent three areas of linguistic study: morphology, syntax, and semantics (note that she leaves out phonology); consider her examples also as a hierarchical order from least to most important. Consider whether her structuring of her examples is effective in strengthening her argument. Examine the last sentence's effectiveness as a conclusion, noting the irony of the phrase "speak up."

Discussion Questions

1. How does Lakoff define *women's language* in the opening paragraphs of her essay? Why does she claim that its use makes women "communicative cripples"?
2. According to Lakoff, what are the specific components of women's language?
3. What is a "tag question"? Why does Lakoff feel the use of tag questions is a weak form of communication? Does she relate any situation where their use would be acceptable to her?
4. How does Lakoff see euphemisms for the word *woman* changing in meaning through usage? How has the word *lady* changed in meaning in a way *gentleman* has not? How has *mistress* changed in a way *master* has not? What does this say about society's perceptions of women?
5. What other examples does Lakoff give of the "linguistic double standard"?
6. Study the order of the examples Lakoff presents in her essay. Is there a pattern? How does she build her argument? How does the final sentence serve as an effective conclusion?

Writing Assignments

1. Consider Lakoff's contention that the use of the tag question by women makes them ineffective communicators. Do you agree with her stand, or is she simply embracing male norms without looking at the *value* of women's language? Is the tag question really allowing the speaker "to avoid commitment" or is it simply intended to invite dialogue, to create relationship rather than disagreement? Write an essay exploring these various interpretations of this one linguistic behavior.
2. Lakoff analyzes several pairs of words that have changed in meaning in different ways for the two genders: *lady* and *gentleman*, *master* and *mistress*, *bachelor* and *spinster*. Write an essay examining other pairs of words in the same manner and support or refute Lakoff's thesis.
3. Do you feel that this essay is dated? Have some of the problems Lakoff describes been reduced through increased awareness

among people since the time Lakoff wrote this essay? Write an essay relating which of these situations seem to be less prevalent, which ones still need to be addressed, and whether there are other problems with the gender differential that are more critical.

An American Childhood

ANNIE DILLARD

Begin your discussion by focusing on the personality of Dillard's mother as conveyed in this essay. What traits are revealed by her behavior? What motivations could be behind her actions? Is she an admirable person? Explore the possible deeper meaning behind her actions, and examine what clues we have that this is a very intelligent woman locked in a lifestyle that lacks sufficient challenge for her. Next, examine Dillard's perception of her mother—whether she admires her and whether she sees her as funny, loving, exasperating, or cruel. Look for specific words and sentences in the essay that convey these attitudes. Explore the impact of Dillard's mother on Dillard: what values did she learn from her and what skills did she learn from her? Finally, look at how many of her examples concerning her mother's behavior have something to do with language. Also explore how this early relationship may have influenced Dillard's development as a writer.

Discussion Questions

1. How would you characterize Dillard's mother? What specific behaviors illustrate these characteristics?

2. What do you see as the motivation behind these behaviors? Is "Mother" simply eccentric, or is there a deeper meaning behind her actions?

3. What is Dillard's attitude toward her mother? How does Dillard convey her attitude to the reader? Find specific places in the text where her word choices convey this attitude.

4. What does Dillard's mother mean by an "intelligent apron" or "intelligent pan handles"? What is the significance of these descriptive words in characterizing Dillard's mother?

5. What is the significance of the phrase "Terwilliger bunts one"? Why is this incident an effective opening to Dillard's essay?

6. What does the essay reveal about the mother's influence on Dillard's character? On Dillard as a writer? What specific words, phrases, or paragraphs convey this?

7. What is the significance of the title "An American Childhood"? In what ways was Dillard's upbringing particularly American? What aspects of American culture and values were acted out in Dillard's home?

Writing Assignments

1. Is there a person in your life who has influenced you to the extent that Dillard's mother influenced her? Using Dillard's essay as a model, bring that person to life vividly in an essay in which the individual's influence on you is conveyed to the reader but is not directly stated.

2. Write an essay examining the societal role of eccentric individuals, those who seem compelled to push against conformity and to defy society's rules. What influence do they have on others? To what extent are they the movers of society, keeping that society from stagnating? To what extent are they a destructive force in a society?

3. Write an essay exploring the concept of human intelligence as a natural resource. If intelligent women, such as Dillard's mother, are compelled to stay home and be housewives, could this be defined as a waste of a natural resource? Using Dillard's

mother as an example, how might our society change if intelligence were employed skillfully, at worthy tasks?

Memory and Imagination

PATRICIA HAMPL

Begin your discussion by exploring the memory of the piano lesson narrated in the opening paragraphs of Hampl's essay, noting the specific details that Hampl refers to repeatedly. For example, note the significance of the finding of middle C, the sneeze in the sun, the descriptions of Sister Olive and Mary Katherine Reilly. Next, compare how these details differ from what Hampl reveals later really happened, and explore the significance of these differences. Note how this comparison leads into Hampl's analysis of the role of imagination in the writing of memoirs, as well as how she sees the writing of memoirs as a tool for self-discovery. Note how she defines memory as something stored because it has value and how that value reflects the meaning of the memory. Explore Hampl's definition of a first draft, how it functions for the writer, and how it differs from subsequent drafts; note how she sees a piece of writing as having a life of its own and how the metaphors she uses illustrate this. Finally, bring together these aspects of Hampl's essay to understand her definition of *memoir*.

Discussion Questions

1. What is the specific memory that Hampl relates in the opening paragraphs of her essay? What key details does she emphasize by repeatedly calling attention to them?

2. What details of the piano lesson does Hampl later indicate are fabrications? For example, how does the real Mary Katherine Reilly differ from the child in Hampl's memory? What reasons does she give for altering these details?

3. What does Hampl mean by the statement, "memory is not, after all, *just* memory?" If memory is unreliable, why does Hampl feel its examination is important? Why does she feel the writing of memoirs is worthwhile?

4. Why does Hampl repeatedly refer to the phrase "Question Authority"? How does the reference to this phrase fit with the rest of her essay?

5. What does Hampl mean when she says, "I write in order to find out what I know"? How does she define a first draft? How do these two ideas support each other in the essay? What does Hampl see as the function of memoirs?

Writing Assignments

1. Recall to mind your most vivid memory and write about it in great detail. Then, examine its content for reasons why it remains strong in your memory. Write an essay exploring the revelations you see in your "first draft" (as defined by Hampl) and the reasons why you recall your memory with the particular details that you do.

2. Note Hampl's statement that "our capacity to move forward as developing beings rests on a healthy relation with the past." Write an essay exploring the power of the past to influence each of us today and why it is important for each of us to come to a reconciliation with our individual memories.

3. Relate Hampl's concepts of the function of memoirs to Maya Angelou's "Graduation," and write an essay reflecting on the role of Angelou's essay in giving her a reconciliation with her past. Could Angelou's memory of graduation function for her in much the same way as Hampl's memory of her first piano lesson?

Wounded Chevy at Wounded Knee

DIANA HUME GEORGE

Begin your discussion by exploring the aspects of George's life that make her perspective on the lives of present-day Indians different from those of another white observer or an Indian. Establish what her attitude is and how it might differ from that of other writers interested in Indian culture. Examine her narrative approach to this essay—how she moves back and forth from story-telling to commentary. Examine how the use of the narrative and the vividness of the narrative serves to illustrate her thesis so well. Examine each character she introduces us to: Mark, the children in the Chevy, the aunt in the Comanche truck, Hank, big Bernard. Note how each character description serves her discourse in different ways. Examine the conclusions she draws from all these encounters, and explore how they fit with her own expressed hopes for her granddaughter, Sequoia. Does Sequoia represent a bridge between two cultures, much as the Cherokee chief Sequoia did in his time? Look at the anecdote in the final paragraph and explore its meaning in the greater context of George's essay.

Discussion Questions

1. How does George's attitude toward the Indians differ from that of her companion, Mac? What is the basis for this attitude?

2. What does George mean by "the white liberal-intellectual's romance with all things Indian"? Is it the same thing as "the myths of . . . the smitten hippies"? Why does she feel contempt for these beliefs?

3. What reasons does Goerge give for entering the Indian world when she was fifteen? What was her life like during this time? What reasons does she give for leaving at the end of her five-year marriage?

4. What characteristics of the Indian people does George see as evidence that they are a "people on their way to annihilation"? How are these characteristics manifested in the children she sees in the broken-down Chevy? In Mark, the young man she and Mac take to buy gas for? In Bernard, her ex-husband? In Hank, Bernard's best friend?

5. What present behavior on the part of the Indians does George describe as a modern form of the Ghost Dance? What other examples does she give of modern reflections of past traditions that serve to keep Indian people from finding a place in the modern world?

6. How does the title of this essay serve to enhance its meaning? In what ways does it serve as a metaphor for the lives of Indian people today?

Writing Assignments

1. George looks at Hank and his behavior in the modern Indian's world and imagines what he would have been in a past time, before tribal life was disrupted by white people. Imagine Mark in a past time, and write an essay describing what he would have been like and what place he might have had in a tribal society.

2. Consider George's position as a white woman living in an Indian culture, and write an essay considering the larger issue of anyone marrying into a culture different from the one in which he or she was raised. What difficulties are bound to result? What benefits might arise from the coming together of different cultures in this way? Is it possible for such a marriage to survive in a healthy manner or is the balancing of different backgrounds too much to achieve?

3. Write an essay examining the annihilation of a race. How could it be done or has it been done? Why would anybody want to do it?

A Question of Language

GLORIA NAYLOR

Begin your discussion by examining Naylor's opening section to consider her argument that speech is more powerful than the written word. Examine why this opening section is important to Naylor's essay and how it adds meaning to the later sections. Next, look at the incident at school and how Naylor knew from the boy's voice that *nigger* was a "bad" word. Note how this leads into her analysis of the Black community's use of *nigger* as she learned it within the context of her family. Explore the various specific meanings as related by Naylor and the context associated with each. Note how these examples illustrate the consensual nature of word meaning and how that meaning can be altered. Examine Naylor's analysis of the reasons why the Black community adapted *nigger* for their own use, and explore whether this same technique could be used with other words of negative connotation. Finally, consider the power of using a negative word in a different context; examine the way in which a Black child exposed to *nigger* in a positive context would have some defense against the effects of later encounters with this word in its standard negative context. Consider the degree to which this technique could defuse any word's negative power.

Discussion Questions

1. Why does Naylor consider the written word inferior to the spoken? What gives spoken words their power?

2. When the little boy in school called Naylor a *nigger*, how did she know it was a "bad" word if she didn't know what it meant? How does the relating of this incident illustrate what she says in the first section about the power of the spoken word?

3. How does Naylor describe her home atmosphere? Why is this description important to the rest of the essay?

4. What was different about the use of the word *nigger* in Naylor's home "that caused it to register in [her] mind as something else"?

5. What were the meanings of *nigger* that Naylor learned at home? Were they positive or negative? How did the different meanings change in different contexts? In what ways did the word *girl* have a similar range of meaning?

6. What does Naylor see as the dynamics behind the use of *nigger* in the Black community?

Writing Assignments

1. Consider Naylor's statements about the power of vocal inflection and social contexts to assign meaning to a word. Write an essay analyzing other words in our language that can change meaning in this way.

2. Write an essay considering to what extent vocal inflection is more important than the actual words said. Are there situations where all communication is contained within the inflection (e.g., with babies or pets)?

3. Write an essay comparing Naylor's analysis of the word *girl* with that of Lakoff in "You Are What You Say." How do these two women view the use of this word differently? Could the Black community's model for transforming the degradation of a word be applied to the use of *girl* by men, a practice criticized by Lakoff? Is the consideration of vocal inflection a possible adjunct to Lakoff's argument—that is, a means of identifying contexts where offense is not intended by the speaker?

Reflections on Race and Sex

BELL HOOKS

Begin your discussion by examining the convergence of racism and sexism as defined by hooks. Examine her explanation of how the rape of black women by white men throughout history serves to illustrate this convergence, as well as the fantasy invented by white men of the black man as rapist. Examine her examples of this convergence in the present, particularly in the media's choice of news focus. Explore her interpretation of the politics of the Central Park rape and how this serves her thesis as an illustration of the convergence of sexism and racism. Finally, examine her conclusions concerning the components of the black liberation movement: what does she see as the movement's flaw, and what does she propose instead? What does she see as the feminist component needed to make it a true liberation movement for all blacks?

Discussion Questions

1. According to hooks, what are the ways in which sexism and racism converge? How did/does the rape of black women by white men reflect racist thinking as well as sexist thinking?
2. What is the fantasy about black men invented by white men? How do sexism and racism converge within this belief?
3. What examples of this "sexual project" does hooks see in news coverage today? How does the news media's choice of focus serve to keep the myth alive?
4. What flaw does hooks see in the basic approach of the black liberation movement? What does she suggest as a better model for black liberation?

5. How does hooks see the young black males involved in the Central Park incident as being "victims of the patriarchy"? What does hooks see as the role of black men in realizing a new society that is "less violent and more just"?

6. How does hooks blend narration with other expository techniques to explain her viewpoint?

Writing Assignments

1. Hooks raises the question, "Cannot black women remain seriously concerned about the brutal effect of racist domination on black men and also denounce black male sexism?" Write an essay describing a possible model for how this could be realized.

2. When hooks talks about the images of black men as rapists, she says, "the obsessive media focus on these representations is political." Think of other types of "obsessive media focus" that are also political and write an essay on the power of the media to shape public opinion.

3. Hooks makes a statement about the "pornographic glorification of male violence," connecting it to violence in society such as the Central Park rape. Consider the stand taken by Margaret Atwood in her essay "Pornography" and write an essay on how hooks's insights could be added to Atwood's to realize an even deeper understanding of the effects of pornography in our society.

Anatomy and Destiny

PERRI KLASS

Begin your discussion by looking at Klass's examination of the term *sexism*. First, point out how in the opening paragraph she explains that her medical school professors didn't tell offensive jokes, and how in the next paragraph she relates other, more subtle forms of sexism she did encounter. Next, note how she begins to relate this to feminism by pointing out how female medical students were feminists in that they were aware of and grateful to the women who had gone before them, but that they also wanted to be part of the brotherhood of medicine, which required fitting in. Examine Klass's exploration of the term *feminist* in her high school and college years and then in her medical school years and discuss how the meaning of the word shifted around her until she found herself labeled a *radical*. Examine what Klass means by the statement, "one of the courses everyone gets . . . is an introduction to sexual politics." Explore the difference Klass sees in the young female doctors she works with now and how their definitions of feminism involve a "sense of entitlement." Finally, point out the balance that Klass says women need to make their way in medicine and to make a contribution to it.

Discussion Questions

1. How does the opening paragraph of Klass's essay function in the larger context of her essay? Did the lack of offensive jokes about women in Klass's medical school experience mean that all forms of sexism were gone?

2. What were the subtle elements of sexism that Klass tells us she experienced in medical school? What were the effects on Klass and the other female students?

3. What contradictory desire made it difficult for a woman to declare herself a feminist in a medical school setting? According to Klass, how has this changed today?

4. Did Klass consider herself to be a feminist? How did she define the term differently than other feminists she had known? How did she suddenly find herself being labeled a "radical feminist"? What did this show her (and us) about the range of definition this term can include?

5. In what field of medicine did Klass find a higher percentage of female residents? Why do you suppose this is the case? Why is this an advantage for the female resident?

6. What is the significance of the title "Anatomy and Destiny"?

Writing Assignments

1. Klass examines two words that seem to have varying degrees of meaning for different people: *sexism* and *feminist*. Write an essay explaining how you would define these two words, including any experiences you may have had with people who define them differently.

2. The director of Klass's medical school was upset because she and the heads of other student groups were giving assistance to female and minority applicants and no similar service was available for white men. Write an essay exploring your view of this issue.

3. Consider the scene Klass describes in the operating room where all the participants were women. She says, "there was less yelling, more courtesy, more collegiality and less strict hierarchy." Why do you suppose this was the case? Write an essay on the gender differential in work relationships, perhaps comparing Klass's observations to those of George Eliot in her essay "Only Temper."